INCOMING

BY

JACK "DOC" MANICK

authorHOUSE®

AuthorHouse™
1663 Liberty Drive
Bloomington, IN 47403
www.authorhouse.com
Phone: 1-800-839-8640

First published by AuthorHouse 10/15/2010

ISBN: 978-1-4520-6111-5 (e)
ISBN: 978-1-4520-6112-2 (sc)
ISBN: 978-1-4520-6113-9 (hc)

Library of Congress Control Number: 2010911401

Printed in the United States of America

This book is printed on acid-free paper.

THANK YOU

James Irwin

In the late 1990s, a website named InTheGardenState.com and an editor named Jim Irwin emerged from within the Comcast Cable System. In the early nineteen nineties, Comcast came up with a great idea; create local content servers to provide communities with news and stories from Comcast's Staff and also from area writers. It turned into a smashing success and was a site that all of the local communities proudly called "Their Own."

Being an early subscriber to Comcast Cable in New Jersey, I found out about a "call for local content authors" to contribute material to their web site. I met Jim at an Open House in Union New Jersey and pitched my idea of a Veterans Column. He liked it, and so began my writing career. Jim gave me my first shot at writing to large audiences and inspired me to start writing this book. I would like to thank Jim for believing in me and the idea of a Veterans Column and Comcast for thinking out of the box and providing local content servers to all who would venture into the wonderful world of writing and the Internet.

Kyle Smith

I wish to offer my heartfelt thanks to Kyle Smith for the incredible drawings that he has donated to this book. Kyle can be reached at computersmithart@ gmail.com.

DEDICATIONS

I proudly dedicate this book to:

The 58,192 Americans who gave their lives in "America's Longest War" and especially to Tim Murphy and Pete Mazzillo, my friends from High School who went to Vietnam before me and never returned, and to the 3.5 million Americans who served in the SE Asia Theatre of Operations and the 2.5 million who served on the ground in Vietnam.

In addition, I most proudly dedicate this book to my lifelong and Best Friend, Joseph Glydon. Our friendship spanned the years from high school until his tragic death four years ago. Joe was a friend such as I've never had before nor will ever have again. Although our paths in life took us in different directions, we always got back together again. We rode 50cc motorcycles together in the early 60s on New Jersey roads where tractor trailer drivers feared to tread. Nothing would stop us! We were always there for each other…no matter what. Joe was the best man at my wedding and the experiences and memories that Joe shared with me will be with me forever. Ace, I miss you.

To my wife and lifelong companion Barbara, I thank you for your love for all of the years that we have been together, for your encouragement in writing this book and your eternal patience as you watched me disappear after supper every night into our computer room and write till I dropped, while listening to the sounds of the 60's on my headphones. For Barb and me, it was love at first sight and that hasn't changed in the thirty six years of our marriage.

I have been writing this book for more years than I would like to remember and more years than I can count. I did it because of my passion for writing and my memories of Vietnam. To me, it's as if Vietnam happened just yesterday.

Notes from the author

"In Death there is Silence"
Jack Manick

"Incoming" is a work that is a long time in coming…almost too long. This book has been a dream of mine and at times, an obsession. It has fulfilled my passion for writing while at the same time has set free a demon that's been locked up inside me since 1970.

For the first 25 years after returning from Vietnam, my only discussions regarding my experiences there were with my wife and rarely with others. The feelings, the memories, the smells, the sights and the sounds are as real to me now as they were the day I left Cam Ranh Bay for home.

Late in the 1980s, I took pen and ink to paper and scribed my first notes about Vietnam. Soon thereafter, I transitioned to the word processor. Almost every night, I typed and typed and typed. At times, my wife would find me asleep at the keyboard.

I have been asked to classify this book…is it fact or fiction? Is it a true story or a novel? Memory leakage being what it is and the fact that no two people seeing an event will remember it in the same way, I must classify this book as a "Historical Novel based on a True Story."

Where memory has failed, I have combined events and timelines. Where anonymity was needed, I changed the names of people. My goal has always been to tell a story, based on real events and real people and never to expose or hurt any of the participants.

"Incoming" is a glimpse into the light and the dark sides of war as seen through my eyes, the eyes of a Combat Medic. Most of all, it is the story of the bravery and courage of two hundred men, who struggled day by day and hour by hour to survive in the face of unimaginable odds and inconceivable hardships.

Soldiers are dreamers, they dream about going back home to wives or girlfriends or to Mom and Apple Pie. Incoming is their story…it is our story…it is my story.

ABOUT THE AUTHOR

Jack Manick is a lifelong resident of New Jersey. His active duty military career spanned the years from 1968 through 1971. Trained as a Field Combat Medic, he served in Germany during the second half of 1968 in a Military Hospital and Dispensary, there learning the tools of his trade, then in late 1968 volunteered to go to Vietnam. In the Central Highlands of Vietnam he served with both the 70th Combat Engineer Battalion and the 131'st Engineer Company (LE) (also known as the Vermont National Guard) for his Tour of Duty. After Vietnam, he served with the 24th and 1'st Infantry Divisions until his separation from active duty in 1971.

Jack married Barbara Dailey, in 1973, shortly after graduating from Stockton State College. Six months later, he was hired by the Veterans Administration Hospital in East Orange New Jersey where he worked in their Research Lab for the next ten years. Loving his job but unable to pay the bills on his and his wife's combined salaries, Jack went back to school at night for two years to become a Computer Programmer. Barbara went to school and became a Medical Assistant.

Today, Jack continues to work in the Data Processing Field but his heart remains in medicine and health care.

To date, Jack has written seven specialty Art Books documenting the life and times of artists who have shaped the destiny of the 20'th and 21'st Century, names like Michael Godard, John Kelly, James Coleman, David Garibaldi and others. Along with Richard Enfantino from Enfantino Publishing, they published their first ever book about the life and art work of world famous artist Michael Godard, titled "Don't Drink and Draw." It won the "Best Art Book in 2006" Award by the "USA Book News."

In the late 1980s and early 1990s, Jack wrote a Veterans Column titled "Insights of a Veteran," for Comcast's "IntheGardenState.com", a local content site in New Jersey, and was awarded a "Best Military Site" by Military.com for it.

Jack believes that every day is a "Gift" from a higher power and that it should be lived with conviction and passion. Besides his wife Barbara and dog Kimba, transforming what the heart feels to "Pen and Ink" is Jack's passion and he plans to continue with it for years to come.

TABLE OF CONTENTS AND PREVIEW OF EACH CHAPTER

With a big smile on his face the armorer said in a deep southern drawl, "Boy, if you all have to use that pistol, you be dead before you use up half this ammo! This is a last resort weapon only! "Don't count on it for nothin else." Shit, I said silently to myself! 112

home for food. GIs were blessed with sixth senses and knew when even a single parcel containing food arrived in camp. Once the recipient was identified, the fight was over.

Chapter Twenty Seven: Friendly Fire Friendly fire is not friendly! There is nothing more terrifying, more frightening, more confusing and more wasteful of human life than being targeted and fired upon by your own side. When a soldier is killed in action, it matters not to him or his family whether the bullet or explosive came from a friendly or non-friendly source; the end result is the same.

Chapter Twenty Eight: Nam Pei I sucked in a mouthful of the vile liquid through the long bamboo straw and immediately felt the urge to vomit. The muscles in my diaphragm started to contract violently. It was as if they were trying to expel my guts through my mouth, but I hadn't yet swallowed it.

Chapter Twenty Nine: Freefire The sound of rifle and machinegun fire shattered the silence of an otherwise peaceful evening near the Cambodian Border. Explosions from 81 millimeter High Explosive (HE) Mortar and 40 millimeter grenade launcher rounds joined with the rifle and machine gun fire to create a deafening symphony of sound, color and death to all who wandered into its destructive path.

Chapter Thirty: Indian Country Our three truck convoy left for base camp a little after 5 AM. We always traveled in twos or threes in order to protect each other on the long drive through "Indian Country." An attack on or a breakdown of a single, unescorted vehicle in Indian Country was effectively a death sentence for those foolish enough to tempt the fates.

Chapter Thirty One: Payback is a Bitch Shortly after 8 PM we saw the flash of a B-40 Rocket leaving its launching tube. It provided us with the aiming point that we needed. Gun fire erupted on the berm such as I have never seen before or since. We were not just targeting that area of the rubber plantation where the rocket was launched from; we were targeting everything and anything within the plantation, regardless. Payback, that night was a bitch!

Chapter Thirty Two: Out the Door I felt myself falling downwards towards the open door. Only my handhold on the bar and a foot wedged against the metal seat frame prevented me from exiting the chopper, but my grip was quickly loosening and so was my foot hold.

Chapter Thirty Nine: The Final Battle...A recurring Nightmare The commanding officer came running into the radio room, grabbed the Mike and called out, "Quebec Romeo niner this is Lima Alpha 26, this is 6, what's your status, over?" "They're all over us sir. Most of the men are down! "Can you make it back to camp niner?" "Don't know sir. Were gonna make a run for it sir...I'm dropping the radio...pray for us sir." "Niner...come in niner...this is six." There was no response!

Chapter Forty: Going Home I was going home and I was pissed! I had extended my Tour of Duty for an additional six months in Vietnam and was to be the medic in Medevac Helicopters. I would have gone home for 30 days then returned for six months then home again, permanently. It all seemed perfectly sane at the time, my decision that is. I really needed the money to buy my British Sports Car and if I got killed while on my six month extension, so be it.

Chapter Forty One: Avenel Here I come The flight home was relatively calm until we hit the east coast and a massive snow storm. The DC8 started bouncing around like a Mexican Jumping Bean. I paid no attention to it until I looked out the window and saw the wings flapping like a Sea Gull just taking flight. They were bouncing up and down six or seven feet from the horizontal .People everywhere started screaming. The man next to me was screaming louder than the women. As we continued our freefall, I had a sinking feeling that this was the end for us all. I didn't panic, nor scream nor show any signs of fear. With the calmness of knowing that my death was imminent, I uttered just one word, "Shit."

Chapter Forty Two: Home I put on my Class A Uniform complete with ribbons, borrowed my grandfather's Chevy and set out north on the Garden State Parkway to Upsala College and the Student Union Atrium. As I pushed open the door, I wondered what and who I would find. Would I encounter another "Up Close and Personal" hostile reception like that at the Seattle/Tacoma Airport just days before? Half way across the atrium I saw her. She was reading a book. Slowly, as if something or someone had told her, she raised her head and looked at me. Our eyes met and I smiled. She stood up slowly, then broke out into a large smile and started screaming "Oh my God, Oh my God, it's you" as she ran towards me. I held out my arms and she dove into them. Wrapping her arms around me she gave me a kiss that seemed to stop time. I could feel a passion and an emotion in her lips that I had never felt before. That kiss erased all of the suffering and anger and frustration of the past year.

CHAPTER 0
NVA IN THE WIRE

"The Vietnam War lasted for 14 years and is labeled the longest war in American History. According to available statistics, 1202 medics were killed in Vietnam as a result of Hostile Action and another 202 as a result of non-hostile action."

Jack Manick

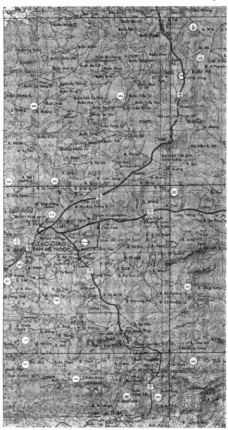

"Lac Thien"

The Concussion Wave tossed me into the air like a rag doll being sucked into a twister! By the time I hit the ground, I was fully awake and wondering what the hell had happened. Shards of rock and twisted metal blasted through the bunker entrance, penetrating my jungle fatigues and embedding themselves in my body. It felt like someone had just shoved a thousand hot pokers in me. It hurt like hell!

Inside the bunker, it was pitch black. I couldn't see my hand in front of my face. With a groan, I forced myself up to a sitting position and like a kid playing blind man's bluff, immediately started searching the ground surrounding me for my weapon. Finding my vintage World War II M-2 Carbine Rifle, I placed it across my lap and immediately pushed the selective fire switch forward, into the "Full-Auto" Position. My heart was pounding like a High School Bass Drummer at a band recital. I thought it was going to rip itself right out of my chest!

"What the fuck is going on," I yelled out to my bunker partner, who was only a few feet away.

"Shut up!" He shouted back. His voice was muffled and it seemed like he was speaking from a long distance away. I was disoriented and in pain but I had to shake it off and quickly...my life depended on it!

Just then, something warm started to run down my cheeks. It was probably sweat, sweat from the oppressive heat here at Lac Thien. I reached up and tried to brush it away with the palm of my left hand, but it didn't feel like sweat, it was too viscous!

Boom! A second concussion wave threw me back up into the air. I landed with a groan. Searing waves of pain penetrated my ears from the noise of the explosion. It was as if a grenade had just gone off inside my head. Lung choking dust and fragments of debris blew in through the bunker entrance. Hoping to reduce my exposure to the rock and shrapnel entering the bunker, I quickly pushed myself backwards towards the wall, pressing my back flat against the sandbags.

Concussion and explosion followed one after another in a never ending series of bone shattering detonations until suddenly, all went quiet. I tried listening for strange sounds outside the bunker, sounds that would tell me what the hell was going on, but my ears were still ringing from the explosions.

Based on my time in country and prior experiences, I knew that a massive bombardment like this was just a prelude to a ground attack! The Gooks would never waste that much ordnance and not come in after us!

"We're in deep shit," I yelled out to my buddy. "They're gonna be coming in now!"

The dead silence outside was suddenly broken by the sound of a high pitched siren. "What's with the siren, what the fuck is going on," I screamed out!

Just then, I caught a glimpse of a shadowy figure running by the entrance to our bunker yelling "Gooks in the wire, Gooks in the wire!"

"Shit," I said to my buddy, "they're not coming, they're here!"

There were about a dozen bunkers spread out in this football field sized area of Lac Thien. Each bunker was about twenty feet long, eight feet wide, seven feet tall, was covered with sandbags filled with dirt and had one and only one entrance. Spaced twenty to thirty yards apart, they were built with their entrances facing different directions. This would prevent the enemy from penetrating the wire, running down a line of bunkers and throwing grenades into each opening. The layout of the bunkers was well thought out but the barb wire protection that isolated the bunker complex from the jungle beyond was almost non-existent. At best, it was no more than a strand or two of wire.

My grandmother could have walked through this wire, untouched, never having scraped her legs on the razor sharp points.

"We gotta get outta here," I yelled out. "Once they get through the wire, we're dead! All they have to do is drop a grenade in here or sit on top of the bunker and pick us off as we run out."

"Jerry just back from Lac Thien"

My memory instantly flashed back to the advice my buddy Jerry gave me early that morning, just before our convoy pulled out for Lac Thien, "If they hit you," he said, "Fight Outside the Bunkers," and so we would!

By the grace of God, Jerry had survived Lac Thien for three months, an eternity by anyone's standards. He told me about the nightly insanity and terror...he warned me to stay away, but I wouldn't listen. I believed his warnings to be nothing more than the ranting of a man who'd smoked too many nickel bags...after all, how bad could it be?

"Jack preparing to Leave for Lac Thien "

"If we stay in here, we're dead," I yelled out to my buddy.

"What do you want to do Doc?" my friend yelled back.

"We gotta clear out any Gooks near the bunker then take our chances outside," I replied.

"OK," I said… we gotta roll two grenades out the bunker about two seconds apart. The first has to go out about five or six feet and the second about fifteen feet and stop. When they go off, they should kill any Gooks on the roof or near the bunker."

"After the second grenade goes off, I go out firing a burst in front of me to kill anything that's still alive. I'm gonna turn left, fire another short burst then left again and spray the top of the bunker as I'm climbing up the bunker wall. You do the same but you turn right after getting out. Don't spray the top or you'll kill me because I should get there before you."

"If we go out the bunker too fast after the second grenade goes off, we're gonna eat shrapnel. Actually, you won't eat it, I will," I said.

"Shit Doc, if we screw up, we're dead."

"No shit!" I replied.

"You gotta get the grenade out the opening." If either of us messes up and it bounces back in, we're dead."

"OK Doc."

Adrenalin had now pumped me up into a near "junkie like state." I was going out of the bunker and fight for my life but, strange at it seemed, I didn't give a damn whether I lived or died!

"OK, we pull the pins together, release the handles together…then we count. I throw mine out on three and you on four. That should give us three seconds before the first one goes off. You gotta throw it out about ten to fifteen feet, no more! If it goes any further it won't do any good. Got it?"

"Ok Doc, shit, I got it."

I could hear the escalating fear in his voice. Mine was no less real.

"Pull Pin"

We each grabbed a grenade. "OK, pull pin."

"Pin pulled Doc."

"Release handle!" I heard the metal handles being ejected from the grenades. Screaming out at the top of my lungs, one….two…three…I leaned out over the bunker entrance and gave mine a light toss. Pulling back from the opening, I felt his body brush past mine as he threw his.

"OK," he yelled.

"Get back," I screamed as we flattened ourselves onto the back of the bunker. I grabbed my carbine which was loaded with two, thirty round back-to-back banana clips. My ammo pouch was already over my shoulder

6

and was jammed with twelve more magazines. I had almost five hundred rounds of thirty caliber ammo on me. I hoped it would be enough.

The first grenade went off and the concussion almost buckled my knees. In the blink of an eye the second one went off. I immediately turned left, pointed my weapon out the door, yelled "let's go" then fired a sustained burst of about ten rounds as I exited the bunker. In the excitement, I forgot to follow my own warnings and wait a second or two after the second grenade went off. If there was any shrapnel that hit me from the second blast, I didn't feel it…I was too pumped up to feel anything. Following close behind me, I heard my buddy screaming as he exited the bunker. I turned left and fired a short burst of five or so rounds.

In the distance, I caught a glimpse of figures, silhouetted by the muzzle flashes and explosions, moving about in the darkness.

A short burst of rounds went off to my right. Looking immediately up and over my left shoulder, I pointed my weapon at the top of the bunker, just above the entrance and fired another short burst. Two, maybe three strides and I was on top of the bunker. I sprayed the top from the front to the rear until my magazine was empty.

I hoped that I'd killed anyone who might be on top but there was no way of telling, it was too dark! About the time I squeezed the last round off, I heard another short burst go off below and to my left. As my buddy came running up to the top, we ran into each other. "Doc?"

"Yeah, it's me. I have to reload."

"Me too. You OK?"

"I'm OK Doc."

I pushed the magazine release lever, pulled out the empty magazine, reversed it and tried to push the fresh one into the receiver housing, but in the pitch black of night, I couldn't see the opening; I had to feel for it. After fumbling for a few precious seconds, I felt it slide in and heard that familiar metallic click, indicating that it was locked. Pulling back on the charging handle, I released it, chambering the first round.

"I'm loaded," I yelled out.

"Me too" was the reply from the darkness.

"I'm going to the far end of the bunker and spray both sides as I walk, then I'll spray the end. You stay here and hold this end."

"OK Doc."

I slowly walked towards the far end of the bunker and sprayed both sides with five and ten round bursts. After emptying one magazine, I ejected it onto the roof of the bunker, went down onto one knee, reached into my ammo bag, pulled out a fresh magazine and locked and loaded it.

I had an idea of where the end of the bunker was but in all the confusion of firing and reloading, I wasn't really sure, so I slowly placed one foot in front of another and didn't rest my full weight on the front foot until I felt something solid under it. On my fifth step, I felt nothing under my front foot so I backed up a step, pointed my carbine downwards and emptied thirty rounds into the area just beyond the end of the bunker. I swapped in a fresh magazine then waited, waited for something to happen.

There was firing all around me and heavy firing in the distance. Green tracers from enemy machine guns lit up the blackness of the early morning hours. Red tracers from our M-60 and 50 caliber machine guns responded. Small explosions from grenades and grenade launchers could be heard everywhere.

"You OK," I yelled out?

"I'm OK Doc. I can't see a damn thing."

"Me neither," I replied. "If you hear or see anything, challenge it. If it don't answer, then blow it the fuck away."

"Ok Doc!"

I heard the thump of mortars leaving their launch tubes… but whose mortars were they? A few seconds later I heard pops in the sky and suddenly, night became day. They were illumination flares.

"Illumination Flares over Lac Thien"

"Charlie owned the night...we owned the day"

"It was a familiar phrase used by the troops in Vietnam. Borne of the type of warfare chosen for us by the powers to be in Washington, D.C., it had great meaning to many of us. On this night, in this place in Vietnam, it was "Spot On True!"

A quick visual scan around me revealed a number of people in the distance, on top of their bunkers. I scanned as quickly as I could, knowing the flares would soon burn themselves out. About fifty yards away, I saw men in strange uniforms running in my direction so I aimed at them and emptied my thirty round magazine. Two or three of them dropped to the ground. I reloaded.

Just then, the flares went out!

My buddy and I remained separated at either end of the bunker for what seemed like hours. We watched, waited and prayed that the next bodies to come by would be friendly.

"I'm coming back to you," I yelled out, as I crawled back to the other end of the bunker. "Let's sit here, back to back till its light, this way we cover each other and they won't be able to get us."

"OK Doc, that's a good idea."

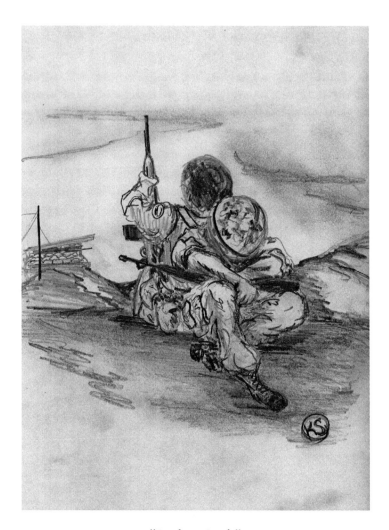

"Back to Back"

When the first rays of light broke over the horizon, I could see enemy bodies scattered everywhere. Four of them were close by our bunker, two in front and two to the right of the entrance. "Let's check out these bodies. I'll take these two, you take the other two."

"OK Doc."

I walked up to the nearest body. He was lying face down and was wearing a tan uniform with black rubber sandals. The back of his shirt was stained with blood. Alongside him was an AK-47. I walked up and kicked away his weapon then watched him intently for a few seconds. There was no movement. He's probably dead, I thought. I should probably roll him over to make certain but what if he's playing possum? This could end up in a hand to hand contest and that was something that I wanted to avoid so I fired a burst of three rounds into him and three into his buddy a few yards away.

"What are you doing Doc," my buddy screamed out?

"Do you want to take a chance that these guys are just playing dead?" A few seconds later, I heard two bursts of fire go off in rapid succession!

"Making Sure"

It was over. We had survived the night. A quick check of our convoy personnel revealed a few scratches and scrapes and minor shrapnel wounds but nothing serious. I was the most seriously injured of the group.

I treated the injured then tried to patch myself up. I had puncture wounds in at least a half dozen places. Luckily for me, the fragments were large enough to be seen and I pulled them out with a pair of forceps. It hurt like hell trying to get them out but worse than the pain of pulling them out was the pain that I felt when I poured rubbing alcohol over each puncture. Searing waves of pain shot through my body the likes of which I'd never felt before. It was as if I'd just stuck my finger into a wall outlet. The pain was excruciating!

My hands were covered with blood, blood that I wiped off my face a few hours earlier. I guessed that the explosions had damaged my eardrums. There was little that I could do to treat them except jam some cotton into my ear canals to keep any additional dirt from entering.

The lieutenant in charge of our convoy asked if I wanted to be Medivaced out because of my injuries. Although painful, my wounds were not life threatening and would heal once I was back at camp, besides, the convoy needed a medic and I would never desert the guys who I came here with unless I was near death. I took my medical oath to the men seriously when I said that I would protect them with my life.

I refused the Medivac!

It was time for us to go. Our convoy had to get back to Camp before dark. I shook hands with the guy who I shared one of the scariest nights of my life with and we hugged. "Take care man," I said with a lump in my throat.

"You too Doc, and thanks." I gave him the fisted hand salute as our convoy departed. I never knew his name and never saw him again.

CHAPTER 1
THE RIDE HOME

Our convoy pulled out for the long, dangerous trip back to Camp. After traveling less than two hundred yards, the lead truck entered the dark green, unforgiving jungle that surrounded Lac Thien and, like Lemmings, we followed close behind.

The adrenalin rush from the firefight only hours before had dissipated, and with it my ability to mask the pain from my wounds. With every bounce, dip and suspension crunching hole that our truck dropped into, I grimaced in pain.

"Leaving the dirt road in Lac Thien and entering the bush"

"Into the Bush"

There were no roads here, only paths through the jungle that looked like goat trails. Our convoy wound its way through undergrowth so thick that we literally had to stay within sight of the rear bumper of the truck in front of us, lest we get lost. In many areas, the vegetation was so thick that we couldn't see the truck in front of us. Sudden stops or slowdowns by any vehicle in the convoy often led to bone crunching collisions. We were like bumper cars in a blind arcade!

"The jungle envelopes us"

In some areas, the vegetation actually came in through the open windows of our truck as we crawled through the matted undergrowth and vines. Conditions were ripe for an ambush at any point in our jungle trek. I was just waiting for someone to stick an AK-47 through the open window of our truck and waste us.

Two torturous hours later, the jungle suddenly parted and the terrain changed from a lush green into a rocky, lifeless landscape that looked like the surface of the moon. It was so uneven that I was convinced a mountain goat couldn't traverse it let alone our trucks, but somehow, they did.

'The road near camp. This is one of the better parts of superhighway QL 21 that stretched from Camp Swampy to Lac Thien"

During the long drive back to camp, the dust and dirt blowing through the cab of my "Deuce-and-a-half" combined with the coagulating blood from my puncture wounds and created a half dozen or so hideous, raised, ant hill like protrusio ,rom my body. It was a nasty sight!

Six hours later, we passed through the gates of Camp Swampy and into relative safety. I was glad to be home. Here, I knew that it would be difficult for the gooks to get through the multiple layers of Barb, Concertina and Trip Wire that surrounded us. I was looking forward to a good night's sleep!

"Camp Swampy Wire"

The feelings of security provided by the massive amounts of wire was however a false one at best! A determined enemy could only be slowed up by such measures…never stopped!

Inside the medical bunker, I was greeted by one of my best friends… fellow medic, JC. After removing my blood stained and perforated jungle shirt, he took a quick look at me and said, "What the fuck happened to you?"

After telling him, his response was, "you gotta be shittin me. Hit the showers then come back and I'll clean your wounds then sew you up."

In the shower, men stared at me as though I were a Leper. "Hey Doc, what the fuck happened to you?"

My answer was "Lac Thien." No other explanation was needed.

I scrubbed my scabs with a washcloth and a bar of Lux Soap until the reddish brown protrusions came off and fresh blood started to flow again. Back at the medical bunker, JC cleaned my wounds with peroxide and sterile water then sewed me up, but the damage had already been done.

The open wounds had festered for more than twelve hours with dirt from combat the night before and from the long, dirty drive back to camp.

I injected myself with a massive, double dose of procaine penicillin and took double oral doses of penicillin for the next thirty days, hoping to fend off the inevitable infection. I didn't want to be Medivaced out to a hospital, which was the normal procedure for men who contracted massive infections. Most men, whom I Medivaced out for that very same reason, never returned to the unit. They were all sent home and I didn't want to go home.

That night, I lay on the wooden framed canvas cot in the medical bunker and tried to sleep but couldn't. Every time I closed my eyes, I felt my body being tossed up into the air from the explosions the night before. Uncomfortable with lying on a cot, I slid off onto the wooden planked floor for the remainder of the night. There I relived the explosions and firefight and the words that I uttered less than 12 hours before, "Pull pin… release handle… 1…2…3…throw."

I wondered how my buddy from the bunker last night was doing. Was he still alive? Would he make it through another night? I never did get his name. What a fucking war!

Somewhere between my concerns for my buddy at Lac Thien and my flashbacks, I fell asleep. I was awakened by Paul Skerritt, my buddy from the radio room when he came on shift at about 5 AM.

"Hey Jack, what are you doing on the floor?" he yelled out.

He repeated his question again and again until I awoke. With difficulty, I rose to my feet. Everything on my body ached, except for possibly my fingernails. "What are you doing on the floor," he repeated? I had no answer.

Just after sunrise, I was driven to base camp, where the battalion surgeon examined me. After irrigating both ears, he peered inside with his Otoscope and confirmed what we both knew to be true, both eardrums had been damaged by the explosions.

"It'll take some time to heal," he said. "We need to keep them clean."

He put in antibiotic eardrops and plugged my ear canals with cotton. I would have to remove the cotton daily and put in fresh drops.

Back at camp, my ears healed quicker than I expected. Within two weeks, both ears and the puncture wounds in my chest were healing nicely. Within a month, I was physically sound but mentally, I would flash back to that night at Lac Thien for years to come.

CHAPTER 2
FOUR YEARS EARLIER

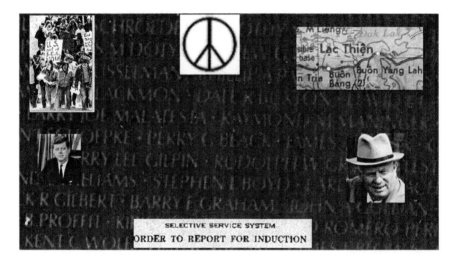

"The 60's"

Four years earlier, I was a part of the 60's generation...that fun loving, inquisitive, soul searching, disbelieving, protest ready, part hippie, part straight, group of individuals who challenged authority, ignored dogma and worshipped rock n' roll.

We were conformists and we were non-conformists...we sported crew cuts and we grew pony tails...we wore polished oxfords and we strapped on Hippie Sandals...we dressed in Leisure Suits or we pulled on a pair of beaded jeans...we protested and we accepted...we lived in communes and we lived with our parents...we were inducted into the military and we left for Canada...we burned our draft cards and we fought in Vietnam. We were a generation in search of itself!

The "Establishment" labeled us as either "Straight" or "Hippie." To them there was no in-between. You were either "with" the Establishment or "against" it.

Martin Luther King Jr., John F. Kennedy, Nikita Khrushchev, Civil Rights, Riots, the Cuban Missile Crisis, bomb shelters, hating Communists and being drafted were all part of our everyday lives. We watched as Martin Luther King and John F. Kennedy struggled to make life better for all Americans…we mourned at their tragic assassinations.

In high school, we were taught to hate Communists and reject Communism. Communism, we were told was the single greatest threat to the existence of the American Way of Life. Pictures of Nikita Khrushchev pounding his shoe on the podium of the United Nations General Assembly and those of Russian Ships carrying nuclear missiles to Cuba unfolded before us on the evening news. Fear, tension and foreboding were part of our lives.

The "Beach Boys," "Mamas and The Papas," "Rolling Stones," "Jefferson Airplane," Phil Oakes, Bob Dylan, Barry McGuire, "Four Tops," "Martha and the Vandellas," James Brown, Wilson Pickett and the "Fifth Dimension" were but twelve of the scores of incredible groups that produced the sweetest music on earth in the 60's. Songs like "Eve of Destruction" and "Draft Dodger Rag" protested our involvement in the war while "The Age of Aquarius" proclaimed our new era of self-awareness. Music and lyrics reflected the joy, hope, fear, turmoil and changes that were taking place in America.

Our moral principles were drummed into us by our parents and reinforced by our teachers. These principles were challenged daily by our peers on college campuses, in high school classrooms, at soda fountains, on school busses, at athletic fields and public and private forums as small as a two-person conversation or as large as an encounter at Woodstock. We were torn between our teachings and our friends, between our hopes and our fears, between the wisdom of our parents and the inexperience of our youth, between our hopes for peace and the realities of war.

For young men of draft age, there was only one issue, Vietnam! Would we be drafted? What would we do if we were drafted?

These were monumental questions for an 18, 19 or 20 year old to fathom, let alone to answer. Our parents, like most parents, hated the war. They couldn't understand its purpose (we still can't) yet believed for the most part that military service was an honorable duty. They lived through and served in "The Last Good War," World War II, where objectives, strategies and policies were clear, where the outcome of losing the war was catastrophic and where commitment and sacrifice was expected by all. They tried to apply those principles and ideas to Vietnam and came up short. Some parents hoped to keep their sons in school and thereby avoid the draft, others believed that volunteering for the armed forces was the duty of their son(s); still others believed that if drafted, their son(s) should serve. Few encouraged draft resistance or draft dodging.

Automatic military exemptions were given to married men with children, as were full time students. Men hurried to the alter and chose to immediately start families, hoping to have that first child before the draft board snatched them up. Others chose the "2S" Student military deferment route. Enrollments in college, graduate and technical schools were up. High School graduates sought sanctuary from the Selective Service in college; college graduates sought the same sanctuary in graduate school. Alumni of graduate schools sought a last ditch hiding place in post graduate school. For all but the married man with children, however, it merely delayed the inevitable.

The Selective Service System was like a giant wood chipper, with no heart, no conscious, no soul, only an insatiable appetite for men. As the scale of the war intensified, so did the efforts of the Selective Service. More men were needed, monthly draft quotas increased; the massive wood chipper was running at supersonic speed, trying to fill the need for ever larger troop commitments in Vietnam.

We were terrified, scared and confused. Parental and peer pressure was incredible, "go/don't go," "enlist/evade." Nightly, we watched news footage of military operations in Vietnam. Cameramen caught in the midst of firefights captured the terror, confusion, pain, loss and courage inherent in such confrontations. Phrases like "Body Count," "Body Bags," "Kill Ratios" and "Fields of Fire" became familiar to us. Saigon, Khe Sanh, A Shau Valley and Pleiku were no longer just names on a map of a country located 12,000 miles from the east coast of America, they were places where Americans were fighting, suffering and dying.

Time, Life and Newsweek gave front-page coverage to our finest moments and our worst nightmares. Protesters protested it and soldiers fought in it. It was a time of great confusion for our country but especially for those of us of draft age.

For most eligible men, the wait to be drafted was short. In August of 1967, the wood chipper found me. I was going to college part time at night. This did not qualify me for a 2S student deferment, my classification was 1A (Ready to serve). As I read the now famous "Greetings from the President of the United States Letter," a cold chill ran through me. Little did I know that my "Vietnam Odyssey" was about to begin.

"A Sample Greetings from the President of the United States Letter"

For the past 6 months, I'd been going to the chiropractor because of back problems. Much of the time I walked hunched over like an old man afflicted with Arthritis. What was I to do? How could I possibly survive the physical requirements of the military with my back being in such bad condition?

My chiropractor wrote a letter to the Selective Service, describing my condition. I hand carried it to my induction physical in Newark, New Jersey in October of 1967. There, I handed it to a physician who after reading it, promptly crumpled it into a ball and threw it into a nearby garbage can saying, "We'll fix your back problems for you son!"

I was speechless! He hadn't examined me, how could he make such an assumption? After completing my series of eye, ear, heart, lung, foot, butt and everything else exams, I was pronounced, "Fit as a fiddle and ready to go." As I hobbled out of the physical exam building towards my waiting bus (to take me back home) I reflected on my newly acquired physical status, "Fit as a Fiddle!"

In 1967, 1968 and 1969 rejections of armed forces induction candidates due to physical problems were rare. Men with flat feet, men who were grossly overweight, men who were underweight, men with heart murmurs...all went. The joke of the day was that if you had two eyes, ears, arms and legs, you qualified. Examining physicians told candidates with flat feet that they would be given arch supports, overweight candidates would be put in special "fat platoons" and the weight run off them, underweight candidates would be fattened up. Whatever was wrong with you, the Army or Marines had a fix for it.

A candidate standing next to me had only one testicle. He was told that one was sufficient. During physical exams, some men tried faking homosexuality; others tried making themselves sick by making rectal suppositories from a bar of hand soap then inserting it … giving them a low grade fever. Any and every trick possible was tried. During the early to mid 1960's, some of them got away with it, but examining doctors soon learned the tricks. Fool me once shame on you, fool me twice shame on me. The doctors were never shamed again.

Between August 1964 and February 1973, 1,766,910 men were inducted into the armed forces by the Selective Service. This figure excludes volunteers.

I never thought about draft dodging or going to Canada. I knew that if called, I would serve. Since I was declared physically fit, I decided to explore my options for enlisting in one of the armed services. I spoke to the Navy, Air Force and Army Recruiters. I bypassed the Marines because I wasn't sure that I could make it through their basic training. My first choice was Navy and nuclear subs, but the six year commitment was more than I was willing to donate to the cause of freedom and peace. The Air Force wanted four years and the Army three. If I enlisted in the Army, I would get my choice of jobs and they would postpone my induction until January of 1968, allowing me to complete my college semester, so I chose the Army and enlisted. My selected job was "Combat Medic."

I completed my fall semester at Middlesex County College just before Christmas. The day after completing my General Chemistry Final Exam, I went to speak to my Chemistry Professor, Doctor Spano. He was a great teacher and I considered him to be a good friend and mentor. I consulted with him every step of the way after receiving my draft notice. During my last discussion with him, he tried lifting my spirits by telling me that my final grade was an "A". The "A," he said stood for Army. I managed to crack a small smile. His parting words were to take care of myself and come home safely. Did he know something that I didn't?

In early January, I reported to the Perth Amboy, New Jersey Selective Service Office at 6 AM, there to be transported to the Newark Induction Station. At 11 PM that evening, a bus load of us departed the Newark Induction Station for our next destination, Fort Dix, New Jersey and basic training.

CHAPTER 3
FORT WHERE?

I completed basic training in April 1968. It was a grueling, challenging, heart breaking, eye-opening experience for a twenty year-old who was overweight, out of shape, always sheltered by his grandparents and who exuded the confidence of a turtle walking past a soup factory. In the eight short weeks that spanned February and March, I was painfully transformed from a one hundred eighty five pound amorphously shaped Pillsbury Dough Boy into a finely sculpted, one hundred fifty pound, self assured soldier. Never had I faced such challenges. Basic training forced me to depend on, count on and trust in the only person who I could turn to in times of need, and trust in times of doubt, me! Never was I more proud of my accomplishments, my graduation and my uniform.

At the conclusion of graduation ceremonies, I eagerly returned to the barracks, where my unopened orders for Advanced Individual Training awaited me. I would be bound for Fort Sam Houston in Texas for twelve weeks of medical training. There, I would be taught the basic skills necessary to become a "Field" or "Combat" Medic and upon graduation, would be qualified to function equally well in a hospital, dispensary, or battlefield. At least that's what I thought!

I grabbed the nine by twelve inch manila envelope off my bunk, tore off the end and pulled out my orders. With the speed of a cat hopping off a hot frying pan, I scanned the document, looking for my name. About half way down the page, I saw it, "Manick, Jack, A." As I read the text to the right of my name, my jaw dropped open like a Venus Fly Trap looking for its next victim, only this time I was the victim.

The words read, "EM (enlisted man) to report to Fort Leonard Wood, Missouri." Fort Where, I said to myself? Shouldn't it say Fort Sam Houston Texas? I read the ten simple words over and over again, hoping to make sense out of the bastardized, abbreviated army version of a sentence. Why did it say Fort Leonard Wood? Maybe it was a typo or a transcription error. Maybe I was being routed to Fort Sam Houston via Fort Leonard Wood, just like the airlines do when they route you to your final destination via intermediate stops, maybe!

Being told never to question orders, I didn't, but I still had a bad feeling about it. After packing my duffel bag, I and thirty or so other basic training graduates boarded a Greyhound Bus bound for the Philadelphia Airport. The ride to Philly was relatively short and awfully quiet. Most of us just stared out the window, chatted quietly or tried to sleep.

As the bus neared the airport, I started feeling a bit nervous. This would be my first ever plane flight and I was scared, plenty scared. I shouldn't have been, after all, the army had trained me to handle difficult and life threatening situations so this should be a breeze, right? Not so! Images of crashed, burning jetliners and mangled bodies flashed through my mind, images that I had seen on television over the past years, images of planes that had crashed on takeoff or landing. I felt as if I was living the last few seconds of my life.

Would the crash of my plane make the evening news? Would my body be burned to a cinder or simply reduced to "Chopamatic" sized pieces that would be scooped into a plastic garbage bag? In a battlefield, with a weapon in my hand, I had at least a modicum of control over whether I lived or died but in a plane; I was totally dependent on the pilots, the mechanics and God. I felt helpless!

As I sat at the gate and stared at the other waiting passengers, I wondered if I was the only "first time flier." They all looked so calm and composed. I tried not to show the fear that had welled up inside me; after all, I couldn't let the civilians see fear in the face of one of their military personnel, so I tried to act Kool.

My seat assignment was on the aisle, about half way into the coach section. After stowing my saucer cap and overcoat in the overhead compartment, I sat down, buckled my seatbelt and waited… and waited… and waited. I wasn't quite sure what I was waiting for, until the front door to the plane suddenly closed, sealing us inside. I listened intently as the chief stewardess reviewed the safety procedures with us, including water landings. What the hell did water landings have anything to do with our "Over Land" flight to St. Louis, I thought? Shit! That scared me even more.

Finally, I heard an engine start and we started moving backwards. Shouldn't we be going forward, I thought? A few seconds later, we stopped our backwards movement, paused for a moment then started forward.

Well, I thought, at least we're going in the right direction. After five to ten minutes of stop and go, a voice came over the PA.

"This is the captain, cabin attendants, please be seated for takeoff."

Oh shit, I thought, here we go.

I imagined that my takeoff experience would be similar to that of the Coyote being strapped into an Acme Rocket Sled that was about to accelerate from zero to 500 miles per hour in three seconds, but it wasn't. It was a nice, smooth acceleration. It wasn't what I expected it to be.

My concentration was centered on the window, two seats to my right. I stared at the buildings and objects that flashed by, trying to judge how far down the runway we'd traveled and how much of the concrete pavement still remained. After what seemed like an eternity, the front of the plane began rising and the coach section followed. It was a rather pleasant feeling. The landing, hours later, was just as smooth and uneventful. I'd always been terrified of flying and it turned out to be a breeze.

After checking in at Fort Leonard Wood, I questioned the sergeant at the reception desk, asking if this was an intermediate stop on the way to Fort Sam Houston or if medical training was being taught in Fort Leonard Wood.

After staring at my orders for what seemed like an hour, he said "You got bad orders, you should' a been sent to Fort Sam, but don't worry, as long as you're here, we'll make you an engineer."

"Sergeant," I said, "when I enlisted, I was guaranteed Medical Training and that's what I want."

"You a wise guy private," he said in a nasty tone?

"No sergeant, just looking to get the training that the army and I agreed upon. Sergeant, I'd like to speak to the commanding officer about this."

With that, he bolted from his chair with my orders in hand and stomped out of the room. Within a minute or so, he returned and beckoned at me to follow.

We entered the office of the lieutenant in charge, where I promptly came to attention and saluted. Peering at me across a large, wooden pock marked desk was a slovenly dressed 2'nd Lieutenant who appeared to be in his early twenties. He had a look on his face that said "I really don't want to be here."

I explained my situation to him and in a nasty tone he exclaimed, "I can change these orders. I can keep you here if I want to, Private!"

The intonation on the word Private made me feel like I was little more than a mass of dog poop on the bottom of his shoes that he hadn't yet scraped off. In basic training, I treated all officers with respect and they returned the courtesy. Here, it seemed like a one way street. I was surprised.

Realizing that if I didn't speak up, I would remain there and be trained as an engineer, I said, "Sir, my enlistment papers guarantee me medical training," at which point I pulled out a copy from my vinyl document carrier and handed it to him. It seemed to take him forever to read them. I wondered if he was purposely taking his time just to annoy me or if he was looking for a loophole in the document, one that would allow him to keep me there. Maybe he was reading impaired. No matter, my contract with the army was iron clad and legally binding on both parties and I could not imagine him finding a crack in it.

Finally, his gaze broke from the document and he stared at me. His face was grimacing with anger and his lips were twitching. It was as if someone had just stepped on his pet Goldfish!

"OK private, we'll cut you a new set of orders."

"Thank you sir" I said as I snapped to attention, saluted then left. I felt like cracking a large smile as I left his office but decided that would not be a good move, so I just kept a straight face.

The sergeant outside told me to report to a transient company while I awaited my new orders to be cut. Nothing was instantaneous in the army, especially cutting new orders. For the next six days, I waited in an old wooden barracks with a dozen or so "short timers." These men had just a few days left in the army and were waiting to be discharged. Most of them were sick of the army and just wanted to get home to continue with or start up their lives. I tried to keep a positive attitude in this environment, where so many men were so pissed off.

"Fort Leonard Wood Barracks"

To keep us busy, we were assigned work projects like cleaning up yards, lots and streams on the base. It was busy work, crap work. Any lousy assignment that no one else wanted, we got, but I didn't care. I knew that I had another 34 months to serve and I just wanted to get to Fort Sam. Six days later and yet another plane ride put me into San Antonio and Fort Sam Houston.

CHAPTER 4
FORT SAM

April in San Antonio and Fort Sam was warm and sunny…May was hot and sunny… June was blazing and sunny. It was a welcome change from the freezing temperatures, rain, snow and mud of Fort Dix in January, February and March.

My medical training here would be intense, graphic and "Hands On." The "Hands On," unfortunately meant, hands on the twenty nine other members of my class. We learned to start IV's, administer injections and draw blood. Our untrained, unpracticed and unsteady hands caused us to stick needles into bone, ligaments and tendons rather than muscle when giving each other injections and to miss, collapse or butcher arm veins when trying to draw blood or start IV's. By the end of week four of our twelve week course, our clumsy, inept and brutal efforts resulted in massive bruises and multiple puncture marks on our arms and butts. We looked like a group of "track marked junkies" rather than medics in training. Since practice makes perfect, however, we punctured, stuck and probed each other repeatedly, trying to perfect the skills that might one day save a fellow soldier's life.

Training was a combination of class instruction, field instruction and Physical Training. The heat of San Antonio made the class room experience a challenge. As the temperature continued its upward climb over the twelve week training course, it was increasingly difficult for us to keep our eyes open in the air condition-less classrooms. Instructors would walk up and down the rows of desks, slamming wooden meter sticks onto the desk of offending sleepers, snapping them instantly back to consciousness. It was however, a losing battle. The tendency of our bodies to fall asleep in the heat was overpowering. Try though I might, I too joined the ranks of the sleep offenders.

In class, we memorized anatomy, physiology, bacteriology and virology. We bandaged and splinted each other for hours and days on end, until we looked like mummies. Movies on amputation, sucking chest wounds, abdominal wounds, trench foot and gangrene made us sick. Pressure points, morphine use, bed pan and urinal use and on and on, day after day, the skills and knowledge were pounded into us. We even learned how to make a hospital bed with the sheets folded in a crisp 45 degree angle. By the end of the 12'th and final week of our training, we thought we knew it all... we didn't!

During the training day, we all wore the standard army cotton OD Green fatigues and black leather boots. Our headgear consisted of a helmet liner instead of the traditional baseball cap. These liners formed the internal support mechanism for the steel pots (helmet) that fit over it and that we wore into combat. It consisted of a fiberglass shell with a canvas and leather web harness and headband. It was lightweight and somewhat comfortable but it was also something else, it was a heat sink. The dark green colored shell absorbed the heat from the sun's rays, as any dark colored object would, and transferred the energy to the airspace beneath, superheating it. It literally cooked our heads. After eight weeks of training, my hair stopped growing. It didn't start growing again until six weeks later.

One of our field training exercises was to construct makeshift boats from wood framed canvas litters and sheets of canvas. We were then supposed to ford a river with them. It was yet another exercise in futility. During our river crossing, my boat sank and those of us in it, who were non-swimmers like me, struggled to make it safely to dry land.

During simulated combat field exercises, we carried each other in Firemen Carries or dragged each other around while on our hands and knees. We were given instructions on how to erect large hospital tents and we spent many hours erecting them only to have them partially or totally collapse on us. It was very frustrating.

At the beginning of our training, one man from each barracks was selected to be a "Barracks Sergeant" and four were selected to be "Barracks Corporals." These men were chosen for these posts most probably because their boot shining, clothes starching and sock folding abilities far exceeded that of the rest of us. It had nothing to do with their potential leadership qualities. On their sleeves, they wore sergeant and corporal stripes that were sewn onto black elastic armbands. These elastic rank bands could be put on and pulled off the sleeves of a fatigue shirt or field jacket much like a garter at a wedding.

While these jobs, in the army's view, were no doubt important in building leadership skills, most of the barracks sergeants and corporals soon transformed themselves into little dictators, obsessed with their temporary rank and intoxicated by their perceived powers over us. We soon learned to dislike them.

My barracks sergeant was Sergeant Neil X. His clothes were starched to a cardboard like consistency and he could polish a pair of combat boots into a patent leather like finish that could blind a sightless man in a dust storm. At morning inspection, the crease in his OD Green, cotton fatigue pants was sharp enough to cut a tree in half at fifty yards.

We obeyed these mini-dictators as if their rank was real and permanent. In reality, we tolerated them because we had no other choice. At graduation, half of our class was promoted to PFC (Private First Class). Sergeant Neil was one of them. I was another. Never was I as proud of anything as I was of that simple, yellow colored "V" shaped piece of cloth sewn onto my sleeve. The day that I received it, I must have grown four inches in height, just from pride. I was as happy as a pig in a mud wallow.

Even though Sergeant Neil and I were now on equal rank stature, I never approached him to tell him what an ass he was during training and how he had made so many of us so miserable. When we saw each other for what I thought was the last time, we nodded at each other, each recognizing the others achievement in being promoted. Little did I know that this would not be my last encounter with him.

After graduation, my orders were to report to the replacement depot in Frankfurt Germany for further assignment to the 97'Th General Hospital. Arriving at Rhein Main Military Airport in Frankfurt, I was immediately bussed to the replacement depot Mess Hall for chow. It was evening. As I neared the end of the serving line, my eyes beheld a sight that brought an enormous smile to my face. There, standing behind the line of servers was a soldier who was collecting empty stainless steel serving dishes and putting them on a cart. His fatigues were wet and covered with food debris and he looked very tired. It was PFC alias Sergeant Neil.

"Hey Neil," I yelled out. He turned his gaze towards me, smiled and just shook his head as if to say, yeah, they got me. At Fort Sam, neither he nor any of the other acting sergeants or corporals had to pull KP, like the rest of us. Seeing him wet, dirty, tired and on KP made up for the twelve weeks of crap he gave us. While everything that goes around does not always come around, this time it did! I never saw him again.

Chapter 5
The 97'th General Hospital

Germany Collage - A section of The Vietnam Veteran's Wall is in the background. In the foreground is A USAREUR(US Army Europe Pin)… my unit, a Conserve the Fighting Strength Pin(The Medics Motto), a Peace Sign(symbol of the 60's), The #13 Strasse that I used to take into the center of Frankfurt from the Hospital, me in Frankfurt and a small portion of the "Order to report for Induction Letter"

The 97'Th General Hospital was shaped like a large "H ". Three stories high and covered in white stucco, it was as clean inside as it was outside. My duty assignment was the Surgical Intensive Care Ward. It was a great work assignment and I loved my co-workers, my job and Germany. My primary work responsibilities were to take care of Post Operative Patients, maintain the equipment and keep the ward spotless and as close to sterile as possible.

I learned advanced patient care as well as how to maintain and operate respirators, autoclaves, aspirators and a myriad of other equipment. The respirators proved to be a real thorn in my side. After each use, they had to be disassembled, cleaned and re-assembled. The Bird Respirator was a nightmare to disassemble and reassemble because of the multitude of strange shaped plastic parts that had to be disassembled then reassembled in a specific sequence. It required "Erector Set like skills" and a good memory. Since I never successfully completed any erector set project at home, it took me weeks to master the Bird.

Bed pan duty was something I never got used to. It was a necessary part of hospital duty and was the most disgusting part of my job.

I was given a specific set of instructions on how to perform this. They were clear and concise and had to be executed sequentially. They were as follows:

- Remove bed pan from the patient and slide it immediately into paper bag especially made to house it
- Walk across the hall to the "Utility Room." The Bed Pan Sterilizer is located on right hand wall. (It was made of stainless steel with pipes and valves in various places and a large handle that protruded from the center)
- Read operating instructions on front of device. The instructions read as follows:
- To open, Grasp stainless steel handle and pull towards you
- Remove paper cover from bedpan and discard
- Slide bedpan into slot on door with opening facing away from you and the narrow end facing down
- Close door until you hear a click, indicating it is locked
- Using actuating handle/flushing valve, rinse the contents multiple times until all fecal and paper content have been washed down the drain
- Open steam valve and sterilize for 20 minutes
- Close steam valve and allow the pan to cool for 5 minutes before removing
- Remove bed pan

The process was simple, oh so simple and the instructions were complete and self explanatory. Nothing was left to chance. This would be a piece of cake and I was ready.

My first opportunity came sooner than I expected. After the patient made the deposit, I slid the bedpan out from under him and holding it at arm's length, quickly inserted it into the bag. I didn't want to look at the contents, the smell was bad enough. Taking my prize quickly across the hall, I opened the door to the bed pan machine, removed the paper cover and quickly slid it into the machine in the prescribed manner. Closing the door, I breathed a sigh of relief, literally. The hard part was done. The rest was just a matter of executing a few simple instructions, or so I thought.

I pulled down on the flushing valve once and let go. I could hear the water rush into the device. I then flushed it a second, a third, a fourth and a fifth time. The more the better I thought. It should be clean by now but I had to check to make sure before turning on the steam. If it wasn't and I steamed it, it would literally bake the contents onto the metal and make it almost impossible to remove. Standing in front of the bed pan cleaner, I grasped the long stainless steel door handle and gave it a tug. Nothing happened. I tried again, this time exerting some additional force. Nothing!

"Shit, it must be stuck," I thought. I grasped the handle with both hands and gave it an enormous tug. The door flew open and in that split second, a mass of water, feces and toilet paper came rushing at me. There was nowhere to run, no place to hide and no time to react. It hit me in the chest and almost knocked me to the floor!

The mixture of water, fecal matter and disintegrating toilet paper quickly spread across the floor. I shouted something profane, probably "Shit" or "Fuck me" or "Mother fucker," I don't remember which. Within seconds the medics and nurses from my ward across the hall came running into the room and stopped dead in their tracks. There I stood, soaked in water and covered with feces and toilet paper, with a look on my face that was most likely priceless. Most tried to hold back their laughter so as not to embarrass me any more than I already was, others couldn't help it and burst into uncontrolled laughter.

Sergeant Gaeta, my Wardmaster remained. Surveying my feces covered white uniform, he vainly tried to form a mean look on his face so as to discipline me but he just couldn't. He smiled at me and said, "Manick, what the hell did you do?" I explained and he just shook his head in disbelief saying, "after one or two flushes, you need to open the door to make sure that the contents have flushed down the pipe. Five or six times in a row are too much, especially if the drain has gotten clogged like it did here."

"Go and get some surgical scrubs, take a shower and come back when you're done."

"Thanks Sarge," I said as I stumbled off. The only saving grace in this embarrassing episode was I didn't have to clean up the fecal/toilet paper mess on the floor.

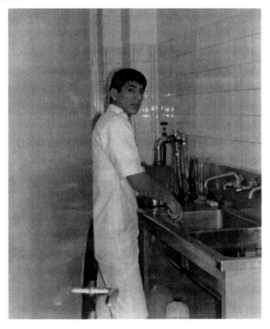

"A fellow Medic using the Bed Pan Sterilizer"

The food in the hospital was excellent. The German Chefs who cooked for us were gourmet cooks. Never had I been offered so many meal choices and all were delicious. Our barracks were old but in good condition and our small, two man rooms were comfortable.

Most of my off time was spent in Frankfurt. The Strasse (Trolleys) was my primary transportation mode into the city, until I bought a five speed bicycle. I loved to ride the Number Thirteen Strasse (or my bicycle) into the center of Frankfurt and have lunch or supper at the Bratwurst and Rheinwurst Pushcart Vendors. They would usually set up outside the Haupt Bahnhoff (Main Train Station and/or subway station). The Wurst was broiled over a bed of white hot charcoal on a Hibachi like grill and served on a small semi-hard roll. It was beyond delicious. To this day, I've never tasted its equal.

In college, I studied German and expected that it would help me but alas, the Germans spoke too quickly and my dialog was limited only to simple sentences, common words and phrases. The "locals" were not terribly friendly to us GI's, only the U.S. Dollar or German Mark opened a communications dialog. That however, was a small price to pay for being in such a great place. Life was good, the countryside beautiful, the food great, my off time exciting and my body weight increasing.

The 97'Th General Hospital was divided into functional areas called wards. Each ward had a Wardmaster (High ranking sergeant) to supervise the military non commissioned staff. Sergeant Augustine Gaeta was mine. He was a rather large man, in his late forties with almost jet-black hair and sporting an enlarged waistline. He was a consummate military and medical professional, seeking to uphold all military rules and regulations and religiously teaching us the skills necessary to provide the best possible care for the patients.

Before the start of each duty shift, we had an inspection that included a physical inspection of our person and a status report of patients who remained on the ward from the previous shift. We wore clean, white uniforms that were starched to a cardboard like consistency and highly shined black leather shoes. During these daily inspections, Sergeant Gaeta paid close attention to the luster and shine on our shoes. His personal inspection of us started at our haircuts and ended at our shoes.

While completing his inspection of me, he would slide his right foot next to my left, comparing the luster and brilliance of his shoes with mine. After staring at my shoes for what seemed like an eternity, he slowly shook his head in disappointment then looked me square in the eye and moved on to the next person in the inspection line. Day after day, week after week, try though I might, the shine and gloss on my shoes never approached the mirror like finish of his. I never learned his secret of creating that shine but after three months, a miracle happened. A buddy of mine discovered an alternate method to achieve that same shine with minimal effort. The secret was Glocoat Floor Wax. After spit shining my shoes with polish, cotton and ice water, I applied the floor wax. The results were dramatic and breathe taking. My shoes shone with the brilliance of a million-candle power spotlight. It was cheating but I didn't care!

I had him now!

At our next daily formation, he inspected my uniform, then moving his eyes to my shoes; he slid his shoe adjacent to mine. I dared not look down. My eyes instead were focused straight ahead and on his expression. He continued to stare downwards then, as his eyes met mine, he broke into a smile and moved on to the next person in line.

Later that day, I shared an elevator with Sergeant Gaeta. As the elevator door closed, I slid my right shoe up against his left, looked at his shoe, then looked up at him shaking my head. He smiled, the door opened and I left. I finally got the best of him!

"Nurses...Miss Dobbins and Miss.? Hiding from the camera"

The female nurses on our ward were young, smart, intelligent, friendly and beautiful. Most were civilian RN's, contracting to the US Army. Our head nurse was an army captain and a man. I don't remember his name, just as I've forgotten the names of most of the nurses. Miss Dobbins, Frausto and Jane Altemose are the only names that remain in my memory. They were all dear friends of mine and I shall always treasure the time that we spent together.

In late September a new medic came into our midst. His name was Curry. He was quiet and soft spoken and always had a serious look on his face. When he spoke, it was in a low tone, slowly and deliberately. Curry was an excellent medic. He always called me "Stick" and I never knew why. It certainly wasn't because of my low body weight.

During one of our day shifts in the hospital, a couple of the other medics and I were engaged in a conversation regarding Vietnam. One of our group remarked that he wouldn't mind going to Vietnam. Curry, overhearing this, walked over to us and asked us if we had any idea what we were saying and the consequences of what we were asking for. His face was contorted as he spoke to us and if possible, more serious looking than normal. The other medics looked at him, puzzled by his question. "Of course we know," was their answer.

"You don't know and you don't want to find out" was Curry's response. He then turned and walked away. Up to that point in time, none of us knew that Curry was a Vietnam Vet, now we knew.

"Jack in front of barracks"

Political rhetoric in 1968 told us that we had to "Stop the Communist Aggression that was taking over South East Asia." If we didn't stop it there, they said, it would be in LA the following Tuesday. Well, that's a minor exaggeration, they never mentioned LA! South Vietnam was under Communist attack and if it fell, all of South East Asia would go with it. Then on to LA!

I was a twenty year old with no worldly experience beyond that of my secluded and protected one and a half years of college. The political rhetoric meant nothing to me; I took it with a grain of salt.

I knew about the casualties in Vietnam, the KIA's and the body bags. I never heard about the MIA's and POW's, that information was kept under close wraps. My information came from Vets just returning from Vietnam and being stationed in Germany or from what I read in the Stars and Stripes Military Newspaper. As a medic, going to Vietnam, I thought, would be where I could do the most good at saving lives, so I volunteered.

Two weeks later, I was promoted to Specialist Fourth Class and one week later received my orders for Vietnam.

CHAPTER 6
NEWARK TO CAM RANH BAY
(PART 1)
SAN FRANCISCO HERE I COME

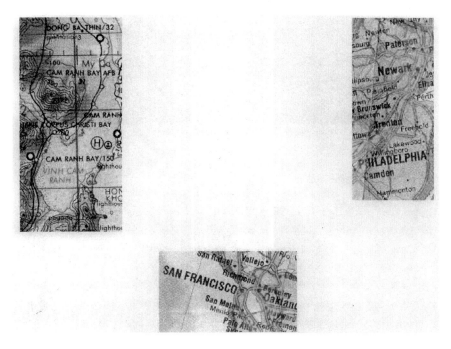

"Newark to Cam Ranh Bay, San Francisco here I come"

My thirty day leave passed all too quickly. At home, no one could understand why I volunteered to go to Vietnam. Why not stay in a safe place like Germany, they asked? Why take the chance of being killed?

With emotions at home running at peak levels, I just wanted to say good bye and get going. As the car I was in, pulled away from my grandparent's house, I didn't look back, didn't wave, I couldn't.

My orders read, " Asg to: US Army Oversea Replacement Station, Fort Lewis, Washington for further assignment to WOBR VN Trans Det EN APO San Francisco 96384." The date was January 4, 1969. The orders did not specify how I was to get to Fort Lewis, so I chose to fly from Newark to San Francisco then catch another flight from San Francisco to Seattle. There would be a seven hour layover in San Francisco, during which time I would visit my best friend Joe Glydon, who I hadn't seen in three years.

Joe and I attended Woodbridge Senior High School together. We were best friends because we were so alike, yet so different.

There was chemistry between Joe and I that neither of us could explain. It kept us tightly bonded as friends, for life.

In High School, we both were mild mannered, intuitive and non phys ed oriented. We tried to avoid or minimize participation in high school sports that involved violent physical contact like "Crab Soccer" or "Dodge Ball."

Crab Soccer was a bastardized form of soccer that was probably invented during the Spanish Inquisition as an alternate form of torture to the "Rack."

It involved two teams of players who sat on the hardwood floors of the School Gymnasium in "Crab-Like Fashion" and kicked or attempted to kick a four foot leather ball around on the floor until it crossed that area in the gym that was considered the opposing team's goal line. In reality, it rarely resembled an organized soccer game. It was in fact a testosterone proving ground where the jocks and animals in class had full and free reign to domineer, dominate, abuse and intimate all who would oppose them.

When the jocks could not kick the ball, they kicked anyone and everyone around them, knowing that there would be no repercussions for their actions. This was our Coliseum, complete with gladiators, hungry lions and Christians. As soon as the game commenced, Joe and I slowly crab walked backwards, away from the insanity. We hoped that our strategic withdrawal would not be spotted by the Gym Teacher or the other participants. Our goal was to get to the corner of the gym where the large folding doors were retracted and remain hidden there for the remainder of the game. Most times, no one took notice of our withdrawal, they were too busy competing for the testosterone championship…other times we became victims of the beasts.

Dodge Ball was another sport that we hated. There was nowhere to run and no place to hide. The best strategy was to get hit early and by someone who was not a Neanderthal.

Our Gym Teachers, Mr. Holloway and Mr. Lupo picked the sides, trying to put equal numbers of Neanderthals and homo-sapiens on either side, otherwise the game would be a slaughter from the get go.

For reasons yet unclear to me, the Neanderthals on either side always seemed to be the ones throwing the ball. They seemed to draw pleasure in not just eliminating opposing players but injuring them with their cannonball like throws. These testosterone giants were fearless in the gyms. At first glance, they appeared to be the perfect fighting machine, fearless, ruthless and with no sense of mercy or compassion. In point of fact, few of these Neanderthals ever served in the military. They seemed to be experts at escaping and evading the draft. Where did they hide? Did they lie to avoid being drafted? Did they marry and immediately have children to avoid induction? Did they run across the border into Canada?

The truth is known but to God and to them. It was in fact the Christians from the coliseum who were drafted or enlisted and served, many never to return again.

During the warmer months in high school, we were forced to run laps on the "Cross Country Course," two laps to be exact. This course was little more than a goat trail that started on flat terrain then wound its way upward through a heavily wooded area then down a steep slope to the start/finish line. It was almost a half mile long.

Joe and I hated to run. Our running skills rivaled that of two tortoises in high gear on a cold winter morning. As a result, we were always at the end of the pack of runners. Punishment for being one of the last five to finish the two lap run was to run another lap. I did that once and so did Joe. We vowed never to repeat that so we formulated a plan, a diabolical plan. It was simple in concept and flawless in execution.

We followed the pack to the top of the hill on lap one and as the trail passed through the forested area, we ducked into the woods and hid in the underbrush. While the rest of the pack continued their run, we recuperated from our one eighth mile run. No one saw us as we ducked into the woods. They were all too busy running to notice what we had done.

When the pack returned for lap two and the last man in line passed us, we jumped out and started running behind him. Fully rested, we effortlessly stayed behind them, then made our move to pass the five individuals in front of us. We then fell back into the pack and finished the run. We made ourselves look very, very winded so no one would suspect.

It was a brilliant tactical move, borne of desperation and fueled by good old American Ingenuity. We repeated it every time we ran the course. No one ever figured it out and we were never caught!

After high school graduation, I went to College in New Jersey and Joe to the San Francisco Art Institute. This was my only chance to see Joe before going to Vietnam. I wanted to surprise him so I didn't write and tell him I was coming. That was a big mistake!

I flew "Military Standby" to San Francisco aboard a United Airlines DC8. My seat assignment was in the last row, next to the galley and across from the bathrooms. The seats in my row butted up against a metal bulkhead, making it impossible for me to recline my seatback. The two seats to the right of me were unoccupied which meant I had no one to talk to except those passengers waiting to get into the bathrooms.

With no one to talk to or commiserate with, I started to feel isolated, frightened and a bit depressed. Thoughts flooded my mind…was this a one way trip for me…where would I be assigned…would I be captured… would I die…what was dying like?

Never had I felt so down, so depressed, so frightened and so helpless. I thought it ironic to be traveling to a foreign country, to fight a war, whose purpose I didn't understand, whose outcome I was unsure of and be rewarded with a seat next to the Outhouse.

No one spoke to me. People on the way to the bathrooms just passed by me as if I didn't exist. If they had to wait for toilet access and they happened to look my way, they stared right through me as if I was part of the bulkhead. For the next hour I just sat there, silently staring into the seat back in front of me, wondering why I was being treated like dog poop on the bottom of someone's shoes.

An hour and fifteen minutes into the flight, a stewardess who had been walking back and forth for the last hour stopped next to me, bent down at the knees so that we were face to face and said, "Hey soldier, what's your name?" She was an attractive brunette in her late twenties or early thirties. I was surprised that she was taking the time to stop by and say hello. No one else had!

"Jack," I answered in a low tone.

"Are you going to Vietnam," she asked? Holy shit, I thought, how did she know? I wasn't wearing a sign saying "Going to Vietnam," yet the look of fear and helplessness on my face must have told her the whole story. It was the same look that she must have seen on the faces of untold thousands of soldiers who had preceded me on the same path, to Vietnam!

She asked if she could sit next to me. Almost speechless, I quickly replied "Yes" as I moved aside to let her into the seat next to me. Why did she want to sit next to me, I was after all nothing more than a low ranking enlisted man on his way to a war that no seemed to care about and everyone wanted us out of?

We talked for what seemed like hours about everything and anything. Her voice was soft, calm and reassuring. Never again in our conversation did she mention Vietnam. At one point she asked one of the other stewardesses to cover her work while she stayed with me. I couldn't believe the amount of time she was spending with me. I didn't understand why.

Finally, she could neglect her work responsibilities no longer. I thanked her for taking the time to be with me. As she walked away, I realized for the first time that day, that I had a smile on my face. She brought me out of my depression, made my flight more enjoyable and took my mind off my final destination for a few precious hours.

After landing, I was the last passenger to exit the plane. As I walked down the aisle toward the forward exit, I noticed her standing by the door. She walked up to me, gave me a big kiss on the cheek, told me to take care of myself and come back safely. I almost started crying at that point but held back the tears; after all, I couldn't let her see one of America's finest crying. I thanked her again, turned and preceded into the terminal, thinking I hadn't just met a wonderful stewardess but had rather found an Angel in disguise.

It was a miserably cold and rainy day in San Francisco. Regardless of the weather, my objective was to find my friend Joe. The last letter I received from him had a return address of Sutter Street. Stowing my duffel bag in a locker at the airport, I took a bus to the San Francisco Downtown Bus Terminal. There, after asking and receiving directions to Sutter Street, I exited the terminal into a cold driving rain. My winter green uniform, wool overcoat and saucer cap, while providing excellent insulation from below freezing temperatures, offered little protection from the rain.

The beginning of Sutter Street was close by the terminal, which was a relief to me. I didn't relish walking miles just to get to it. I probably should have taken a cab to Joe's apartment but I wanted to save money and figured that it couldn't have been that far away by foot. I was terribly wrong and would pay dearly for it that day.

As I walked, the cold winter rain poured off my flat topped saucer cap, onto the collar of my wool overcoat and down my back causing chills to run up and down my spine. In hopes of stopping the flow of bone chilling water down my back, I pulled up the collar on my overcoat. This, I hoped would redirect the flow of water to the outside of my coat and also provide me with a windbreak from the cold air that was blowing on my neck.

Not so! Instead, it formed a highly efficient funnel that channeled all the water rolling off my cap directly down my back. It saturated not only my overcoat but the wool winter green jacket of my dress uniform, my shirt, underwear and pants. This additional water weight made me feel as though I was carrying a pallet load of cement blocks on my shoulders.

Slowly at first, then in ever increasing episodes, my body started shivering until I was shaking uncontrollably. The pace of my walking started to slow in direct proportion to the added water weight that I was carrying.

I followed Sutter Street as it wound its way up and down the hills of San Francisco. In roller coaster like fashion, the trough of one hill inevitably led to the crest of another which led to the trough of another and on and on in a never ending procession. After an hour and a half of walking, the numbers on the homes were not even close to the number of Joe's Apartment and there was barely enough time for me to walk back to the bus terminal, catch the airport bus and make my connecting flight to Seattle/Tacoma.

I hated to turn around but the army was not tolerant of those arriving late at a designated destination. It was a great disappointment for me to come three thousand miles and not see Joe but it was not to be!

I made it back to the airport just in time to catch my connecting flight to Seattle and Fort Lewis, Washington. So long Joe!

Next stop….. Seattle/Tacoma Airport and Fort Lewis.

CHAPTER 7
JUNGLE TRAINING

My plane touched down on the snowy runway at Seattle/Tacoma International Airport shortly before midnight. I exited through the first class gangway to a terminal that was as dark, clammy and devoid of life as the dark side of the moon. Even the late night janitorial staff had long since gone home to warm meals and comfortable beds. With heads hung low and eyes barely open, my fellow passengers and I stumbled down the maze of corridors like a herd of drunken cattle, blindly following the first passenger off the plane to what we hoped was the baggage claim area.

The sound of high heel shoes striking the hard ceramic floor reverberated in the echo chamber like confines of our walkway. Passengers too tired to lift their carryon baggage, simply dragged it behind them. The rhythmic "clacking" sound of metal and plastic luggage feet dragging across the uneven tile joints reminded me of the sounds that a train's wheels makes as it passes over uneven track joints.

Shops on either side of the jet way were dark; their lights having long since been turned off. Finally, the corridor opened into an immense area where large circular metal carousels were lined up next to each other. Suddenly, a flip board above one of them came to life. The rapid, chaotic movement of the flip cards continued for five or ten seconds until it finally spelled out our airline and flight number.

Like cattle drawn to a watering hole, we approached the metal giant and waited for the first pieces of luggage to appear. Time seemed to stand still until finally, the first bag dropped onto the stainless steel carousel and others quickly followed. My luggage was easy to spot, a large Olive Drab Duffel bag with the name Manick, Jack written across the center in black permanent ink. As it drew near, I grabbed the canvas handle with my right hand and in one fluid motion, hoisted it up onto my right shoulder. In Lemming like fashion, I blindly followed the other passengers out of the baggage claim area.

Immediately outside, but still within the terminal was a small white wooden booth. Above it was a sign that read "Fort Lewis." Inside, a half asleep sergeant was seated in a metal folding chair, his head supported in the palms of his hands and anchored to the desk by two vertically stretched arms bent at the elbow. Dropping my duffel bag to the floor, I startled him awake. Removing my orders from a package of paper, I handed it to him. After staring at them for at least 30 seconds, he ripped off one copy and told me to sit down and wait for transport.

Once again, I would be arriving at a military installation in the wee hours of the morning. I hated it. It happened at Fort Dix for basic training, at Fort Leonard Wood and now here.

During the day, Army installations are at best, large, busy and impersonal places. At night they change into something lonely, ominous and spooky.

After a thirty minute wait, my ride arrived. Exiting the terminal, I was greeted by a blast of arctic like air, snow and a howling wind. The drive to the fort was brief and devoid of traffic. Passing through the main gate, the tires on our vehicle crunched the ice-encrusted snow below. Outside the plowed areas, the snow appeared to be knee deep or more. "Shit," I said to myself.

I hoped that my stay at Fort Lewis would be a brief one, maybe a day or two to process the paperwork. As usual, I was wrong!

At the Reception Center, I presented my orders to a sergeant at the desk. He pulled off a set of orders and told me that my stay there would be two weeks, during which time I would take an "Intensive Jungle Training Course."

"A what," I said in a surprised voice as he handed me a pile of paperwork to fill out. "No one ever told me about a Jungle Training Course. I thought that Fort Lewis was just a way station, a Gas Station so to speak, on the road to Vietnam. "

"Shit................!"

How could anyone in their right mind want to conduct a Jungle Training Course under such conditions? A tropical setting, like Fort Polk, Louisiana would have made perfect sense but how could they possibly prepare me to survive in a tropical jungle by training me in this frozen hell?

The next morning I turned in my military clothing with the exception of my field jacket, baseball cap and gloves. I was issued three pair of jungle fatigues, two pair of jungle boots, socks and green underwear. The jungle fatigues, constructed of a lightweight ripstop nylon material, were extremely durable, porous, lightweight and were designed to dry quickly after becoming wet. They were as different from my previous issued 100% cotton fatigues as day is to night. The trousers contained two standard pockets and two cargo pockets. The Cargo Pockets were appropriately named, for they were designed to carry large amounts of material. Inside and anchored to the bottom of each pocket was a 1 ½ foot long nylon strap. It resembled a long, flat shoelace and I later learned that it was used to anchor shifting cargo in the pocket to your leg.

The jungle shirt was worn over the pants (not tucked in like the cotton fatigue shirt) and contained two top and two bottom pockets. The pockets were slanted and contained button down flaps to keep the contents in. This uniform closely resembled those worn by "Airborne Troops" in World War II. I liked the look.

The jungle boots were unusual in their construction. Normal combat boots were all leather and had a flat composite sole. The uppers on these strange looking boots were nylon-reinforced canvas. The lowers were still leather but with lugged soles and heels, much like that on the rock climbing shoes that I'd used in a different life. Designed specifically for hot, wet climates, these feather light boots dried quickly after being immersed in water thanks both to the porous uppers and the two drain holes in the leather lowers that allowed water to drain and wet feet to breathe. Though brilliantly designed, these new boots would cause me grief and pain for weeks to come.

This new clothing and footwear issue was ideally suited for tropical climates. In the snow and ice of Fort Lewis in January 1969, they were a disaster!

At 6 AM the following morning, we were awakened and ordered to fall out onto the street in front of our wooden barracks, wearing our newly issued jungle fatigues, gloves, baseball cap and field jacket. I didn't get to the barracks until almost 3 AM so by the time they woke me; I'd had all of two hours sleep. Stumbling out of the barracks, half asleep, I fell into formation on the snow-covered road.

Within seconds, the icy cold air passed through my jungle pants, shocking me awake. The longer I stood in formation, the worse it got. Slowly, oh so slowly, my teeth started to chatter as the cold worked its way upwards from my legs into my torso. Moments later, I was unable to control the staccato like gnashing of my upper and lower teeth. With my teeth chattering so much, it was difficult to form intelligible words.

The cold was far worse than anything I'd ever experienced in Germany. All that I could think about was getting warm and drinking something hot. What had I gotten myself into? Where was the Vietnamese Heat that I so desperately wanted?

The first day was a nightmare…a frozen nightmare! Most of our activities were outside. How my companions and I survived that day without frostbite is still a mystery to me. After returning to the barracks at day's end, we discussed how best to keep warm the following day. The group consensus was to put on all three pair of our issued jungle fatigues, one pair on top of the other. This layering, we hoped, would keep us warm. We were wrong!

In formation the next day, the icy cold wind penetrated the multilayered tropical clothing like a hot knife through butter but the added bulk of two additional uniforms made it difficult to walk, so we waddled around like Pillsbury Dough Boys with hemorrhoids. It was a pitiful and amusing sight.

By the morning of day three, we were out of ideas and expressed our concerns about freezing to our instructors. They promised us "Cold Weather Gear."

Marching us into a supply building, we expected to be issued wool pants and parkas; our smiles soon changed to frowns as they handed each of us one pair of rubberized, chest high coveralls. These, they insisted would keep us warm and dry. We slipped them over our jungle pants, under our field jackets and walked into the freezing temperature outside.

Within seconds, the rubberized coating froze solid, making it difficult to walk. There was no flex in the frozen rubberized material. As I walked, the coating started to crack then broke off into small pieces, making a terrible noise. The coating that did not fall off proved to be as effective a conductor of cold as any metal smelted by man. It did however have one positive attribute; it reduced the air infiltration to my body. This then was our "cold weather issue" and we would suffer with it for the remainder of our time at Fort Lewis.

The majority of the remaining ten days were spent outside, shivering and trying to stay warm. The most important part of our training was the familiarization and qualification with the army's newest weapon, the M-16 Rifle. During basic training, I used the M-14 Rifle. The M-16 was significantly lighter and made of black plastic and metal. It didn't have the clean lines and character of the M-14, was butt ugly and more closely resembled a child's play toy than a weapon of war. I hated it.

We were transported to firing ranges deep in the wooded hills of Fort Lewis, in large, open backed trucks. During these half hour drives, we huddled together on the frozen, wooden bench seats trying to gather warmth from each other and reduce the numbing effects of the bitter, wind driven cold. At the ranges, we tried to "Zero" or sight in our weapons. We couldn't fire this new weapon with our gloves on because we couldn't feel the trigger, however, removing the glove on our shooting hand proved disastrous. Sweat laden palms and fingers instantly froze to exposed metal parts. As we released our grips from the frozen metal weapons, layers of skin were left behind. There were, however, no other options. In order to qualify with the weapon, we had to shoot "Bare Handed."

By day's end and in the days to come, Band-Aids covered the palms and fingers of most of the men, a testament to the arctic like environment and our absolute need to train in it.

In addition to the cold and the "peeling skin syndrome" that we all suffered through, I had problems with my newly issued jungle boots. The nylon ankle support straps dug into my ankles as I walked, causing them to bleed. Most of the time, I hobbled around looking like I was constipated. Three days later, I went to the dispensary and showed them my bloody ankles. They issued me a medical exception to wearing the jungle boots and gave me two pair of the standard military issue leather boots. After putting them on, I was once again able to walk, pain free. This was however, a stopgap measure. Once I got to Vietnam, I would be forced to wear jungle boots but unbeknownst to the medics at Fort Lewis, there was a simple "Fix" for the Jungle Boot Issue, a fix that was shown to me when I reached Base Camp. Within fifteen minutes of "Applying" the fix, both pair of my jungle boots were wearable and quite comfortable.

It was quite simple actually. "Take your boots into a shower, get them wet and beat them with a baseball bat for ten or fifteen minutes. The beating would break in the nylon and as a secondary benefit, soften the leather. "It worked!

On day thirteen, we were all given "Last Will and Testament Forms" to fill out. It was a very sobering experience. Up to that point, Vietnam was merely something that I saw on the evening news, read about in the newspapers or heard on the radio. It was a distant reality with no substance. All too soon, that would change. After signing my "Last Will and Testament," Vietnam took on a personal note. For me and for us, it was as real as it gets!

On day fourteen, we graduated from our Jungle Training Course at the North Pole. Shortly thereafter, we stuffed our gear into duffel bags and were driven to the airport. There, we boarded a Charter DC8 Airliner bound for Vietnam.

Our first stop was Hawaii. We arrived there shortly after midnight. It was merely a refueling stop but we were allowed to get off the plane to get some fresh air and stretch our legs. It was a beautiful, warm, star filled evening. I hoped to see Hawaii during daylight hours, but that was not to be… our next stop was Clark Airbase in the Philippines.

Arriving there at 5 AM, we were greeted by steam bath like conditions and a thermometer that hovered a bit over 100 degrees. The sheer magnitude of the heat was incredible. In less than six hours we had gone from freezing to frying. Was this a prelude of what was to come in Vietnam?

After refueling, we boarded, waited on board for an hour or so then disembarked. We repeated this musical chairs process multiple times and were finally told that the runway at Cam Ranh Bay (our final destination) was damaged by the crash of an Air Force jet carrying a full bomb load. Once the damage was repaired, we would depart. The rest of the day and into the early evening, we waited on the tarmac. Finally, a truck picked us up at 9 PM and took us to a local hotel for the night. Before going to sleep, I put my Ricoh 35mm Camera under my bed in the hotel room and fell fast asleep. I awoke to a banging on the door. Someone was shouting that the plane was ready to leave; everyone was aboard except me and my roommate. They had forgotten about us. He kept yelling to Hurry, Hurry, Hurry. Well, I hurried and left my camera behind, under the bed. I hope someone got some good use out of it.

 Our next stop… Cam Ranh Bay, Vietnam.

The mood of the flight so far, was quiet and reflective. Our conversations were short and low key. We tried sleeping but the apprehension over our final destination prevented this. Hours later, a voice came over the intercom notifying us that we were approaching Cam Ranh Bay. We crowded around windows, hoping to catch a first glimpse of our home for the next twelve months. Tents stretched out for what seemed like miles. Clouds of black smoke rose from the ground below. Were they under attack? Were we landing under fire? The flight crew reassured us that Cam Ranh Bay was not currently under attack and that the fires below were simply the burning of human waste.

CHAPTER 8
- WELCOME TO VIETNAM

Exiting the plane, a massive wave of foul smelling, superheated air, hit me head on like a ton of bricks, then I heard the words that would forever be burned into my mind and heart, "Welcome to Vietnam Gentlemen." Standing at the bottom of a steeply pitched metal stairway was a sergeant dressed in faded green jungle fatigues. In his right hand he held a clip board and like a traffic cop at an intersection, was pointing to his left saying "Board the trucks to your right."

I decided it best to hold onto the handrail as I descended so I grasped it with my right hand and tightened my grip. In less time than it takes a bullet to exit the barrel of a gun, my hand shot upwards in response to the superheated metal. The burning sensation in my right hand was intense. It felt like I had just stuck my hand into a bed of red hot charcoal. I was in country less than five minutes and I'd already burned my hand. Was this an omen of things to come?

Knowing that the handrail was red hot, I descended the steps slowly and tried sliding my hand along the top of the rail to stabilize my descent rather than grasping it. As I neared the tarmac below, I felt the first drops of perspiration running down my face. The heat and humidity of Cam Ranh Bay far surpassed the steam bath like conditions I'd left behind at Clark Air Base. I felt like I was going from the frying pan into the furnace.

I climbed aboard the first empty truck in the column and slid my butt along the wooden bench seat on the left side of the truck until I was as far forward as I could go, just behind the cab. The two bench seats filled quickly with soldiers and the overflow either stood or were forced to sit on the hot, metal floor. After the last man was onboard, the tailgate was lifted into place and locked by the driver. I thought we were ready to depart but instead we sat there, in the blazing sun, going nowhere.

The truck drivers gathered near the center of the convoy and started talking. I wondered what the hell they were talking about. They just stood there for what seemed like hours while we baked in the trucks.

Because all metal surfaces on the trucks were superheated, it was impossible to touch them. A touch usually meant a burn. Those of us sitting on the wooden bench seats were lucky, no metal contact. Those who chose or were forced to sit on the floor, squirmed and moved about like Mexican Jumping Beans, shifting their butts around every few seconds, trying to find a cool spot, trying not to burn themselves. Some tried kneeling or crouching. Those who kneeled burned their knees. The crouchers soon developed muscle cramps and spasms, forcing them to stand and stretch. Once the spasms ceased, they resumed their crouching positions. The "Floor Dwellers" looked like they had "Ants in their Pants." I felt sorry for them!

The sun quickly took its toll on us. No one was immune from its effects! Within minutes, I sought refuge from the blazing rays of the sun by bending my body over at the waist and hanging my head down as low to the floor as I could manage. The sweat from my face and head that began as droplets a few minutes ago turned into torrents and poured downwards to the red hot floor below. Hitting the superheated metal, it instantly evaporated, leaving behind telltale white patches of salt.

My eyes started to sting and burn. I tried wiping the sweat away from them with the sleeves of my jungle fatigues but it was a futile effort. As quickly as I wiped away one watery deposit, another one formed. Soon, the lenses of my eyeglasses were covered with a white translucent deposit of salt that I could not see through. I tried removing it but succeeded only in streaking it and making it worse, so I gave up!

Everyone in the trucks suffered, each to varying degrees. We weren't accustomed to the tremendous heat, humidity and intense sun, after all this was January, a winter month. At best, our previous military assignments were in moderately cool or cold environments. In less than twelve hours, we went from freezing to frying, from being accustomed to a low cool sun to a high, blazing, summer sun. Even though most of us were between eighteen and twenty five years old and in good physical condition, adapting to this new climate would be traumatic.

Finally, the driver's conference broke up and our truck pulled out. The sun was relentless! It beat down on exposed flesh and quickly changed it from a creamy white to a bright pink color. The only saving grace to our first convoy was the breeze that was generated by our vehicles as they sliced through the superheated air.

Our newly issued, dark green jungle fatigues contributed to our distress by acting as "Heat Sinks," gathering the infrared energy from the sun, transforming it into radiant energy and dissipating it into our bodies. We felt like lobsters in a pot of boiling water!

Our mini convoy drove out of the airport and onto a series of interconnecting roads. Some were blacktop, some gravel and some dirt. Along these roads and in the vast expanses between them, were hundreds and probably thousands of tents, bunkers and a few corrugated metal buildings. Most were neatly lined up in rows; the rest scattered about in no apparent pattern. Each structure or tent was surrounded by a wall of sandbags that extended to a height of approximately four feet. The soil in Cam Ranh Bay was primarily sand and I couldn't help wonder how the tent stakes held in such loose sandy soil.

Heavy construction equipment was everywhere. Some sat idle in open spaces, fenced in areas or on flat bed trailers while others were preparing construction sites. grading roadways, hauling dirt, sand and gravel. Cam Ranh Bay was a beehive of activity. Dump trucks, road graders, front-end loaders, earthmovers and bulldozers were moving about in all directions, each performing its specialized task. Thick black smoke poured from their exhausts and dissipated into the hot, thick, moisture-laden air. The smell of burning jet fuel, burning feces and diesel exhaust combined to permeate the air with a sickening odor.

A troop carrying convoy passed us going in the opposite direction. The soldiers in the trucks were laden with weapons and equipment. As each truck passed by us, the soldiers all gestured at us, some giving us a "Thumbs Up", others a "Clenched Fist" while others formed a "V" with their index and middle finger. I wasn't really sure what these greetings meant so I just waved back.

Along our route of travel, I saw men dressed in faded green uniforms and scuffed up boots. They had deep, dark, rich looking sun tans, the kind that beach goers and sun lovers would kill for. Their movement was slow and deliberate and seemingly oblivious to the heat and smells. With our bright green uniforms, polished jungle boots, pale skin and innocent looks, we stood out, in stark contrast to these vets who had been in country for many months.

I wondered how I would survive the incredible heat and humidity for the next year. How could any human being survive such heat for more than a few hours much less an entire year?

Our trucks stopped in front of a large corrugated metal building. "Everybody Out," was the word from the driver, "Report inside the building."

Above the doorway was a sign that read, "22'nd Replacement, Welcome to Vietnam."

We entered the building, handed our orders to a sergeant standing at the entrance and were told to sit down and wait while they processed us. The temperature inside the building was significantly cooler than the furnace like conditions outside. I felt air movement across my face and arms. Looking around, I noticed large pedestal mounted fans interspersed among a sea of neatly line up folding metal chairs. The air currents generated by these welcome giants increased the rate of evaporation of the sweat on my skin and clothing and cooled me off. Compared to the hellish like conditions outside, this was paradise!

As I sat and waited for my fate to be determined, I wondered what my year in Vietnam would be like. Where would I be assigned? Would I be in the field for my entire tour? How would I perform under fire? These questions and more flooded through my mind. The answers did not. There was quiet talk among those of us who had just arrived, you know, small talk…your name, where your hometown was, how much time you had left in service, etc. There was no loud talk, no bragging, no tall tales. We were here to await our assignments and our possible future fate. We were scared and we knew it!

Finally, my name was called. Walking up to the desk, I was handed orders assigning me to the 70'Th Combat Engineer Battalion. I had anticipated being sent to an infantry unit and was somewhat surprised by this assignment. My role in the infantry would be clear but what would I do in a combat engineer unit? I was told that transport would pick me up the following day to take me to the 18'Th Engineer Brigade Replacement Depot, from there I would be transported to the 70'th Combat Engineer Battalion located in the Central Highlands.

After all assignments had been handed out, we were given a "Welcome to Vietnam" talk. I paid close attention to the details of this speech, realizing that every tidbit of information might one day save my life. Next, we filled out more paperwork.

At Fort Lewis, less than twenty four hours earlier, I had filled out reams of paperwork. I hated paperwork! What did they do with the mountains of forms that we signed? Where were they stored? If they ever needed to retrieve a completed form, could they ever find it again? What a waste of time and money!

The paymaster was next. I was issued two months back pay, in U.S. Dollars. It was great to be paid, but what the hell would I do with all that money in Vietnam? It was a soldier's nightmare, a pocket full of money and nowhere to spend it!

Our next and last official stop of the day was a large metal framed building, a transient barracks. We were told to grab a bunk inside and wait there until someone from our assigned unit came for us. For most of us that wouldn't be until the following day. Inside, rows of bunk beds seemed to stretch to the horizon. Our duffel bags had been delivered and were thrown into a huge pile outside the building. After rummaging around for a while, I found mine and carried it inside.

For me, tomorrow's trip would only be an intermediate stop, for others it might be directly to their assigned units. Since my transportation wouldn't arrive until the next day, I decided to take a walk. My only instructions were to stay on the base. I chuckled to myself at that statement. Why would I voluntarily leave a military base, in a war zone, with no weapon and no destination in mind? Never happen!

I asked for directions to the PX (Post Exchange) and was told that it was a short, ten minute walk away. The heat however, made the ten minute walk feel like a ten hour forced march. By the time I arrived at the large corrugated metal building with the letters PX painted on the outside, I was soaked to the bone with sweat.

Inside I found a 1960's like Department Store complete with bathing suits, dress pants, shirts, neckties, brightly colored Hawaiian Shirts, sandals, shorts, electric lamps, refrigerators and stereos. The first thought that ran through my mind was "what the hell did they need these items for in a war zone?" Were they crazy or was I missing something?

After wandering the aisles, I stopped in the jewelry section. There, I purchased a diamond pendant for my cousin Debbie. I thought she might enjoy the gift and if things went south for me, at least she would have something to remember me by. The pendant cost me one month's E-4 pay (Specialist Fourth-Class $175.00).

I continued strolling down the aisles when suddenly, from among scores of GI's in the building, I noticed a familiar face, one from my recent past, a fellow graduate of Woodbridge Senior High School. What the hell was he doing here? As I moved closer, his eyes met mine. He stopped, stared at me for a moment then erupted into an ear to ear smile.

"Holy shit man, what are you doing here," he said?

"What are you doing here," I replied, shaking hands with him. The questions were rhetorical. We smiled like two boys who had just been handed their first Daisy BB Guns. If smiles could kill, the VC and NVA were in deep shit today.

What were the odds that I would meet a fellow high school graduate twelve thousand miles from home in a war zone? Was it coincidental? I'm not much on organized religion but this was spooky and sure seemed to be the act of a higher power.

We talked for a long while. He had a deep brown tan and was wearing faded, washed out jungle fatigues, indicating he had been in country for a long while. "Today is my last day in-country" he said, "Tomorrow, I'll be back in the world." I wasn't quite sure what "Back in the world meant," but I thought it somehow meant the USA. My heart felt heavy. I was saddened to see him for such a short period of time but was happy that he was going home. He had survived his tour!

We walked out of the PX together, speaking of old times in high school, times that were no more than four years old but seemed like an eternity ago. We shook hands and said goodbye. He wished me good luck and I wished him the same as we parted ways, each walking in a different direction. After a few seconds, I stopped and took one last look at this disappearing figure, and wondered if I would ever see him again.

"LST on Beach In Cam Ranh Bay"

Walking back to the barracks, I chose an alternate route. With my poor sense of direction and no map, taking an alternate route back was a less than stellar decision on my part, but I figured what the hell…how lost could I get? Five minutes later, the panorama changed from buildings and tents to a large, smooth sandy beach that stretched for miles. Behind it was an enormous bay.

Less than half a football field away, I saw an LST (Landing Ship Tank) sitting on the beach. It looked like large gray rectangular whale stranded on the sandy soil. Its bow was firmly planted on the sand while its stern floated peacefully far out into the calm waters of Cam Ranh Bay. The large bow doors were open and through them, supplies and equipment were being offloaded directly onto the beach. I had never seen an LST in person. It was much larger than I thought it would be. This and other similar amphibious craft, I knew, made possible the Pacific Island Hopping and the North African, Italian and European Amphibious Invasions of World War II. My father had served aboard LST 1103 during the Second World War, participated in the Invasion of Okinawa and survived the Kamikaze Attacks and typhoons in 1945. Now I could fully appreciate the stories he told me about his experiences on the LST.

I turned onto the next road that seemed like it would take me back in the general direction of the replacement depot. Along this road was an area about two hundred yards long that was stockpiled with supplies as far as the eye could see. Wooden crates were stacked one upon the other to a height of fifteen or twenty feet. It was an impressive sight.

"Jack at Cam Ranh Bay with Stacked supplies in background"

Fifteen minutes later, I arrived back at the barracks. Inside, I plopped down on my bunk, tired from my thirty minute walk in the sun. Some of the men were sleeping, others read books, and still others engaged in poker or dice games. I never played poker or dice so I just spoke to the guys around me. We talked about the units to which we were assigned, home towns, time left in service, sports, anything that came to mind, anything to take our minds off of what we all were thinking.

Shortly after leaving for the PX, those men remaining in the barracks were taken to have their US Dollars exchanged for Military Payment Certificates (MPC) or Funny Money as we called it. MPC closely resembled Monopoly Money. It was smaller in size than US Currency and was often colored red or blue. This was the currency used by US Armed Forces in Vietnam. It was legal tender within Vietnam Only. US Dollars (greenbacks) were forbidden to be used by armed forces for purchases within Vietnam except at the main PX in Cam Ranh Bay and those in other bases that were departure points for men going home.

I didn't find out about the currency exchange until the next day, when it was too late. I thought that wouldn't be a problem. I was wrong!

The next morning, a pickup truck from the 18'Th Engineer Brigade Replacement Depot came for me. I threw my duffel bag into the rear of the truck and climbed into the cab. I was his only pickup from the replacement depot. The drive lasted about fifteen minutes. As we turned and twisted our way through what seemed like endless hard surface, gravel and dirt roads, I was amazed at the size of this base.

Suddenly, we slowed and came to a halt in front of a tent, surrounded by sandbags. "This is it," my driver said.

"This is what," I asked, looking at a tent that sat in the middle of nowhere.

"This is the 18'Th Engineer Replacement Depot Tent, go in and wait for someone to come for you."

"You gotta be shittin me," I said as I grabbed my duffel bag and hoisted it out of the back of the truck. In a cloud of dust, the truck sped away, leaving me stranded next to a falling down brown tent. I had expected to see another corrugated metal building like the one at the 22'nd Replacement Depot; instead, my destination was a tent, covered with an inch of dust that looked like it had been standing there for thirty years. The quality of my living accommodations was rapidly deteriorating!

Close by the tent and protruding from the sand below was a small sign that was leaning over at a forty five degree angle. I had to crook my head in order to read it. In very small, washed out letters, it read: "18'Th ENGR Repl." Had the sign been any smaller or angled any more, it would have been suitable reading only for ants or scorpions.

I picked up my duffel bag, flipped open the entrance tent flap and entered. Inside, were ten bunks, lined up five on each side of the tent. The outside temperature hovered near the one hundred ten degree mark. Inside the tent it was hotter!

The smell inside the tent was foul and stale. I likened it to smells that early Egyptian Tomb Robbers must have experienced when they first cracked open a hermetically sealed tomb.

I threw my duffel bag onto a nearby bunk, kicking up a huge cloud of lung choking dust. Moving to an adjacent bunk I slowly sat down and just stared at the tent wall, wondering what I'd gotten myself into.

I was sweating profusely and was extremely thirsty. Within seconds the micro fine particles of dust penetrated my nose and mouth and settled into my nasal passages and throat. The thick brown slurry that had just formed in my mouth generated a pungent, disgusting taste. I was dying for a drink of water or any liquid, anything to quench my thirst and wash the crap from my mouth. I had been issued no equipment, no weapon, no canteen…nothing! There was no water in the tent and I carried none with me. While at the replacement depot, I assumed that wherever my next destination was to be, that water would be available. That was a bad assumption!

I couldn't stand the smell inside the tent so I wandered outside. I visually searched for signs of water, maybe a water tanker, but to no avail. The blazing sun outside the tent was just as bad as the dead, superheated, dust filled air within the tent. After a few minutes of being exposed to the direct rays of the sun, I decided to go back inside. There, I waited and prayed for someone to come, preferably with something to drink, and rescue me from this dust filled inferno.

I fantasized about ice cold Cokes and Pepsis, ice cold anything would be great. Any liquid however, cold or warm would be acceptable. There I sat, hot, dusty, dirty and thirsty, with nothing to drink and a pocket full of illegal currency. Not exactly how I envisioned my second day in country to be.

An hour or so later my prayers were answered. The tent flap opened and in came a live body dressed in bright green jungle fatigues. He introduced himself and we chatted for a while. His name was Fred and his destination was the same as mine. Fred had come in the day before and was returning from the Enlisted Men's Club where he had just downed a few cold beers. He asked me if I was thirsty. Thirsty, I was ready to suck the sweat off a roaches back, that's how thirsty I was.

"Fred"

"Yes," I answered in a gravely, dust choked tongue. I then proceeded to explain my financial predicament. Fred said that he would buy me any drinks I wanted and would help me to exchange my greenbacks later. What a Guy! He saved my life.

The walk to the Enlisted Men's Club was short. All I could see before me were tall, cold glasses of soda. Inside the club, it was cool and dark. I ordered Cokes, ice cold Cokes and must have consumed gallons of it. I drank until I was supersaturated, then drank some more. Never had cold soda tasted so good. Fred and I talked for a while then headed back to the replacement tent.

As darkness fell, the temperature dropped to about eighty five degrees. After an uneasy night's sleep, we were picked up early the next morning and driven to the airstrip. There, we boarded a C-130 Transport through the open, rear doors.

The cargo bay was a large open area with an aluminum floor and canvas straps stretched across its width. We were told to sit down on the floor, grab a floor strap and hold on. I didn't see the rationale behind grabbing the floor strap so I chose to ignore it. The engines started up and the plane began to vibrate. The noise of the engines was ear deafening and reverberated throughout the cargo cabin. Conducting a conversation was almost impossible. You had to shout directly into the ear of the person you wanted to speak to then try to read their lips as they answered. This wasn't going to be a smooth, noiseless, vibration free flight like the one that brought us to Vietnam.

The pitch of the engines increased and we started moving forward, gathering speed quickly. As we reached takeoff speed the front of the plane lifted quickly and we immediately went into a steep climb. I started sliding backwards on the floor and as the angle of ascent became ever steeper, my backwards speed increased. No one was sitting directly behind me to stop my rearward progress so I reached down for the strap nearest me and missed it. As I continued my rearward movement across the floor I quickly approached the closed cargo door and reached for the next strap on the floor. My fingers, now bent in the shape of a fishhook, wedged themselves between the strap and the metal floor. I closed and locked my grip around the strap just before my arm reached its fullest extension. With a quick jerk, my rearward motion stopped. I was now sitting about twelve feet farther rearwards in the plane than the spot where I initially sat down...so much for me not listening to instructions. I would never question or disregard instructions given to me in an airplane again!

After leveling off, my heart rate started its slow return to normality. Looking around, I noticed four parachutes hanging from the bulkhead walls, two on either side, but where were the rest? In the event that we had engine trouble and had to bail out, what would we do? Would we draw straws for the four chutes? I asked the flight engineer in a form of sign language, about the lack of visible parachutes.

He bent down and yelled into my ear " the C-130 was very safe and could absorb a tremendous amount of punishment before going down… besides the parachutes were not designed for passenger use; rather they were for the crew."

Shit, I thought, I could just see the crew bailing out and leaving us behind. I prayed for an uneventful flight.

Less than an hour later we landed at a military airport just outside Ban Me Thuout in the Central Highlands. A ¾ ton open back truck from the 70'Th Combat Engineer Battalion was waiting for us. We threw our gear into the back and climbed in just as the driver sped away leaving a cloud of dust behind in our wake. Our next stop was base camp.

This was my first chance to see Vietnam outside of an American Base. The area around the airport and Ban Me Thuout was a combination of affluence and poverty. The French Influence was obvious in the brightly colored homes and the beautiful silk dresses worn by the Vietnamese Women of French Descent. The poverty stricken lived by the roadside, in shacks constructed of scrap lumber, discarded cardboard from C-Ration Boxes and other containers. The contrast between rich and poor was incredibly stark and heart breaking.

The US Military influence dominated everything. Dust and mud encrusted military trucks and jeeps were on the move everywhere, carrying troops and equipment. Civilian motor scooters and motorcycles darted in and out of the military traffic like dolphins before the bow of a ship. Three wheeled Lambrettas, stuffed with Vietnamese civilians lumbered along the road at speeds slow enough to make a tortoise blush.

The smell of wood burning fires was everywhere.

Passing out of the city limits of Ban Me Thuout, we turned off the paved blacktop roads and onto those made of gravel and dirt. Our truck moved very quickly along the pothole laden, wildly dipping, dirt road. I thought the speed that we were driving at to be excessive for the poor road conditions. Huge clouds of dust kicked up from our vehicle and covered Fred's and my uniform. Within moments, we both started coughing profusely.

I yelled down at the driver, "Why are you driving so fast?"

"It makes it harder for the Gooks to hit us, we make less of a target," he said. What's a Gook, I said to myself?

Five minutes later, our driver yelled back at us, "Base Camp up ahead."

CHAPTER 9
BASE CAMP - THE ARRIVAL

There it was, on my left, Camp Jerome (Base Camp), looking so much like a fort from the American West of the mid 1800's, complete with guard towers.

It appeared to be between three to five hundred yards long and at least as wide. Surrounding it on all sides were large open areas devoid of trees and brush. The distance between the outer walls of the compound and the nearest trees or bushes appeared to be at least two hundred yards. This area was cleared in an attempt to deny cover to an approaching enemy and provide a great field of fire during the daylight hours. Unfortunately, the enemy in this area of the Central Highlands rarely attacked camps in daylight hours.

"Looking into base camp through the Concertina Wire"

As our vehicle approached to within fifty yards of camp, I noticed the beginnings of multiple layers of barbwire. It seemed to surround the compound and ran almost uninterrupted to the dirt wall that marked its outer boundary. The wire was divided into distinct layers and types. The layer farthest from the compound lay close to the ground in what appeared to be a tangled web. Strangely enough, it was called "Tanglefoot." I likened it to a spool of nylon wire from a 21'st century weed whacker that once removed from the device, tangles itself in every possible direction. This layer appeared to be between five and ten yards deep. The intent of Tanglefoot was to literally trip up the enemy causing them to fall into it. In point of fact, it rarely tripped up the VC or NVA for whom it was intended but did a great job on us when we had to enter it to do repairs.

A couple of yards of open area separated this from the next layer, a single layer of Concertina Wire. Concertina is barbwire that is fashioned in such a way that it forms a coil, much like that of a "Slinky Toy" when stretched open. It appeared to be about three feet in diameter.

A few yards of open ground separated this layer from a triple Concertina layer consisting of two coils of Concertina laid on the ground, one in front of the other and a third on top of the first two.

Another short open space distanced this from a five foot high barbwire fence. Each strand of wire in this fence was spaced close together, possibly eight inches or so.

A last open area separated this fence from the final layer, a double apron barbwire fence. This was essentially another five foot high barbwire fence with the addition of strands of wire that ran forwards and backwards from the top of the fence to the ground about six feet from the base of the fence. Looking at it from the side, it resembled a V Shaped arrowhead with the tip pointing upwards.

From my perspective, it was a vast maze of flesh ripping wire that I thought impenetrable. I was wrong!

Between the inner most layer of wire and the outer walls of the compound were metal posts that were about fifteen feet high and were spaced at intervals of twenty five yards. They appeared to have floodlights on top of them.

The outer boundaries of the compound were made of huge earthen Berms (walls), eight to ten feet high. Protruding from them at varying intervals were Guard Towers made of wood and concrete. Tightly packed against their outer walls were multiple layers of gray or green sandbags. These towers stood like silent sentinels, looking out on the wire and the no-man's land beyond it.

I wondered who would be foolish enough to attack or skilled enough to penetrate a camp with such formidable defenses. My answer would come sooner than I expected.

We rapidly approached the main gate of the compound when suddenly, I heard the piercing, screeching, metallic sound of brakes locking and felt my body being lifted off the wooden bench seat and thrown forward towards the cab.

Instinctively, I reached out with my left hand, trying to grab onto something that would stop my forward momentum but my reactions were too slow. My left shoulder slammed into the back wall of the cab with a thud. I groaned! Less than a heartbeat later I was thrown across the truck towards Fred, who like me had been thrown forward towards the cab. I felt like a stuffed animal being kicked around by an angry child. All I could do was go along for the ride.

I took no more than two steps before I crashed into Fred. He grabbed and held onto me, preventing me from taking what surely would have been a fatal plunge out of the truck. Our vehicle screeched and skidded to a halt in a large cloud of dust. As I returned to my seat and sat down, I felt my heart pounding. I looked across at Fred; his eyes were open as wide as mine.

"Thanks man," I said. He nodded a "You're welcome" back to me.

As I rolled my eyes upward, trying to relax and shake off this incident, I noticed a large sign. It read "Camp Jerome."

Just inside and to the left of the gate was a small wooden shack, slightly larger than a phone booth. Inside, a guard slowly made his way out and walked towards us. His skin was tanned to a deep brown color. He wore faded jungle fatigues that were impregnated with what appeared to be multiple dark oil stains…his boots were scuffed such that no evidence of the original polish remained. In his right hand, he gripped a dust covered M-14 Rifle, balancing it near the trigger housing with its barrel pointing downward. He paused briefly in front of our vehicle, searching for the unit designation that is painted on the bumpers of all military vehicles. The designation on our vehicle was covered with a layer of mud and dust, making it impossible for him to read the designation beneath. Recognizing the driver, he made a quick "come on in" gesture with his left hand. This motion seemed to require a great deal of effort on his part. It was as if something had sucked all of the energy from his body and he was running strictly on "Battery Power."

With a lurch, our truck once again started its forward motion, driving past the guard and into the compound. We drove a short distance and turned left onto one of the many dirt roads that all seemed to originate at the main gate. This time he drove slowly and carefully, a welcome change from the drive here.

On either side of the road, I noticed V shaped drainage ditches. They were dug to a depth of three to four feet and appeared to run its entire length. Tents, large enough to sleep twelve to twenty men, were pitched everywhere. Each tent was surrounded by a four-foot high wall of sandbags and like our guard's clothing, was a dirty brown color.

Adjacent to most tents were curious structures that looked like they belonged in a children's playground rather than a battleground. They were half tube shaped metal culvert structures that were covered with multiple layers of dirt and sandbags. The height of the half tube was five or six feet with a length of fifteen to twenty feet. These, I later found out, were called "The Hole" and were essentially makeshift bunkers that were used to provide protection for men in the event of rocket or mortar attacks. Since they were totally enclosed by sandbags, they offered greater protection than did the tents which were protected only with a wall of sandbags.

70'th Combat Engineer Base Camp - Camp Jerome
Early 1969 - View from hill in center of compound

"Base Camp early 1969"

The sandbagged walls around the tents were designed to protect the occupants from rocket or mortar rounds hitting outside the sandbag walls. There was no protection from direct hits inside the tents!

As we continued driving deeper into the compound, I realized that something was missing from the landscape but I couldn't figure out what it was. Everything was brown, brown tents, brown dust and soldiers with brownish green uniforms.

Then it came to me, green, there was nothing green and growing in the compound…no grass, no weeds, no plants, no vines, no vegetation, nothing! Where was all the vegetation that should be growing here? This was supposed to be a tropical, green environment yet inside the compound it was as devoid of plant life as was the surface of the moon!

I noticed columns of black smoke rising from different areas within the compound and recognized the rancid smell of burning feces. The temperature here was cooler than Cam Ranh Bay by about fifteen degrees. It was in the 90's but still hot and humid.

As we continued deeper into the compound I noticed vehicles and equipment moving about, their massive tires or metal tracks gripping the dry, hard, surface of the dirt roads, loosening the topmost layer and hurling it backwards from their direction of travel, generating massive clouds of lung choking dust. It transformed every tent, every uniform, and every canvas object that had once been Olive Drab in color to a dirty brown. I had expected to see a lush, tropical Vietnam, what I saw was dust!

Men were moving about the compound, but slowly, much too slowly, almost in slow motion. It was as if I was watching a movie at half speed. Our truck stopped in front of a large tent. Like all of the other tents, it was brown in color. Outside and next to the entrance flap was a small wooden sign with a Red Cross painted on it. The driver yelled back "Medical Tent." Fred and I jumped out, pulled out our duffel bags and carried it into the tent.

Once inside, I dropped it to the ground, drawing the attention of four or five medics standing nearby. After staring at me for a few seconds, one of them approached and said "New Medics?"

"Yep," I answered.

"Come on in and I'll introduce you to everyone." After a round of introductions and hand shaking, I felt a little less alienated. They gave us a quick tour of the Medical Tent.

Half of the available space was occupied by cots; the remainder to medical equipment, supplies and a treatment table. Six foot high metal storage cabinets laden with medical supplies, stood in one corner. The treatment table stood in the center, adjacent to one of the main support poles. Hanging from a hook on this pole were two IV Bottles with their attached tubing and needles.

Boxes of elastic bandages, tongue depressors, cotton tipped applicators, Band-Aids, first aid dressings and other medical supplies were piled in another corner, some ripped open to reveal their contents. Every tent pole had a Coleman Lantern hanging from it. I wondered why so many lanterns were present.

This wasn't what I expected for a battalion aid station. My expectations were more along the lines of a permanent structure, constructed of wood and metal with beds. Here there was only cots and dirt. I wondered how efficiently and safely they could treat their patients under such primitive conditions. I could only stare in disbelief.

Late that afternoon, I was told that no sleeping quarters were available for me in camp and that I would have to temporarily share living quarters with our Battalion Surgeon, Doc E. His quarters were located in an underground bunker, the only one in the compound. The entrance looked like a driveway that was about twenty feet long, twenty feet wide and was dug at a thirty degree angle. Inside, it was spacious, possibly twenty feet by thirty feet with wooden floors, walls, ceilings and electricity. Since there was no ventilation shaft in this bunker, two fans were kept going 24 hours a day. The temperature in the bunker was in the upper 70's, much cooler than the inferno above. Four cots were scattered about the bunker. One had a wooden frame with attached mosquito netting. That one belonged to Doc E. Mine had nothing. Living accommodations in this bunker were plush, compared to the living conditions of those sleeping above ground.

"Doc E,s Penthouse"

Stereo equipment, tape recorders and cameras were strewn about the bunker. Dirty clothes were stuffed into crevices in the bunker wall. Boots covered with an inch of mud and dust lay strewn on the floor in front of his cot. It looked more like the inside of "Delta House" than it did the bunker of the battalion surgeon.

I felt uncomfortable sharing sleeping quarters with an officer, not knowing what to say or how we would get along. My fears were quickly allayed that evening. While unpacking my duffel bag, doc came in, muttered about twenty unintelligible words, removed his boots, pants and shirt, put on the headphones to his tape recorder, turned it on, laid down in his cot, pulled the mosquito netting around him and didn't utter another word to me that evening. So much for the chief medical officer!

That night the bunker was alive with noises. Every time a timber creaked, I awoke instantly, convinced that a rubber sandaled VC or NVA was coming to get me.

After many such awakenings, I glanced at my four dollar Timex Watch and saw that it was almost 6 AM…time to get up and start a new day, my first full day in base camp. I hoped it would be a safe one.

CHAPTER 10
BASE CAMP DAY ONE

"First day in Base Camp"

I climbed out of my cot, weary from my almost total lack of sleep during the night and slowly dressed. My thoughts turned to today, my first full day in base camp and my third day in country. I hoped that it would be productive and incident free. My hopes would only be half fulfilled, productive it was…incident free it wasn't!

Standing up, I glanced in the direction of Doc E….'s Cot. The mosquito netting was down and there was no appreciable movement behind it. I guessed that he was still asleep. It was 6 AM and sick call started at 7 AM. How would he make it there on time if he was still asleep? Shouldn't the battalion surgeon attend morning sick call, after all, he was the resident medical expert?

Before leaving for sick call, I had to shave quickly and get some chow. Unfortunately, I left my shaving cream and mirror back in Cam Ranh Bay. All that I had was a razor and no place to shave. At the 22'nd Replacement Depot, we had bathrooms with sinks, and showers. Here, we had nothing. I decided it prudent to skip shaving this day.

Stubble faced and tired, I exited the subterranean bunker and made my way to the surface. My eyelids were pried apart barely to the thickness of a double edge razor blade, due partly to the change in ambient light from the darkened bunker to the pre sunrise outside but mostly due to my lack of sleep. Growling like a "Tiger in Heat," my stomach demanded food. Unfortunately, I forgot the directions to the mess tent, so no breakfast today. I decided instead to go to the medical tent which was close by and I knew I could find.

Walking there, I surveyed my surroundings. Every smell, except the burning feces, every sight and every sound were new to me. I was a stranger, a novice, a "Cherry" to this tropical paradise and to the ways of war. I felt overwhelmed in the face of the vast numbers of new sensations, sights and sounds bombarding me. I was however, not intimidated by them. If anything, they instilled a resolve in me, a determination to quickly learn about my new environment and learn the medical skills necessary to make me a good medic in the field and those survival skills necessary to keep me alive for the next 362 days.

I tried not to look ahead too far ahead into my "Tour of Duty," tried not to think about what might happen next week or three days from today or even tomorrow. I concentrated on this day, today, day three. My goal was to stay alive until tomorrow, day four.

Arriving at the medical tent, I reported the details of my inability to sleep because of the creaking boards in the bunker to the medics on duty. They chuckled and told me that my reactions were not unusual for a new guy in country. "In time, it would pass," they said. I hoped they were right because I knew I couldn't survive for an extended period of time on less than an hour's sleep per night! They asked why I hadn't shaved and I explained my dilemma… no water, no mirror, no shaving cream. They said it was ok not to shave today and then proceeded to explain the washing, shaving and showering routines in camp. I was led to the nearest source of potable water, a large water tank sitting atop a towable trailer. These strange structures, called "Water Buffaloes," were scattered throughout the compound. Our source of water was the local river.

There were no washrooms here, no sinks and no formal shaving facilities. Anyplace to shave was a good place to shave. A steel pot (helmet) or anything that would hold water was an acceptable sink. Without a mirror, however, I would have to "Blind Shave." I had never before attempted to blind shave and was not comfortable with the idea.

During the past two days, I hadn't had a bowel movement and I had a pressing need to find the "Solid Waste Disposal facility," alias the Outhouse or "Shitter" as the guys called it. This wooden, shed like structure was built for multiple occupancy. Locating the nearest one, I entered to the smell of freshly excreted feces. This powerful and almost unbearable smell almost knocked me over.

A plywood platform, looking like a bench seat at a football stadium, stretched the length of the shitter. Six evenly spaced circular holes were cut into it and six faded, scratched, dirty, white toilet seats were anchored over the holes. Their sole purpose was to prevent butt splinters.

Peering through one of the holes, I saw a 55 gallon steel drum cut in half resting on the ground below. It was nearly full with feces and toilet paper. After finishing my business, I was shown another key piece of sanitation equipment, the "Piss Tube." It was a cast iron pipe, probably 6 inches in diameter that was driven or buried in the ground at a 30 degree or so angle. The open end was about 2 to 3 feet off the ground. This, I was told was where we urinated. Poop in the can, piss in the tube...I got it! Piss tubes were located all over the compound and in great numbers. Shitters were fewer and farther apart.

Returning to the medical tent, I inquired about the presence of the battalion surgeon, after all, it was almost 8 AM, one hour into Sick Call and he didn't appear to be present. My questions drew mass chuckles and smiles from those inside.

The medic standing closest to me leaned over and in a soft voice said "Doc never comes to sick call, he just hangs out in his bunker most of the time, coming out only to eat, shower and shit. He's probably in the mess tent now."

"You gotta be kidding me," I said. "What good is he if he stays in his bunker?" Their responses are unprintable.

"Don't worry bout it, said the medic, "don't mean nuthin!" That was the first time I'd heard that expression, "Don't Mean Nuthin." What did it mean? Looking into my face, he realized I hadn't picked up the Nam

Lingo or dialect and had no idea what that expression meant. "Don't mean nuthin means: who cares, who gives a shit, we don't care, I don't care, nobody cares".

"Oh," I said, "I get it."

It bothered me that our battalion surgeon seemed to be as useless as teats on a bull. He was, in fact, a draftee as were most doctors inducted into the army during the Vietnam War. That however, did not give him the right to ignore his responsibilities. His job and my job were to heal the men who depended on us and give them the best chance of coming home alive. Doc E's only goal seemed to be getting Doc E. home safely. Good thing the medics didn't feel that way!

Sick call usually started at 7 AM and ended at 9 AM but that varied depending on the number of men waiting to see us. We never turned anyone away; no matter what time they came to us for medical assistance. Around mid morning, I was told to report to the supply tent to pick up my equipment issue. Finally, after three days in Vietnam, I was going to get equipment. It was about time!

I was escorted to a tent that looked like it had survived the battle of Gettysburg. There were tears and holes everywhere and because it was not properly staked and tied down, it slumped in the center. I ducked my head slightly as I entered through the open entrance flap.

Almost immediately, my sense of smell was assaulted by a powerful, pungent and nauseating odor. It wasn't raw feces this time but rather a strong chemical smell. There was no ventilation inside except for the meager amount of air coming in through the open tent flap. This did little to vent the noxious smells inside.

How could anyone work in this tent for any period of time and not get sick? As I stood in front of the crudely built wooden counter top, I tried breathing only through my mouth, hoping that by bypassing the senses in my nose, that I could tolerate the smell that surrounded me. It was pointless, however!

Next, I tried slowing down my rate of breathing, thereby limiting the volume of chemical laden air that I aspirated. It worked! I was able to stand there and not feel that uncontrollable urge to barf but there was only one catch, I couldn't talk while doing my "modified breathing routine."

The supply sergeant walked out from behind a pile of equipment in the tent and up to me. He then asked what my job was. Shit! I suppose he needed to know this in order to issue me the proper equipment for my job but that would screw-up my new breathing routine!

Uttering as few words as possible I said, "I am a medic." Forcing me to utter these four words caused me to change my breathing pattern and suck in air through my nose. My facial muscles started to contort and I could feel my diaphragm having the first few twinges of a contraction. I tried to hold back my barf response.

Looking into my eyes, the supply sergeant said in a strong southern drawl, "You OK Boy, you all in pain or somethin?" "Shit," I muttered to myself, another damn question. I motioned "No" by moving my head from side to side. That seemed to satisfy him. I prayed he had no further questions.

Behind him were wooden shelves packed with every imaginable type of equipment: canteens, mess kits, web belts, first aid kits, packs, ponchos, bayonets, jungle boots, socks, jungle fatigues, underwear, canvas ammo pouches, water purification tablets, flashlights, etc. Stacked on the dirt floor were helmets, ten or fifteen high in multiple piles. Folded wooden cots were precariously stacked on top of each other to a height of five feet. Dust covered everything. Every square inch of the tent was utilized for storage of something. It was a packrats heaven!

He issued me an M-14 Rifle, five, twenty round magazines, one helmet, two canteens, one bayonet, a first aid kit, two ammo pouches, one gas mask, one flashlight, one set of web gear, one pack, one aid bag and as much ammunition as I could carry. He offered me fragmentation, white phosphorus and smoke grenades also. I grabbed five frags, one white phosphorus and 3 purple smoke grenades.

I was surprised to find M-14's in use here. I thought the M-16 Rifle was being used exclusively in Vietnam. Apparently, I was wrong. I was told to grab a flak jacket from a pile on the floor. This was my first ever experience with a flak jacket. I had no clue what it was or what it was used for. Grabbing the top one with my right hand, I gave it a jerk and threw it over my shoulder. To my surprise, I found it to be unexpectedly heavy.

It was light green in color with multiple pockets and a zipper front closure. Sewn onto the front were canvas loops, which I was told could be used to attach grenades to. The outer covering was an almost un-rippable nylon. Beneath it were multiple layers of a material, designed to slow down shrapnel fragments from grenades or rockets. It was not a bulletproof vest so against small arms fire it was useless.

In our unit, these vests were only worn on convoys. Sitting in a vehicle, on convoy, with a 20 pound flak jacket on was merely an inconvenience. Wearing a flak jacket on patrol meant that you had to leave some other equipment behind to compensate for the additional weight of the vest. I never wore it on patrol.

I requested that the supply sergeant issue me a handgun. He refused stating that only officers and radio operators were authorized to them. At least that was his excuse for not issuing me one. I was disappointed. I preferred carrying both a rifle and a pistol. If I had to go out after a wounded man under fire, while in the field, I might leave behind my rifle and just carry the pistol. Carrying a man using a fireman's carry or dragging a wounded man was much more difficult when you also had to hold onto a rifle. With a handgun, I could still protect myself and my patient and increase my chances of bringing us both back alive.

Upon completion of my equipment acquisition, I carried it outside and took my first breath of semi-clean air. Dumping my equipment in the medical bunker, I was told to bring my aid bag back to the medical tent so that it could be stocked with medical supplies. My leather aid bag was about the size of a large rectangular pocketbook with multiple zippered pockets. The medics stocked it for me, showing me the standard items that I needed to carry. I could of course customize it to suit my own needs after I'd been in country for a while and had acquired the field experience to know what supplies I needed to carry. For now, however, it was a standard issue consisting of bandages, disinfectant, Band-Aids, aspirin(APC's), water purification tablets, wire mesh for splinting, tongue depressors, cotton tipped applicators, a tourniquet, surgical instruments, an astringent (Benzakonium Chloride) and a suturing set. In addition, I would have to carry 2 cans of Albumin.

Albumin is a "Poor Man's Intravenous" (IV). It is a component of whole blood and when infused into the body, draws water into the circulatory system from outlying tissues. The albumin was housed in a sterile glass container. Attached to it was an IV "Set", consisting of IV tubing and a sterile needle. All of this was stuffed into and sealed in a metal can that was about the size of a soda can but 4 or 5 inches longer. My aid bag had a long, adjustable canvas shoulder strap to which I attached (with surgical tape) two cans of albumin. Its light weight allowed me to carry a couple on my aid bag and its armor protection (the metal can) allowed me to treat it harshly without fear of breaking the bottle.

The lead medic then issued me two boxes of 0.5 grain Morphine Syrettes containing five per box. The syrettes looked like tiny tubes of toothpaste with a needle attached to the end. The needle was covered and sealed by a hard plastic transparent cover. I had to sign for and account for the use of every syrette. I kept one box in the front pocket of my jungle shirt and the other in the rear pocket of my jungle pants, thereby insuring that if one box was lost, the other would be available. The morphine was to be used only when the pain from an injury was unbearable and when its administration would not, in my judgment, adversely affect the condition of the patient.

Late that day, I was told to remove one of my "Dog Tags" from the chain around my neck (we carried two) and lace it into the lowest part of my boot. This required me to take off and unlace one boot, thread the lace through the hole in the dog tag then re-lace it. I asked why and was told that if I were blown up or blown apart then there would be a good chance that they could identify me from the available body parts.

A cold chill ran down my spine. I could only utter one word to myself, "Shit."

For the remainder of the day I watched the activities within the medical tent and hoped for a better evening than the previous one. This was not to be!

CHAPTER 11
BASE CAMP
LOST IN CAMP

"Base Camp Tents"

Supper on day three consisted of a mixture of colorful substances that smelled terrible and tasted like a cornflakes box. It's only redeeming value lay in its ability to wash the three pounds of dust that had settled in my mouth and esophagus into my stomach.

After chow, I returned to the medical tent. It was almost 7 PM and the sun was slowly dropping below the horizon. Except for the muffled conversations of those on duty in the tent and the distant sound of diesel powered electric generators, it was peacefully quiet. The massive construction and transport vehicles that had blotted out the daylight with their mountainous clouds of lung choking dust and resounded the air with their constant metallic, throaty noises, were now silent.

Two of the medics going off duty asked if I'd like to accompany them to their tent for the evening and meet some of the other members of the battalion. Since I had nothing else penciled in on my social calendar, I accepted.

"OK, get your gear and let's go," they said. Walking to the far corner of the tent, I picked up my rifle, web harness, ammunition and flashlight, but something was wrong, the flashlight was too light. Shit, it had no batteries! I was too embarrassed to ask the guys in the tent for batteries… that would make me look stupid, so I chose to fake it.

The "fake it plan" would quickly backfire on me and for this brief moment of "Male Ego Posturing," I would pay dearly this night.

Exiting the tent, I found enough residual light lingering in the evening sky to walk without the aid of a flashlight, but within moments, this too disappeared. With my rifle balanced in the palm of my right hand and my remaining gear slung over my left shoulder, I ran into the abyss, trying to catch up to the shadowy figures in front of me. I hoped that I would not trip over any objects in my path but in the darkness I knew that it was only a matter of time.

The equipment-laden harness banged back and forth against my back as I ran towards the narrow beams of light bobbing and weaving in front of me. I quickly narrowed the distance between us until, miraculously, I was standing behind the last man.

I followed close behind him, watching the beam of light from his flashlight as if it was my own. I knew that if I somehow lost sight of it that I would be hopelessly lost in the compound.

After an eternity of walking in the pitch black of a nearly moonless night, we arrived at the tent. Following my buddies through the tent flap, I once again entered into the world of light. Three light bulbs attached to a span of twisted wire ran the length of the tent, illuminating the inside with a weird yellow glow. The light was a welcome relief from the blackness outside.

Seven men, some laying on bunks or cots, greeted me as I entered. They were dressed in faded, dirty jungle fatigues, olive drab tee shirts and jungle boots. Dust covered everything. Canvas duffel bags were strewn everywhere. Dirty, crumpled clothes lay on the brown clay soil floor. Dust and mud covered foot lockers were located near the foot or alongside each bunk. These worn, discolored, gouged, scratched and scraped wooden boxes reflected the tough living conditions here in Vietnam. Packs, helmets and flak jackets hung from the two main tent poles or were stuffed under the beds. Rifles and bandoleers of ammunition were prominently visible along the head of the bunks or on nearby tent posts. Cots and beds were intermixed and arranged in two parallel rows down the length of the tent. Some sat atop wooden pallets while others rested on the dirt floor. The yellowish glow from the dust-covered light bulbs gave the tent, the occupants and its contents a surreal look. I felt like I'd just stepped into another world.

"Jack outside tent with an M-79 Grenade Launcher"

For the next few hours, we talked, laughed and swapped stories. Before the army, I wasn't much of a socializer. Talking wasn't one of my strong points and integrating into a group of new people went against my normally shy nature. One year after joining the army, I had changed. I hadn't yet earned the title of "Social Animal" but I was light years ahead of the sedate, timid and socially inept college student of 1967.

During my medical training, it was ingrained into me that my job was the most important job in the army. Men's lives depended on me doing my job correctly but I already knew that, that's why I asked to be trained as a medic and that's why my lifelong ambition was to become a physician.

While in training and later working in Germany, the concept of death and dying had little meaning to me. I was in my early twenties and so "Death, to me, was something that happened to old people! "

While in Germany, I never worried about a patient dying on me because of something I did or didn't do. There were always multiple layers of caregivers about. Doctors, nurses and experienced medics were always available to call on for advice or help. Backup was always available. In Vietnam, the story was different.

In most camps, there were no second opinions from nurses or doctors. Doctors were only assigned to large camps and bases and nurses only to field hospitals. In Vietnam, one or two medics, drawing upon their individual or combined knowledge made decisions that made the difference between sick and well, injured and healing and life and death. I wasn't sure that I was ready for such a responsibility so quickly.

Sometime after 11:30 PM, I decided to head back to the medical bunker and get some sleep, but I had two problems: First - I had no idea how to get back to the medical bunker and second, my flashlight had no batteries. My trip here was more a "Blind Man's Bluff" than a path that I could remember. I had merely followed flashlights shone on the ground to arrive here.

I put on my web gear, buckled the belt around my waist and asked for instructions back to the medical bunker. After receiving them, I knew I was in trouble. I would never remember them. As I was leaving, one of the medics asked me if I had batteries for my flashlight. His question took me by surprise. How did he know? Did I look that dumb? Maybe it was because I was "The New Guy, the Cherry" and new guys are expected to know nothing. That night, I would live up to that reputation.

"No sweat," I said, "I'll be ok without it."

They looked at me with a surprised, "You gotta be kidding me" look, then raising their eyebrows, glanced at each other, smiled and said, "Ok, see you tomorrow." Why were they smiling? Did they know something that I didn't?

I turned, opened the tent flap and exited into the black abyss outside. "Now what were those directions, I said to myself?" They said, "Go out to the road and turn right." What road, I didn't remember seeing a road? Since I couldn't see a damn thing, maybe I should just let my eyes adjust to the darkness before proceeding further. After a couple of minutes of standing perfectly still my vision hadn't improved one iota. I waved my hands in front of my face, hoping to catch a glimpse of a finger or palm or something. I saw nothing! My only sensory perception was the hint of a breeze caused by my hands passing so close to my nose.

Knowing that I couldn't stand there all night and too embarrassed to go back into the tent to ask for batteries, I took a deep breath and set off in search of the road. It had to be out there, somewhere. Within seconds, disaster struck. My right foot hooked onto something and I lost my balance. I started falling forward into the blackness. With no visual frame of reference, nothing to focus on, not knowing where the ground was, I instinctively threw my hands out in front of me, hoping to break the fall. Unfortunately, my right hand had a firm grip on the wooden stock of my rifle and my instinctive attempt to quickly raise it while still holding on to the 8-pound weapon failed. Refusing to release the grip on my weapon, I choose instead to suffer the consequences of the fall.

It seemed to take forever until the forces of gravity and the laws of physics regarding a falling object were satisfied. I hit, weapon first with a thud. A sharp wave of pain shot through my right hand, elbow and thigh. From inside the tent I heard someone yell out "You ok out there?"

"Yeah, ok," I replied, as I quickly picked myself off the ground. From within the tent, I thought I heard the sound of muffled laughter.

I was determined to continue along, alone, with no help from anyone. This fall was only a minor setback. Realizing that I had tried to walk much too quickly in zero visibility conditions, I devised a new strategy, walk slowly and feel for obstructions with my feet.

Cautiously extending my right foot, I probed and searched for obstructions. Finding none I put it down then repeated the process with my left foot. After a couple of iterations, I felt confident that I'd developed a foolproof way of walking in the dark. Once again, I extended my right foot, feeling for obstructions and finding none; I shifted my weight to it and forced it down to the ground. I expected it to make firm contact with the hard clay soil. It didn't! There was nothing there but air! My foot kept going down, beyond where the soil surface should have been. My body followed and for the briefest of moments, it felt as if I'd just stepped off the edge of a cliff and was falling face first into an endless black pit. It was an intensely peaceful feeling until my right shoulder and thigh hit the ground, again. A sharp wave of pain momentarily shot through my body. "Shit," I muttered.

Now I was totally disoriented and confused. What had I fallen into? Where was the road? Where was the tent? Shit, I was lost in the compound!

As the pain subsided, I remembered seeing drainage ditches in the compound earlier in the day. These were dug on either side of the road. Pushing myself up into a kneeling position, I extended my arms in front of me and moved them horizontally from side to side and vertically up and down as a child would while playing Blind Man's Bluff, trying to feel something that would confirm what I'd fallen into. Suddenly my hands, held out at arm's length in front of me, encountered something. It was a dirt wall that extended slightly higher than my outstretched arms. Beyond it was a flat area. I had indeed fallen into the drainage ditch.

Crawling out on my hands and knees, I stood up on the flat ground. But where was I, on the road or near the tent? Afraid to move for fear of falling into or tripping on something else, I stood there, motionless, like a Cigar Store Indian and prayed for something positive to happen. Maybe someone would pass close by, someone with a flashlight. Maybe someone in a guard bunker would shoot off a flare and illuminate the area. All I needed was a few precious seconds to get my bearings. The thought of standing there all night was not a pleasant one.

Minutes seemed like hours until I heard the sound of a vehicle approaching. As it came closer, its narrow slit combat headlights illuminated the area. Indeed, I was on the road. I took note of the landmarks that it illuminated and the approximate distances to the road junction. In the dark, the one hundred yards distance between the tent and the bunker seemed to take an eternity to walk. Finally, I believed that I was in the area of the medical bunker but was once again lost. Approaching me from a distance was a bobbing flashlight. Rather than wander about all night I called out, "Yo, can you tell me how to get to the medical bunker?"

"Sure" was the reply. As I walked down the inclined entrance to the bunker, I thanked my unknown friend for guiding me. Inside, the battalion surgeon was asleep. I removed my clothes and crawled into the bunk. Tired, dirty and bruised, I fell asleep. That night the creaking timbers could not awake me from my deep sleep.

Before falling asleep, I vowed to never again let my ego interfere with my judgment. The next day I obtained a supply of batteries for my flashlight.

Chapter 12
Base Camp
Death and shaving

My eyes, though shut, were aware that the ambient light conditions inside the bunker were changing. Rays of predawn light filtered into the bunker entrance. Opening my eyes, I witnessed the daily miracle of sunrise, where blackness is transformed into light and objects formerly unrecognizable take on familiar shapes. The advancing light hinted at, then highlighted and finally illuminated all that surrounded me in the bunker. As a child, I was always frightened by the night, by the creatures I knew lurked in its blackness and were just waiting for an opportunity to jump out and grab me. As a soldier, I learned to respect it and all of its hidden secrets. I was taught not to fear it but to believe in my abilities to coexist within it. My fear, though gone, was replaced by a sense of foreboding and uneasiness. This darkness, I knew, was filled with demons, creatures and a determined enemy. I was glad that dawn was once again beating back the darkness.

Reaching down towards the floor, I searched with my right hand for that most precious of all items to me, my eyeglasses. After a couple of feeling passes I found them and immediately placed them on my face. Without this five-dollar piece of brown plastic and glass, I was helpless and almost sightless. I rose to a sitting position with a groan. The four hours sleep I'd gotten, while solid and undisturbed, was barely enough to keep my sleep-encrusted eyes open.

Hunched over like a man recovering from a hangover, my eyes stared at the mud-encrusted floorboards and the two bare feet resting on it. Wondering why my hands ached so, I raised them from my sides and slowly turned them, palms up. To my surprise, I saw a dark brown crust covering a portion of my palms and parts of my fingers. Raising my hands ever closer toward my eyes, I tried to focus on and identify the strange substance. Finally, it hit me. It was dried blood. My right elbow and right knee were also covered by it. This was part of the cost of my falls the night before.

In an attempt to relieve the soreness in my hands, I tried closing then opening them. The hardened, coagulated blood however, acted like a mat of dried glue, refusing to crack or break. Finally, the crust cracked, broke off, then fell to the floor. I could finally close my hands. After making a fist then releasing it two or three times, my hands felt less sore but those areas from which the dried blood had fallen off, started bleeding again.

Picking up my soil encrusted jungle fatigues from the floor, I quickly dressed. My scratchy, two days growth of beard had to be shaved off so I gathered my double edge razor, a bar of Lux Soap, a towel and my helmet and walked to the nearest water buffalo. After filling my helmet 2/3 with water, I searched for a place to shave. A nearby 3-foot high wooden crate would be my washroom. I balanced my helmet on it, splashed water on my face and soaped up. I still had no mirror so I was forced to "Blind Shave!"

Blind Shaving couldn't be that difficult, I thought. Men had done it for hundreds of years before the invention of the mirror. If they could shave by feel then why couldn't I?

Slowly and with great care, I moved the razor upwards from the lower part of my neck towards my chin, then over my cheeks and under my nose, all the while feeling a strange sensation with each stroke. I paid no attention to it and continued. After every couple of strokes, I felt my face with my fingertips, searching for areas yet unshaven or improperly shaved. I then redirected the razor to those areas. About half way through the process, I began to feel a burning sensation in the areas just shaved. I couldn't imagine what was causing it. Maybe it was the soap.

After shaving off two days growth, I cupped my hands, reached into the helmet, extracted a double handful of river water and splashed it on my face. The burning sensation that had started earlier suddenly intensified and spread throughout my face. I threw handful after handful of water onto my face, trying to rinse away the pain. I grabbed the brand new white towel that I had brought from home, closed my eyes and patted off my face. Slowly opening my eyes, I gazed in disbelief at the towel. It was covered with streaks of bright red blood, my blood!

Shit, what had I done to myself? I pressed the towel tightly against my face for a few seconds, hoping that the pressure would stop the bleeding. There was however no way of being certain since I had no mirror to view the damage. A quick glance at my watch told me it was time to report to the medical tent for sick call. Dumping out the pink water from my helmet, I took the shaving supplies back to my bunker, dropped them off then ran to the medical tent.

As I entered, all conversations stopped and all heads turned in my direction. Everyone just stared at me. I couldn't imagine why!

One of the medics standing closest to me leaned over and in a soft voice said, "Hey man, what the fuck did you do to your face?"

"What do you mean?" I replied.

"There, take a look for yourself," he said pointing to a mirror hanging from one of the drug cabinets. The sight that greeted me was frightening. It looked as though I'd been in a knife fight with someone and lost. There were cuts, scratches, dried and free flowing blood everywhere. I told them about my first attempt at "Blind Shaving" and they suggested that I obtain a mirror before ever attempting to repeat this process, lest I do permanent damage to my face.

Ripping a hunk of cotton from a roll, one of the medics poured isopropyl alcohol over it and handed it to me saying, "Disinfect your face with this. If you don't, the exposed, untreated cuts will turn septic overnight. "

I grabbed the alcohol-saturated cotton from his hands and began rubbing my face with it.

Micro seconds later, waves of pain engulfed my face. It ran down my arms, into my fingertips and almost made my hair stand on end.

I had difficulty focusing on objects. It felt as if someone was plunging hot ice picks into my eyeballs. My face cringed and my facial muscles twitched with each application of the alcohol. Knowing that I had to completely disinfect my face, I continued the process, while grimacing and muttering obscenities under my breath in an effort to offset the pain. Finally, it was done. Once again I patted off my face, and once again the red stains appeared on another towel. The alcohol had reopened those cuts that had previously clotted!

I was handed a small cardboard-encased glass container about the size of a tube of toothpaste and was told to apply the liquid inside to all visible cuts. The label read "Benzakonium Chloride." It was a disinfectant similar to Mercurochrome. This, they said, should clot and disinfect the open cuts. Benzakonium Chloride, unfortunately, when dry, dyes your skin red. The red color does not wash off but rather wears off. After applying it to the cuts and scratches, I must have looked like my great, great , great , great grandfather, a Cherokee Indian, wearing war paint. It would take two weeks before the sun's bleaching and my scrubbing efforts to erase it all. During those two weeks, I was the center of attention and laughter by all who saw me.

Since my arrival in camp, one burning question was on the tip of my tongue…what was the level and nature of enemy activity in the area. Having finally built up the courage to ask the question, the answer was, "the camp takes rocket and sniper fire on a regular basis and sappers occasionally penetrate the perimeter wire and gain entrance into the compound."

"What," I asked, "is a sapper?" A Sapper, I was told is "A North Vietnamese Army regular (NVA) or Viet Cong (VC) soldier trained to infiltrate undetected into the compound, plant and detonate explosives inside the base, then escape unharmed." Sapper attacks were usually done under the cover of darkness and almost always during those wee hours of the morning when perimeter guards were the sleepiest and least attentive.

Hearing the call of nature, I headed in the direction of the nearest outhouse. Along my route of travel and close by the inner most layer of wire, a crowd of men had gathered. As I approached closer, I noticed that they were standing near a small figure lying on the ground. It was the body of a tiny-framed man wearing gray pants, black shirt and black rubber sandals. It was a sapper. He appeared to be in his early twenties. The back of his shirt was stained reddish brown and a large hole was visible in his back just below his right shoulder blade. I asked one of the men standing about what had happened. He told me that this sapper had penetrated the wire during the early morning hours and was spotted as he tried to make his way into the compound. Trying to escape back through the multiple layers of wire, he was shot in the back at close range with a 40-millimeter Grenade Launcher. Because he was so close to the guard when he was shot, the grenade never had a chance to arm itself and the unexploded round penetrated his back, severing his spinal column and killing him.

Most of us just stood there in silence, staring at him. It was almost as if we expected him to move or come alive. This was my first view of death and my first close up view of the enemy. I should have felt glad that he was dead but I didn't. I should have hated him for being there, in South Vietnam because his presence forced me and thousands of others to come here, but I couldn't. I could have felt sadness at his passing but I didn't. I continued to stare at him for a few more moments then I just walked away. The image of his lifeless body stayed with me for the rest of the day and for weeks to come. I wondered if someone would be standing over my crumpled body at some point, staring down at me and saying nothing.

I continued to mechanically perform my medical duties for the remainder of the day, but my mind was elsewhere. It was on the dead soldier. He reminded me of what I probably didn't want to be reminded of, that people die in wars and that it could just as easily be me lying there as him. As I closed my eyes that night and tried to sleep, I saw him lying there, still and motionless.

CHAPTER 13
CONFRONTING MORTALITY

It felt as though a massive electric current had just passed through my body. The muscles in my torso and legs explosively contracted, forcing me up into a sitting position on the cot. I was fully awake yet disoriented. The muscles in my legs and abdomen were twitching involuntarily. My eyes, though wide open, saw nothing but the blackness of the underground bunker. The image of the dead sapper flashed in my mind. I could see his blood stained body, the massive hole in his back, the worn rubber sandals and the open eyes staring into the distance.

After what seemed like hours of trying to fall back asleep, I raised my left wrist up close to my face, trying to focus on the luminescent hands of my Timex Watch. To my amazement, it was only 12:30 AM, less than an hour had passed since I went to bed. "Shit!"

Minutes or hours later, I don't remember which, my mind finally let go and I drifted off to sleep. Within an hour, I was once again sitting up in my cot, wide awake, muscles twitching and the vision of my dead adversary before me. And so it went on for the remainder of the night, a short period of sleep followed by a sudden awakening. At 5:30 AM, I awoke, exhausted and drained but happy that morning was here.

During my morning meal of green colored scrambled eggs, burned toast and coffee, I spoke to a friend of mine about the incident. He told me, "don't worry man, most guys have bad reactions after seeing their first dead body. You'll get used to it and eventually, the nightmares will go away."

I hoped he was right.

From the moment I got off the plane in Cam Ranh Bay, days before, I carried with me a sense of fear. Maybe it was a fear that I wouldn't perform my medical duties under fire or a fear of being captured or the fear of death. It was reinforced by stories that I heard about torture and booby traps. The fear was real and it seemed to be taking over my body and my mind.

I had heard stories about captured troops being tortured by having sharpened bamboo slivers driven under their finger or toenails. Testicles were cut off and shoved into mouths, bamboo poles were pushed into bowels, bamboo cages were built and sunk into rivers and streams such that the POWs in them were barely able to keep their heads above water.

There was no Geneva Convention here! I vowed to myself that I would never be captured alive!

Booby traps placed along trails, awaited tired, unsuspecting or unobservant soldiers. Sharpened bamboo stakes covered with excrement (Punji Stakes) and dug into covered pits were among the easiest traps for the enemy to make. A fall into such a trap would impale a leg or a torso, rip apart muscles, tendons or ligaments and cause all wounds to become infected.

Bullet traps were buried just beneath the surface of the ground. If stepped on, a bullet would be shot through a foot. Soft drink cans and bottles laced with acids and ground glass were sold to unsuspecting GIs, causing massive injuries to alimentary tracts.

Women and children armed with explosives were sent into the midst of US personnel where they detonated them. It was a "No holds Barred" War for the NVA and VC and a "Play by the Rules" one for us. It sucked!

As a teenager, I hated funerals and viewings and always refused to go to them. Most of the time I got away with it but when forced to go to a viewing, I never looked at the body. Maybe I just couldn't accept death as an inevitable end for all of us. Maybe I just didn't want to look at the manikin like body with the folded hands, powdered faces and fake hairdos. In any event, my attitude didn't sit well with my dad or grandparents, but I didn't care. Up to this point in my army career, this fear, this phobia about death hadn't changed. It would very shortly!

Amongst the men in base camp, fear was rarely discussed. It was a taboo topic. We would never admit to each other that we were afraid; after all, we were trained to believe that we were fearless fighting machines, trained to kill; at least that's what the army tried to make us believe. Not being able to discuss my fears with my friends was a real bummer. With no guidance, no opinions to listen to, no words of wisdom to consider, I was left with but one choice, take control of it myself. Those were tall words for someone who hated to go to funeral viewings but I couldn't go on for an entire year living in a constant state of fear.

The men in the battalion who had seen death before seemed unaffected by it. If they harbored fears, it wasn't evident in their behavior or in their voices or in their body language, but what does fear look like in a person's face? How does it affect your body language? I knew that I was afraid, but did it show? Could others tell? No one said anything to me about it. Were my efforts to hide it successful or did I look like a kid just exiting the House of Horrors at the county fair?

During my four hour sick call shift, my work kept me from thinking about such things. Late that afternoon it came to me, "how not to die... protection was the key!" I would wear as much protective gear as I could and arm myself to the teeth. Accordingly, I put on my steel pot (Helmet) and flak jacket and wore them everywhere. My weapon along with an ample supply of ammunition never left my side. This, I was sure, would reduce my chances of injury and would give me a fighting chance to stay alive should weapons fire be required.

"How to confront mortality"

I placed additional rounds of rifle ammunition in the elastic band that held the camouflage cover tight against my steel helmet and doubled the canvas magazine pouches that I carried on my web belt. The added weight of the ammo onto the already heavy helmet seemed to drive my head down into my shoulders. It felt like a concrete block sitting on top of my head. I clipped two grenades to my flak jacket. The total weight of all of this equipment probably exceeded thirty pounds. Even though I was in good physical shape, the added weight took its toll on me in the 95 + degree-days of January.

Wherever I went, men stared. Some smiled as I passed by them. They probably thought that I was crazy yet no one dared approach me and ask why.

On day eleven, one of my friends took me aside and asked "Why are you wearing all that shit?"

After telling him my fears, his comment to me was, "Hey man, there's no way of preventing shit from happening to you here, no matter how much equipment you wear or how much you try to prepare for it, if it's your time to go man, you go!"

His comments hit home like a ton of bricks. He was right!

"OK," I said to him, "fuck it" as I turned and walked back to my bunker. Once inside, I slammed my helmet and flak jacket down onto my cot, emptied the extra ammo from my helmet band, removed the grenades from the flak jacket and said, "Fuck it, if I'm gonna go, I'm gonna go."

My fear of dying was gone. A weight heavier than that of the equipment that I carried was lifted from me. Once I acknowledged that my mortality was not under my control, that death could come at any time, I gained control of my fears, maybe for the first time ever.

My resolve never to be captured alive continued through the remainder of my tour of duty but it was no longer driven and fueled by fear but by the conscious choices of a person who accepted his mortality and the inevitability of his death.

CHAPTER 14
TIME TO GO

The early morning sun penetrated the open tent flaps, waking me from a deep sleep. My T-shirt and shorts were soaked with perspiration from the unrelenting heat. Despite showering the night before, I smelled like a man who'd just returned from a two-week patrol in the bush. The only positive side to my pungent body odor was that it kept me from smelling the burning feces outside. It was a poor tradeoff at best.

Despite the heat and smells, today, my fourteenth day in country was starting on a positive note. I was alive and there were no rats sleeping in bed with me. Having said that, I realized that this was the first day in Vietnam that I started off being thankful for something, the first time that I began to look for the positive aspects in each day rather than dwelling on the negative. In the coming months, this approach would help me to persevere in times of illness and injury and remain calm in times of chaos. I would carry it through the remainder of my three-year army enlistment and in the years since.

Wake up call for the medics was at 6 AM every day. My internal clock always woke me prior to that. There were no morning "Formations" here like stateside. They made too tempting a target for NVA and VC rockets and mortars. Here, you simply got up in the morning, shaved, ate breakfast and reported to your duty station for the day.

Since arriving in base camp I tried to learn as much as I could about tropical and combat medicine. At Sick Call in the morning, I worked with an experienced medic, initially watching and learning from him for the first few days, listening as he asked patients questions, then examined them, feeling, probing, looking for abnormal signs, for points of pain and pressure, for abnormal discoloration, for rashes or growths.

Finally, it was my turn to question and examine and my mentor's turn to watch. I was nervous and fearful of making mistakes. After questioning and examining a patient, I reported my diagnosis and recommendations for treatment to my teacher. If my diagnosis and proposed method of treatment were correct, he would simply nod his head in agreement, if not he would tell me the correct diagnosis and show me where my logic or examining procedures went awry.

Diagnosing and treating illness was significantly more difficult than treating injuries. Identifying an illness from signs and symptoms was difficult enough, treating it with the appropriate medication and dosage seemed to be even more formidable.

After completing my morning medical duties, I was approached by the chief medic and informed that my stay here at Camp Jerome was ending. In one week's time, I would be transferred to one of our outpost locations known as Camp Swampy. Located some 50 miles away, it was home to two units, B Company of my battalion and the 131'st Engineer Company LE also known as the Vermont National Guard. There, I would remain for the balance of my Tour of Duty. Medics were in short supply at that location and I was selected as the candidate most qualified to go. My total medical experience to date consisted of six months working in a hospital surgical intensive care ward and fourteen days here at base camp doing real medicine. It wasn't exactly what I would call a stellar portfolio of experience but it was all that I had.

I decided to take a proactive approach towards my perceived lack of skills. In the one-week's time left before my departure, I would cram as much medical information into my brain and practice as much hands on medicine as I could. This, I hoped, would bolster my confidence and provide me with the additional experience that I so desperately needed.

My first and perhaps greatest task was to commit to memory the names, indications, contraindications and dosages of more than One hundred fifty prescription medications available to us. Prescribing drugs was never covered in my twelve week medical training course, nor was diagnosing and treating illnesses. These tasks were always reserved for physicians. Vietnam, however, was the exception. Here, 95 % of all diagnoses, treatments and drug prescribing were done by medics. Physicians' time was reserved for complicated medical procedures, diagnoses or surgery.

Dispensing prescription drugs was a great responsibility for me. The wrong medication or the wrong dosage could retard or hamper the healing process of an injury, increase the recovery period of an illness or in a "worst case scenario," cause severe allergic reactions or death. This weighed heavily on me as I made preparations to start the learning process. I began by writing one 5 X 7 Flash Card for each drug. On it, I listed the indications, contraindications, dosages, and usage information from the product inserts that came in the bottles.

I carried the flash cards everywhere, studying them in every free moment. While walking in the compound, I concentrated on the cards to the exclusion of all else, occasionally paying the price for my inattention by tripping over tent stakes or ropes or walking headlong into drainage ditches. While in the mess tent, I quizzed myself aloud in between bites or swallows of food, first asking myself a question then trying to answer it. As I did so, men sitting near me slowly got up and moved to other tables, leaving me seated alone. In the outhouse, it was almost as bad, the only difference being that my fellow occupants were bound to their seats until they completed their business. No one ever asked me what I was doing or why I was talking to myself, they just kept their distance and left me alone.

With each passing day, my confidence rose as my knowledge and abilities grew. By noon of day eighteen, I had committed the drugs to memory, compiled a list of most common illnesses and injuries and learned their treatments. During my work shifts in the medical tent, I asked for and was given every "hands on medical procedure" that came by and was carefully watched and critiqued on each. I felt good about what I'd accomplished in less than a week and was confident that my newly acquired knowledge and skills would be sufficient as a starting point for the job ahead. I was ready to go.

Exiting the mess tent after noon chow, I was stopped by a sergeant wearing a scowling, angry look on his face.

"You Manick?" he growled.

My last name was boldly embroidered in heavy black cotton on my jungle shirt and was clearly visible to anyone looking at me. His stupid question annoyed me. I was about to ask him if he was having a problem reading the name label on my shirt but trapped that evil thought before it left my mouth. Instead, I answered with one word, "Yep."

"You gonna need a driver's license before going to Camp Swampy," he snapped back at me.

Drivers license, I thought, what the hell do I need a drivers license for in a war zone. Unable to control my annoyance at his stupid question, I blurted out, "I already have a driver's license from the state of New Jersey."

"Not a civilian license, you moron, an Army Drivers License," he barked back with an increasingly hostile tone.

"What's the difference?" I retorted, "A license is a license"! If looks could kill, I would have been standing next to Saint Peter.

After a few seconds of glaring at me in silence, he said "Listen wise guy, be here tomorrow at 10 hundred hours for your driver's training and road test."

"OK," I said as he turned and stomped away in a huff.

I couldn't believe it, men were being injured and killed here and Sergeant Bilko wanted me to get a driver's license. What bullshit! Who was going to stop me on the road and ask to see my license, certainly not the VC or NVA? It was a new height in bureaucratic stupidity!

"The Medical jeep that I learned to drive a standard transmission on"

At the medical tent, I told the guys about the license. "Ever drive a "standard", one of them asked.

"Nope," I answered.

"OK, we'll get you some training now, Stubby will take you out. Stubby, alias Robert D. Stubblefield, was the driver of our medical jeep.

"Let's get to it," Stubby said, as we walked to the jeep parked outside. I jumped into the driver's seat and surveyed the controls on the dashboard and floor. Some were familiar but most were not. "Where's the ignition key?" I asked.

Trying to hold back a smile, Stubby said, "There ain't no key." "See that switch?" he said, pointing to a green lever on the dashboard, "Turn it to the left, put the jeep in neutral and depress the starter pedal on the floor. It's just to the left of the clutch. Pump the gas pedal a couple of times until it starts." As the jeep roared to life, a big smile came to my face.

"The shifting pattern is on the dashboard; push down on the clutch, put it into first then release the clutch and give it gas."

I looked at the drawing on the dashboard. It was an "H" shaped figure with 1'st and 3'rd on the top left and right and 2'nd and 4'th on the bottom left and right. Reverse was off to the side, all by itself. This would be a piece of cake.

It all sounded simple enough.....clutch...first gear...release clutch and give it gas. I depressed the clutch and eased the gearshift lever into where I thought first should be. Releasing my left foot from the clutch in one fast motion, I simultaneously jammed the accelerator pedal to the floor with my right. The engine started screaming and the jeep jumped forward like a bucking bronco just out of the chute. The front end rose upwards then rapidly fell back to the ground as the jeep quickly accelerated. Within seconds, it reached maximum speed in first.

"Ease off the gas," he yelled! "Push in the clutch, put it in neutral and stop the jeep." As we came to a complete stop, Stubby looked at me and said, "Listen, you've got the basic principles right but you gotta release the clutch gradually and give it gas gradually. You're gonna melt the engine doing it this way."

After three hours of practice, I was driving around the inner roads of the compound with no problem, incident free. Tomorrow's road test, I thought, should be a breeze.

Standing in front of the medical tent the following day, I waited for my driving instructor and jeep to arrive. In the distance, a large truck approached. Nearing the medical tent, it slowed then stopped. I kept looking for the jeep. It was a little after ten and it should have been here by now!

"Come on, get in," I heard someone shout out. I looked towards the massive truck and saw a man waving at me from the open window. "Come on, get in," he said again, "I'm your driving instructor."

Oh shit, I said to myself, "Where's my jeep," I yelled out?

"Couldn't get the jeep," he said with a smile, "this is just as good!" I smiled back at him and muttered a few choice four-letter obscenities under my breath as I climbed up into the elevated cab. I couldn't believe he wanted me to drive this 2-½ ton monster. The confidence that I had built in my driving abilities yesterday suddenly burst like an inflated balloon in a pin factory.

Inside the cab, the first thing that caught my eye was the immense size of the steering wheel. It looked like a Hula Hoop. After scanning the remainder of the cabin, I noticed three additional problem areas: first, the switches on the dashboard were unmarked and different from that of the jeep; second, the shifting diagram was missing; third, there were lots of unmarked levers on the floor next to the gear shift. A big lump formed in my throat. Oh hell, I thought, this was going to be a nightmare.

After a two minute block of instruction, my instructor said, "Start her up." I pushed the starter button on the dashboard. With a roar, the massive diesel engine came to life, spewing a thick, black cloud of smoke into the air.

"Start off in second gear, first is too low," he said. I put her into second gear, gradually released the clutch and simultaneously depressed the gas pedal. To my surprise, it eased forward without any jerks or jumps. "When you shift, do it by feel, don't just try to jam it in, coax it in," he said. "Don't worry, if you make a mistake, you'll find out right away."

For the remainder of the morning we drove around the roads in the compound. Sometimes I ground a gear, other times I put it into the wrong gear but I learned quickly.

"The Hill"

Finally, it was time for the last part of my driving test. I had to drive the truck to the top of a large hill located in the center of the compound, shifting at least once on the way up. The road was twisty, steeply inclined and had almost no shoulder. On one side, there was a drop off, on the other, a high embankment. After successfully making it to the top, I would be given my license. It sounded simple enough.

I put the truck into second gear and accelerated up the hill. The weight of the truck fought the steep grade of the road as we slowly picked up speed. After traveling about fifty yards, we reached maximum rpm in second gear and it was time to shift. Even though I'd never shifted on a hill before, I couldn't imagine it being different than shifting on a level road surface. I pushed in the clutch, removed my foot from the gas and moved the gearshift lever to where I knew 3'rd gear should be. An arm tingling vibration from the gearshift lever and an ear piercing noise from the gearbox was my reward for a missed shift. I couldn't believe it. I'd easily shifted into third gear twenty or thirty times before while driving on the level roads below.

Two… three… maybe four seconds had elapsed from the time I initially tried shifting into third. With each passing second, the truck's forward momentum was decreasing. I, however, was too busy trying to find third gear to pay much attention to my ever decreasing forward momentum.

I tried shifting into third again, gently coaxing the gearshift lever forward; five…six…seven seconds had elapsed. Another metal-to-metal grinding sound and a tingly hand, punctuated my second attempt. I was out of time!

The truck came to a complete stop and for the briefest of moments; I sat in the cab staring upwards towards the top of the hill. A microsecond later, we started rolling backwards down the hill, in neutral.

"Oh Shit," I muttered as I quickly turned my head to the left, looking into the large side view mirror attached to my door, trying to see where we were headed. On such a narrow road, I knew that there was no room for a steering error. A plunge off the road and down the embankment would surely result in a "Roll Over" and almost certain death for us both. With my eyes glued to the mirror, I tried keeping her on the road. At first it wasn't difficult because we were rolling slowly, but that quickly changed as the 2 ½ tons of steel and rubber picked up speed at an alarming rate. In all of the confusion of trying to stay on the road, I forgot the brakes!

My instructor started yelling, "Hit the Brakes, Hit the Brakes," as the truck flew backwards down the hill at an alarming rate of speed. Without taking my eyes off the side view mirror, I slammed my right foot down to where I thought the brake pedal should be. I got lucky, it was there.

The rear brakes locked and slowly reduced our downward speed but the back end of the truck took a frightening turn towards the right and the drop off. I pulled hard left on the steering wheel then reached over, grabbed another portion of it and continued pulling. My arm muscles strained with each pull as they fought the resistance of the manual steering mechanism. After three or four iterations of cranking left on the steering wheel, it reached its full left hand travel and locked. This, I hoped, would reverse our direction away from the drop off and bring us back on the road, but I was wrong. It had no effect!

Realizing that the uneven braking of the left and right rear wheels was controlling our direction and not the steering wheel, I released the brakes. With the rear wheels free and the front wheels already turned hard left, the rear end of the truck suddenly veered in the opposite direction and smashed into the dirt abutment on the opposite side of the road. The impact forced my body forward, impacting my chest on the steering wheel. Rebounding back into the seat, I turned the steering wheel to the right, trying to straighten up the truck and put it back in the center of the road. Unfortunately, our speed had once again increased to a dangerous level and I had no choice but to hit the brakes again. It was an instant replay of the previous time. The rear wheels locked and sent us towards drop off. Once again, I released them and made another steering correction. After what seemed like an eternity of braking and making steering corrections, we came to a full stop, at the bottom of the hill.

For the next few minutes my instructor and I remained motionless in the cab. Neither of us spoke, we couldn't. Sweat poured down my face and my heart pounded like a buck mink in heat. I turned towards him and him towards me. His eyes were the size of golf balls. He had the look of a man whose life had just flashed before him. Mine surely had!

"OK," he said," up the hill again but this time keep it in 2'nd gear only, no shifting." I couldn't believe that he wanted me to try this fool hardy routine again. He was either very brave or very stupid. I was very scared.

```
U.S. GOVERNMENT VEHICLE                    CARD NO
OPERATOR'S IDENTIFICATION                      0042-70

NAME OF OPERATOR                    DATE ISSUED    2 0 FEB 1969
        Manick, Jack A.
         BIRTH    COLOR OF    COLOR OF    HEIGHT    DATE EXPIRES
 SEX     DATE     HAIR        EYES                  WEIGHT
  M                Brown       Brown      5'9"      165

 BIRTHPLACE                        SOCIAL SECURITY NO.
   Rahway N. J.
         The holder of this card is qual. to operate US Gov. vehicles
         and or equip. spec. subj. to the restrictions set forth

 Name and location of issuing Unit
   HHC 70 Engr Bn APO 96297
 NOT TRANSFERABLE                  SIGNATURE OF OPERATOR
                                     Jack Manick

         W/Glasses
 RESTRICTIONS:  Good in Vietnam Only
                       QUALIFIED TO OPERATE
        Type Vehicle or Equip Capacity    Qualifying Offical
   Trk Util M151         1 ton
   Trk Util M718         1 ton
   Trk Cgo M37 B1        3/4 ton
   Trk Cgo M35A2         2½ ton
```

"My License"

We made it to the top without incident and he signed off on my license. His next comments were, "let's swap positions; I will drive her back down."

For the remainder of the day I reflected on how close we both came to dying just to satisfy an administrative requirement. What a crock of shit!

The following day, a jeep pulled up in front of my tent. It was my ride to Camp Swampy. I said goodbye to the friends I'd made, threw my duffel bag in the back, put on my flak jacket and steel pot and climbed into the passenger seat. As we exited the compound and turned right onto the dirt road, I locked an 18 round magazine into my rifle and chambered the first round. I lay the rifle across my lap with the barrel pointing outwards and wondered what my new assignment would bring me.

Next stop… Camp Swampy

CHAPTER 15
OUT TO THE BOONIES

Our jeep exited the main gate and quickly picked up speed, leaving Camp Jerome behind in a cloud of dust. Like a man possessed by "John's Barley Corn," my driver suddenly started swerving our ¼ ton vehicle back and forth across the road, first left then right then left again in what seemed like a never ending series of violent turns. I soon realized that he was trying to avoid the swimming pool sized potholes that extended down the road as far as I could see. It looked more like the cratered surface of the moon than a major transportation artery leading to Ban Me Thuout, the capital of the Central Highlands.

Despite his heroic efforts, we fell victim to more than half of the cavernous openings that we sought to avoid. Each encounter was a bone rattling, teeth clenching, white-knuckle event that I was not prepared for.

The first hole was the biggest and by far the worst. It appeared to be large enough to swallow a Pee Wee Baseball Team. As we entered it, the front end of our jeep dropped sharply downwards into the void. A heart beat later the front tires crashed into the rock hard soil at the bottom, flattening out the suspension and throwing me and my driver forward towards the windshield. The steering wheel limited his forward movement to a few inches. I however, wasn't as lucky. Helmet and head first, I smashed into the collapsible windshield with a thud. My head penetrated deeply into the webbed harness of the 8-pound steel helmet, stretching its canvas straps and safely dissipating the energy of my forward momentum. I let out a loud groan.

The inertia of the jeep and the recoil action of our front springs ejected the vehicle into the air like a kid on a pogo stick. A second or two later we came crashing back to earth in a kidney shattering impact. My body was thrown out of the seat and towards the outside of the jeep. Instinctively, I reached down with my only free hand, my left one, hoping to grab onto something that would keep me from being ejected. By a stretch of luck or a "twist" of fate, my fingertips grasped onto a metal bar that formed part of the seat railing and held on with a tenuous grip. I pulled myself back onto the seat, got a better grip and held on.

For the next ten or fifteen minutes, we bounced around like bull riders in a rodeo. Each encounter added to the cumulative pounding that the road was inflicting on our minds and bodies until finally, the holes were no more. The poor condition of the roadbed surprised me. One of the major responsibilities of our engineering battalion was to guarantee that the transportation infrastructure within a 50-mile radius of base camp was functional and drivable. This road was terrible!

"Hey man," I said to my driver, "what's up with the road, it's terrible"?

"Too much heavy traffic," he responded. "These roads are graded, filled with gravel and rolled daily, but the hundreds of heavy military and civilian trucks on it every day just tear it up again. It's a losing battle!"

With the worst part of the ride seemingly behind us, I began to relax somewhat and was able to take in the countryside. It was intensely beautiful, peaceful and serene. We passed by hardwood forests, fields of scrub brush and vast expanses of waist high, sun dried grass. The trees looked much like those that surrounded my childhood home in Iselin, New Jersey.

As a young boy of eight or nine, I loved to explore the woods surrounding our house, fish in the nearby streams and most of all, "Play War Games." Five or six of us would get together, "choose up sides" for our upcoming battles then run away and hide behind trees or bushes. Scurrying from bush to bush or tree to tree, we tried to conceal ourselves as we searched for the enemy. After spotting them, we jumped out, aimed our toy rifles at them and yelled 'bang, bang, you're dead", "bang, bang, you're dead."

Sometimes we'd grab our chests as if being hit, drop our rifles, fall to the ground, and lie there until the shooting stopped or until we figured we'd been dead long enough. Other times we just kept shooting with neither side taking casualties. The outcome of the battles depended on our moods at the time. Quite often, arguments ensued between opposing sides regarding who shot whom first and who was supposed to be dead but it didn't really matter because we all went home for supper that night. Now, the consequences of "bang, bang, you're dead" were frighteningly real and the results alarmingly permanent.

Besides an occasional bird, I saw no other evidence of life, friendly or otherwise since leaving base camp until we rounded a right hand bend in the road. Suddenly homes and people began to appear, first in dribs and drabs, then in increasing numbers as we drove ever closer to the suburbs of Ban Me Thuout. Most homes were small by our standards, about the size of a single or double sized garage. Some were fashioned from rough or smoothly hewn lumber, some from stucco and some from combinations of wood and corrugated metal. The smaller, cheaper and less well-built homes had roofs of straw or thatch while the more substantial ones tin or tile.

Shanties began to appear. Made of scrap lumber and cardboard boxes, they were about eight to ten feet long and six to seven feet wide…just enough to fit one or two people. They were less of a home than a shelter from the sun. As we passed by these crudely built structures, I could clearly read the words "C Rations" printed on the cardboard cartons that formed the walls. Surprised and shocked, I couldn't believe that people lived in structures made partly from our discarded food ration boxes. It was a level of poverty that I never expected to see.

Motorcycles, motor scooters, large and small civilian trucks and military traffic began to appear on the road, first in ones and twos, then in increasing numbers. I recognized the small 50 cc Honda Motorcycles because I had purchased a similar "bike" five years earlier when the motorcycling bug bit me. Loaded to capacity with two people, they darted in and out of traffic likes bees in a field of flowers. Their drivers were "Kamikaze" like. With their 50 cc engines screaming, they ventured into opposing lanes and tried to pass slower, heavily laden vehicles. In many instances, operators and passengers narrowly missed being decapitated by the protruding side view mirrors from approaching trucks. As soon as they had cleared the truck's front bumper, they suddenly cut back in front of them. I cringed as I watched their suicidal maneuvers, expecting at any moment to hear the sound of screeching brakes and that terrible metal-to-metal sound that comes from a collision, but I heard none.

We pulled up close behind a three-wheeled Lambretta Mini Bus, packed to overflowing with passengers. Its high pitched, two-stroke engine poured a thick blue, sweet smelling smoke into the air. "Strap Hangers" precariously dangled from its sides and rear. With their feet firmly planted on the rear deck, these daredevils extended their bodies to arm's length and swung to and fro in a syncopated motion, like the pendulum on a clock. Those hanging off the side nearest opposing traffic, narrowly missed being hit by oncoming vehicles, often pulling themselves back in just before being smacked by an oncoming side view mirror, fender or truck bed. A misjudgment, a lost grip by a straphanger or a "bad call" by a motorcyclist would guarantee some unlucky individual(s) a face first impact into oncoming or a fall into trailing traffic thereby earning themselves the status of "Road Pizza."

Traffic slowed then came to a standstill. For what seemed like an eternity, we just sat there and sucked in the exhaust fumes from the Lambretta in front of us. I couldn't believe that we were stuck in a traffic jam, in a war zone, twelve thousand miles from home. Go figure!

For the next ten or fifteen minutes, we played stop and go, until we reached a major intersection and turned right. A small road sign at the junction read "QL21." I wasn't sure whether this indicated the name of the road or designated the speed limit but from my observations of the total lack of regard by Vietnamese Drivers for any rules of the road, it had to be a road designation. Slowly, the number of homes and the volume of vehicular traffic diminished as we headed away from Ban Me Thuout and into the boonies. Soon, we were alone again.

The sides of the road were lined with large flowering bushes that filled the air with a sweet, honeysuckle like smell. With the rays of the morning sun warming my face, I closed my eyes and took in deep, slow breaths of the sweet fragrance. For the briefest of moments, my mind and body were transported to a place that was peaceful, warm, fragrant and safe. I wished that this feeling and this fantasy would last forever but this was not to be. The next bump in the road forced my eyes open and jolted me back to the reality of QL21.

I couldn't help noticing that we were passing by fixed objects along the road at a rapid pace. A quick glance at the speedometer confirmed this. We were doing in excess of 45 mph. "Aren't we going a bit fast"; I inquired of the driver in a voice loud enough to be heard over the engine sounds.

"No way," he said. "The faster we go, the harder it is for the gooks to hit us."

The road twisted through forests and fields, past banana and rubber plantations and close by small villages. Forty-five minutes into our trip, we approached a village of elevated thatched homes built on a hillside. Each was suspended five to ten feet above the ground on large, thick, bamboo poles. Ladders extended from the elevated decks to the ground below. Between the road and the village was a lush, beautiful field of corn that appeared to be knee high. As I kept staring at the village, my driver yelled out, "It's a Yard Village."

"A what," I said?

"A Montgnard Village," he responded.

I'd heard about these "native Vietnamese" in our "In country" orientation. This was my first close up view of one of their villages. It wouldn't be my last.

In our drive so far, I'd seen no signs, except for the military traffic, that a war was raging here. The villages that we'd passed by seemed to be intact. There was no evidence of bombing or burning or napalm. I saw no destroyed vehicles, no defoliated areas. Everything looked normal, until we crested a hill and headed downwards into a deep, green, beautiful valley that ended at a river. Half way between us and the river, the road split into two parallel sections. The fork to the left seemed to end at some type of structure whereas the other went straight into the water.

"One of the blown bridges on QL21"

We took the fork to the right and as we drew closer to the river, I recognized the structure to our left. It was the remains of a concrete bridge whose span was partially collapsed into the river.

As if reading my mind, my driver exclaimed, "It was blown by the VC a few months ago during Tet. All of the bridges in the Central Highlands were blown during that time."

About thirty yards from the river I began to feel a little anxious. I hoped that my driver wasn't going to try and cross. As we drew closer to the river, I could see that one side of the bridge span was totally collapsed into the river while the other remained anchored to the concrete bridge abutment. Returning my attention to the rapidly approaching river, I realized that we were going to cross.

"Are you gonna cross," I asked with a concerned tone?

Smiling back at me, he answered "yep."

"How deep is the water? You know that I can't swim, right," I said?

"Oh shit Doc, you didn't tell me that you couldn't swim," he replied, with a big smile on his face. Then he started laughing. I wasn't amused.

"It's ok Doc. Don't get worried. Its dry season and the water level is low. It's not more than a few feet deep and there's gravel on the bottom so we won't get stuck. By the way, don't worry if water starts coming in the jeep!"

"What do you mean water starts coming in," I said with a sense of panic in my voice. I thought you said that the water wasn't deep?" Without answering, he downshifted into 1'st and slowly entered the river. My eyes were glued to the front tires as they sank deeper and deeper into the water. A quarter of the way across, water started squirting in from around the brake, clutch and accelerator pedals and started creeping up the outside of the jeep until at mid river it started pouring in over the bottom of the door openings.

My driver was completely unfazed by the water rising at his feet. Out of the corner of my eye, I saw him glance over at me once or twice. Each time he wore a big "shit eatin grin" on his face. He was enjoying watching me squirm as the water level rose. Once it started pouring in over the door openings, it rose quickly until it was above the top of my boots and rising up my pant legs. How high would it go, I thought to myself? What if the jeep stalls out? What would I do if I had to jump out? Could I swim if my life depended on it?

About 2/3 of the way across the river, the water level inside, crested just below the level of the seats and slowly started to recede as we approached the far bank. I breathed a sigh of relief as the front tires finally emerged from the river and we started our climb onto the road beyond. Another fifteen minutes of driving led us to yet another rubber plantation. Upon exiting it, the landscape opened up to large clear area that spanned both sides of the road. About one hundred yards distant and on the left hand side of the road was a military compound. To the right was a large flat area dominated by a massive dark gray rock deposit. "Welcome to Camp Swampy," my driver yelled out.

"Camp Swampy as seen from the air"

The camp appeared to be about two hundred yards in diameter, was roughly circular in shape and situated in the center of a large open area on the left side of the road. From inside the compound, large volumes of gray smoke and brown dust rose into the air and hung there like an early morning fog on a cool San Francisco morning. Like base camp, this smaller compound was surrounded by protective layers of barb and concertina wire, but the volume and number of layers of wire here seemed to be more than double that of Camp Jerome. A ten to twelve foot high earthen Berm formed the outer perimeter of the compound. Imbedded in it were numerous elevated and ground level guard towers and what appeared to be bunkers that were used as living quarters. The land that surrounded three sides of the compound was cleared of all undergrowth and obstructions for a distance of at least two hundred yards, providing a good field of fire and an excellent "Kill Zone."

"Layer upon layer of wire surrounded Camp Swampy and sought to protect the men within. To a determined enemy sapper, however, this was merely an inconvenience"

We turned off the road, past a guard bunker and a guard who waved us through. To our left was a massive array of machinery the likes of which I'd never seen. Each piece of equipment seemed to be feeding the next piece in line. This strange set of interconnected machinery generated an ear piercing noise and mountains of thick gray dust. Emerging from a conveyer belt at the top of the last piece of equipment was golf-ball sized pieces of gravel. It didn't take a Ph.D. to realize that this was a rock crusher.

Construction vehicles and equipment were everywhere. We pulled up in front of a large, sand bagged bunker situated in the center of the compound. "OK Doc, this is it, the CP is inside and so is the medical bunker, report to the company clerk inside."

Grabbing my duffel bag and equipment from the back of the jeep, I said, "Thanks for the ride."

With a big smile on his face, he replied "Anytime Doc."

"HQ Bunker for the 131ˢᵗ Engineer Company LE (Vermont National Guard)"

"B-Company"

A large wooden sign outside the bunker read "Company B 70'Th Combat Engineer Battalion, Camp Swampy." I reported inside.

"I'm the new medic, Manick," I said as I handed the company clerk my orders. He browsed the papers then looked up, shook hands with me and said, "Welcome to B Company, Doc." A sergeant and a lieutenant approached me and introduced themselves.

"Boy, are we glad to see you. One of our two medics is leaving for home tomorrow and you came just in the nick of time." I wasn't sure whether to feel happy that they were glad to see me or scared that they were going to throw me into the thick of things right away. I felt both.

After brief introductions to the other members of the Command Post Staff, I was taken through a set of doorways to the medical bunker. Two men stood at the far end of the room. Their faded fatigues and thin bodies told me that they were near the end of their Tours of Duty.

The room was about fifteen feet by fifteen feet with walls and ceilings constructed of heavy-duty beams and covered with wood planking. Electrical wiring ran along the outside of the beams to switches and outlets. Two canvas framed wooden litters were stacked to resemble bunk beds and occupied one corner of the room. Along one of the short walls was a waist high metal cabinet containing lots of drawers. A jar of rubbing alcohol, a stethoscope and a blood pressure cuff lay on its flat working surface. Pushed up against the adjacent wall was a seven-foot high two door metal cabinet and at the far end of the room was a ventilation shaft. Next to the shaft was a hallway that led in two directions, one into another room (the radio room) the other to the outside.

After brief introductions, the medics told me I'd be sleeping in the medical bunker that night until permanent quarters were found for me in one of the bunkers in the Berm. "Besides," they said, "one medic always had to sleep in the medical bunker at night while the other in his bunker in the Berm." This way it reduced the chances of both medics being killed during an attack." Logically it all sounded fine until I realized that I was now factored into their "Death Equation."

They asked me what I thought about my drive in from base camp. "It was OK, "I said.

"How'd ya like the river crossing, they asked with big smiles on their faces?"

"Scared the piss out of me," I said.

"Don't worry; you'll get use to it."

We went into the adjoining passageway, through a mass of threaded wooden beads that hung from the ceiling to the floor and into the radio room. Sitting on a folding chair with his feet up on a table was someone who I assumed was a radio operator. We shook hands, exchanged pleasantries then moved on to the outside of the bunker.

A common passageway led from the radio room and medical facilities to the outside. It ran straight for ten to fifteen feet then made a right-angled turn (forming an L shaped corridor) and ran another ten feet to the outside.

"Why the L shaped," I asked?

"It prevents Charlie from throwing a grenade directly into this part of the bunker. With the "L", they have to come into the passageway up to the bend in the L, then turn inwards to throw the grenade or to have a straight shot at us."

His words left me speechless. He was so calm, so emotionless and so matter of fact when he said them. It sent a cold shiver down my back.

"Welcome to the boonies doc and by the way, we need to break you in real fast so you'll be going out with the crews tomorrow working at remote sites. It'll be your first taste of the boonies." Oh shit, I thought, I was being thrown into the deep end already!

That night, I lay on one of the two litters in the medical bunker, but I didn't sleep much. My thoughts were of the following day and my first trip into the boonies where I might be called upon to put my skills to work. Men's lives would now be in my hands. There would be no medics standing behind me to tell me if my diagnoses, techniques and decisions were correct. It was all up to me now. I prayed that I was up to the task.

CHAPTER 16
CAMP SWAMPY DAY 1

"Rise and Shine Doc, it's five AM."

To my relief and standing in front of me was a man wearing faded Jungle Fatigues. "Gotta get movin, Doc," he said, "we pull out in an hour. Its 5 AM now. The mess hall is open. Grab some chow, shave, hit the can and fill at least two or three canteens with water. It's gonna be hot out there today. When you're done eating, I'll take you to the armorer to get you a sidearm."

Wow, I thought, a handgun! It would be a welcome addition to my M-14 Rifle and would provide me the added protection that I needed should I need to go out into a "hot zone" for a wounded man.

As we entered the Mess Tent, I saw one of the medics whom I'd met the night before sitting on a wooden chair just inside the tent opening. In his left hand was a metal canteen cup filled with small white tablets. He pulled one out, handed it to me and said, "You know the routine doc."

I recognized it as one of the two types of anti-malarial pills that we were required to take. This one, Dapsone, was taken daily and had no reported side effects. It's "once a week" big brother anti malarial pill was round, orange colored and about size of a "nickel." This innocent looking beauty struck fear into the hearts of the bravest men in the compound. It violently and painfully flushed out an alimentary tract within hours of taking it. Everyone hated it!

To avoid the "Orange Death" pill, men would bypass chow when they knew the medic was handing them out, preferring instead to eat C-Rations or food from home…if they had any…or just go hungry. The medics were ordered by the battalion surgeon, to make sure that every man was handed this pill and took it. After surviving the gut wrenching cramps and extreme episodes of diarrhea that befell me after each of the four times that I took this weekly pill, I stopped taking it. I chose instead to accept the possibility of contracting malaria. In addition, I stopped forcing others to take them. When it was my turn to hand them out in the mess tent, I did so and watched with a smile as men shoved them into their pockets, buried them under portions of food that they didn't intend to eat or just threw them into the garbage can. I really couldn't expect them to take it if I refused to do so. This act of kindness on my part made me lots of friends at Camp Swampy, friendships that would pay off in many ways in the future. Years later, I found out that neither of these two anti-malarial pills were FDA approved when they were forced upon us. They were, in fact, experimental drugs at the time and we were the lab rats.

Chow that morning was the usual mixture of creamed, dried, watery, moldy or bug infested mixtures that were overcooked, undercooked or burned. Since it was all that we had, I shoveled it into my mouth and swallowed it, trying not to pay too much attention to any portions of the food that exhibited movement or showed imbedded, identifiable insect parts. It was a normal meal!

Ten minutes later, I was standing in the armorer's bunker. It was a converted army Conex (buzzword for corrugated metal shipping container) covered on top and on three sides with three to four feet of earth. The fourth side contained a door that was protected by a four foot high wall of sandbags placed about six feet in front of it.

As I took my newly issued handgun from the armorer, a big smile crossed my face. "Thanks," I said, looking at it like a kid with his first BB Gun. Along with a holster, he gave me three extra magazines and fifty rounds of ammunition.

"Can I have more ammo," I asked?

With a big smile on his face the armorer said in a deep southern drawl, "Boy, if you all have to use that pistol, you be dead before you use up half this ammo! This is a last resort weapon only! Don't count on it for nuthin else!"

That searing statement wiped the smile off my face.

I hadn't planned to use it as my primary weapon; that was always the function of my rifle. This pistol, however, would allow me to leave my rifle behind and go out after wounded men in a "Firefight," and carry or drag them back to safety while still being able to defend us. I strapped on the holster, loaded the magazine with seven rounds, shoved it into the pistol and exited the tent.

"I'm with the Vermont National Guard," my companion said as we walked to a waiting line of trucks.

"The what," I said?

"Yep you heard it right doc. The 131'st Engineer Company, LE (Light Equipment) shares Camp Swampy and its work assignments with the

70'Th. We were called to active duty last year and we've been here for about 6 months."

"I always thought the purpose of the National Guard was to help out in crises in the states, never to fight in a full blown war," I said. "I can't believe that you guys got activated and were sent here."

"Neither can we Doc, neither can we."

He explained that the work crew that I was going with was composed of members of both units.

"We're goin out to do some bridge demolition and cleanup today," he said. "The heavy equipment is already on the road. Because it's slower, it has to start out about an hour before the main group so we can get there at about the same time."

"What heavy equipment," I asked.

"On this job, we need two cranes to remove the debris from the riverbed after we blow the concrete span. It's loaded with rebar (steel reinforcing rods) and we need to blow it into small enough sections so that the cranes can remove it and put it into dump trucks. The trucks just cart it away and dump it somewhere. The idea is to leave only the two concrete bridge abutments, one on either side of the road, standing.

Gravel is then dumped into the river between the abutments and leveled with bulldozers. This will form a solid riverbed. Over the gravel, we install a bypass. I'll walk you through the process as we do it. This job will probably take a couple of weeks. By the time we're done Doc, you'll be an engineering and explosives expert."

We walked back to the medical bunker where I got my flak jacket, steel pot, aid bag, 3 canteens filled with water and rifle.

Our convoy was composed of jeeps, dump trucks, deuce and halves and flat beds carrying dozers. "This is it Doc, hop in," my friend said pointing to a dump truck. I climbed up into the cab, threw my equipment on the floor and locked in one eighteen round magazine into my M-14.

"It should take us about a half hour to get to the work site," he said as he pushed the starter button and the diesel engine roared to life. Vehicles in front of and behind us fired up their engines.

From behind us, a jeep pulled alongside my door and the Convoy Commander shouted up at me, "are you ready?" My driver told me to tell him we were good to go so I gave him the thumbs up sign. After waiting for what seemed like an eternity, we started moving, winding our way out of the compound and onto QL21.

Even though it was only a little after six in the morning, the temperature was well into the eighties. The first beads of sweat that had formed on my forehead minutes earlier began their slow migration into my eyes. I took a large gulp of water from one of my three canteens.

We arrived at the bridge site to find two large cranes waiting for us. As soon as the column came to a halt, four heavily armed men jumped out of the ¾-ton lead vehicle and were quickly met by a waiting officer. Although I couldn't hear the conversation, I saw the officer tap one man on the shoulder and point in a direction away from the demolished bridge site. The soldier then walked off about thirty yards and disappeared into a maze of scrub brush and hardwood trees. In like fashion, the remaining three men marched off in different directions, each disappearing into the trees and undergrowth that surrounded the work site. These four guards were posted at the corners of an invisible square shaped defense perimeter that surrounded us by one hundred yards. It was our early warning system and we hoped it would prevent, slow down or warn us of any approaching enemy. The knowledge that a defensive net surrounded us, allowed the engineers to concentrate on their work assignments rather than worry about being shot. It was however a false sense of security.

By 1969, the only remaining VC and NVA in our area were the smart ones, those not dumb enough or inept enough or clumsy enough or unlucky enough to get themselves killed or captured, but we didn't know that. By 1969, our enemy couldn't be seen if they didn't want us to see them and couldn't be heard if they didn't want us to hear them. They could have easily penetrated our defenses at the bridge site and inflicted severe casualties if they wanted to, but we didn't know that.

Our guards were engineers, not experienced foot soldiers. Although they had all gone through basic combat training early in their military careers, they were none the less men whose job it was to build compounds, buildings and bunkers, to construct or reconstruct bridges and to create, maintain or restore roads. If they were from the Vermont National Guard then the situation was made all the worse, for here was a unit composed primarily of middle and near senior citizen level engineers, snatched out of their secure lifestyles and sent to a war-zone where the average mean temperature far exceeded the highest temperatures seen in their home state.

Because of a lack of physical conditioning, many suffered in the dusty, dirty, hot bug infested months of the dry season and the mud filled, disease infested months in the wet season. For many of these National Guarders, their last formal military training was a decade or more ago. They went from walking with their families in downtown Burlington Vermont on a Sunday afternoon, to guarding a bridge site in Vietnam the next. It was a sad way to fight a war.

Once posted, the guards at our bridge site would stay at their positions until the work for the day was complete and the work crew was packed up and ready to leave. Twice in the morning and twice in the afternoon, the ranking sergeant at the work site would check on each man, delivering fresh water to them as needed. None of the guards carried a radio. Portable radios were in short supply. Infantry units had first call on them.

Engineer units were always low on the equipment acquisition priority list. We usually got the equipment, rifles, mortars and machineguns that no one else wanted and made do with what we had. Without a radio, however, the guards could only warn us of impending danger with gunfire. Unfortunately, the deafening noise of heavy equipment operating at a worksite often drowned out the sounds of nearby gunfire.

In addition, each guard was positioned so far out from the work site that if he were overpowered or needed help, we'd never know about it. I admired and respected those who sat in the blazing sun for hours on end, trying to keep us safe. In less than two weeks, I would be put into a similar position, only in my case, there would be no help!

"Today, we're gonna blow that collapsed concrete span and tomorrow we'll start removing the debris," my friend said, "then we'll install culvert in the riverbed and top fill it to a level even with the old road surface and repave it".

"Why not just rebuild the bridge," I asked.

"We're not bridge builders and Baileys are hard to come by," he said.

"What's a Bailey," I asked.

"It's an expandable metal bridge that you put together like an erector set. We just assemble it and anchor each end to the two concrete bridge abutments that still exist. The Gooks really screwed up when they didn't blow these abutments."

Having said that, my friend slowly walked to the rear of a ¾-ton truck and reaching inside, pulled out a grayish/tan colored, brick shaped object and threw it into the air towards me yelling, "Hey doc, don't drop it, it's an explosive."

Oh shit, I thought as I quickly repositioned myself to catch the approaching object. It sailed towards me in a high, slow arc. My eyes were glued to the approaching explosive and for the brief second or two that it remained aloft, I kept telling myself "don't drop it, don't drop it"!

I reached out with both hands, captured it and quickly pinned it to my chest in a death like grip. Laughter rang out around me. With a big smile on his face, my friend walked back to me saying "relax Doc, it's harmless without a detonator." He grabbed the explosive that I held tightly against my chest and tried taking it from me but my fingers refused to part with the deadly package.

"It's OK Doc," he said as he continued to tug at it. Finally, I released my grip.

Taking it into his hands, he ripped open the paper wrapper, broke off a handful of the clay like material, and threw it forcefully to the ground. I closed my eyes, expecting the worse to happen, but it didn't.

"See, I told you Doc, it's OK. Don't be pissed, we play this trick on all the new guys."

As I slowly opened my eyes, I saw smiles on all of the faces around me. "You guys got any more surprises for me today," I asked. No one answered.

The engineers quickly removed what appeared to be scores of the gray bricks from the truck. On the outside wrapper of each brick, I could clearly see two letters printed, "C-4."

"Come on doc, we'll show you how to blow this bridge."

With that, they proceeded to place the bricks in a straight line, one butted up against another, starting on the outer edge of the bridge for the entire 80-foot span. Sandbags, filled with dirt, were then placed over the entire length of the C-4 bricks to force the explosion downwards into the concrete; otherwise most of the explosive force would be directed away from the concrete. This process would be repeated multiple times on the bridge surface until it was all reduced to rubble.

The officer in charge of the work detail then yelled out, "Clear the bridge, Clear the Bridge."

After everyone was off, one man approached the line of explosives and inserted a cylindrical shaped metallic detonator into the first brick in line. He then attached a line of wire to it and ran it back a distance of fifty yards to a detonator box.

As we crouched down behind a dump truck I heard ", Fire in the hole, fire in the hole," closely followed by four long blasts on a truck horn. Ten seconds later, the earth shook violently. Within seconds, pieces of concrete reigned down upon us. Most were the size of marbles.

"Get under the truck," my friend yelled as he pulled me to the ground and drug me under. Fifteen seconds later, it was all over.

We pulled ourselves out from under the truck and walked back to the bridge. I expected to find it gone. Instead, I found a spaghetti like mass of reinforcing rods with large chunks of attached concrete. For the remainder of the day, this process continued until the entire span was reduced to a mass of twisted rebar and concrete. The cranes then lifted the tangled masses and placed them into the waiting dump trucks for removal to a dump site. By day's end, my ears were ringing from the scores of explosions.

The heavy equipment left our worksite at about 4 PM. We followed an hour later. The detonations and cleanup would continue for another twelve days. I wasn't accustomed to being in the direct sunlight and heat for an entire working day. By the time I climbed into the cab of our truck at day's end, I was drained of all my energy. The ride back was pleasant and uneventful. I dropped off my equipment in the medical bunker and went straight to the mess tent. I was famished. I didn't care what they were serving, what it smelled or looked like. With the help of my Red Devil Hot Sauce, I ate everything that was put on my tray, no questions asked.

Afterwards, I took a shower, collapsed into my cot in the medical bunker and fell into a deep sleep. Tomorrow and for the twelve days to follow, I would return to the bridge site until the riverbed was cleared of debris and the bypass completed.

CHAPTER 17
NEVER MESS WITH DOC

"The fine line between life and death in Vietnam was often determined by a man with Twelve Weeks of medical training and a burning desire to save lives, even at the cost of his own."

Jack Manick Vietnam 1969

Months ago, when I first arrived in base camp, I was issued an M-14 Rifle. I trained with the M-14 in Basic Training and knew it to be a powerful and accurate weapon. Its best feature, however, lay in its ability to operate no matter how dirty the moving parts became. If there was any downside to the M-14, it was in its weight…11.5 pounds compared to its successor, the lighter 7.8 pound M-16, but the M-16 would not be available to us until mid 1969.

Because of the combined additional weight of the M-14 and its ammunition, it reduced the amount of medical supplies, water and food that I could carry when on patrol so I went on a hunt for an alternate weapon…one that was lighter in weight. I found it in a vintage World War II M-2 Carbine that I bought from a Special Forces guy who I knew. It was a perfect weapon for me, light in weight and able to put out a lot of firepower. It was just what I needed, unfortunately after purchasing it; I found that he had no ammo for it.

Since this was no longer an approved weapon by the US Military, ammunition was no longer available for it through normal supply channels. I could however, get it on the "Vietnamese Black Market" but I felt uneasy about getting involved with them and the possible consequences. As fate would have it, I found a soldier in Camp Swampy who had a supply of four or five thousand rounds of the precious 30 caliber ammunition, so I approached him and asked if he would give it to me. The dilemma was simple, and so was the solution… he had the ammo and no weapon and I had a weapon with no ammo.

After politely asking him for the ammo and even offering to pay for it, his response to me was "Fuck Off." I explained to him that I would put it to good use and once again he refused, using another colorful variation of his previous response so I gave up but having done so, placed a mental check mark in my mind next to his name. As things always happen for a reason, three weeks later he came into the medical bunker where I diagnosed him with Gonorrhea. I informed him of his condition with a straight face and in a strictly professional manner. Inside I was busting out with laughter.

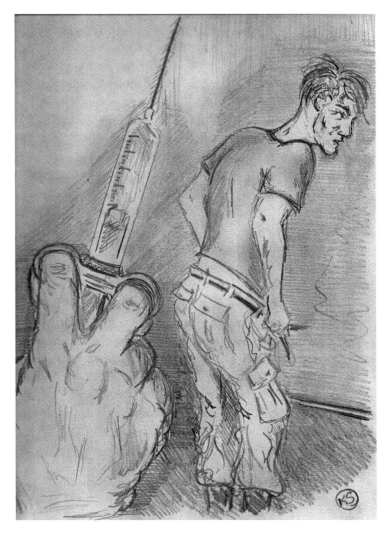

"Drop Em"

The medical treatment for Gonorrhea required an injection of a double dose of procaine penicillin into the buttocks. I promptly mixed up the milky white suspension and aspirated it into two ten cc syringes.

I explained the procedure to him and told him to drop his pants. It was payback time! Before injecting him, I made a minor adjustment to the tip of the needles. I burred them over on the metal surface of the drug cabinet forming a tiny "U" Shaped Hook on its tip. This modification would not prevent me from inserting the needle into the muscles of the buttocks nor injecting the penicillin, however, coming out would be a different story.

The hook shaped tip would carve a widened path through the buttock muscles as I removed it, causing my friend a bit of discomfort and bleeding. Sitting down for the next few days would be a less than pleasant experience for him.

I plunged the needle into buttock number one then pushed down on the barrel as forcefully as I could, injecting the penicillin into the muscles very quickly and very painfully. I then pulled out the syringe quickly, causing additional discomfort. I repeated the process on Buttock number two then told him that he was good to go.

After seeing the grimacing on his face, I knew that my message had gotten through. I would never refuse medical treatment to anyone, regardless of what they had done to me, in fact, I would, willingly give up my life to save a man, even this one, but in this case I was just sending him a little reminder that "You shouldn't mess with Doc."

Later that day, he walked into the medical bunker, carrying three cases of thirty caliber ammo.

"Here's that ammo that you wanted Doc, no charge."

"Thanks man, I appreciate it," I said, as he turned and left the medical bunker. I cracked a little smile.

Later that month I walked into the mess tent, just having returned from a short range patrol. I was starved and would have eaten anything including the silverware. We had a new Mess Sergeant in our camp and he was serving chow that night. Bacon was an item on the menu. Bacon was a rare commodity in camp and after receiving a couple of slices, I asked for a couple more. In a rather nasty tone of voice, the Mess Sergeant promptly told me where I could go. I didn't think that my request was unreasonable so I said nothing to him in response but proceeded to add his name to my "Mental Check List."

In an almost instant replay of a few weeks ago with the 30 caliber ammunition, the Mess Sergeant walked into my medical bunker with a "dripping Penis." He had "The Clap" (Gonorrhea). I smiled silently to myself as I prepared the injections only this time I did not burr over the needles. I did however tell him that this medical treatment episode would have to go on his permanent health record. For a career soldier like the Mess Sergeant, that would have dealt a death blow to his ability to be promoted in the future. He pleaded with me not to enter it into his permanent health record.

Not wanting to ruin his career, I put no notations into his medical records. I never asked him for anything in return. That night, he cooked up a pound of bacon and brought it over to my bunker. We became fast friends and I continued to eat bacon as long as he was there.

Never mess with Doc!

"Just back from patrol and taking a break in the medical bunker"

"Take it like a man...Jack and Larry Van Fossen goofing around"

"A new patient"

CHAPTER 18
OPERATION MID-WAY

"Yeah though I walk thru the valley of the shadow of death, I shall fear no evil for I am the meanest mother fucker in the valley"
Famous saying engraved on Zippo lighters in Vietnam

Two medics were all who could be spared, two medics to care for the health and well being of more than two hundred men at camp. It was a form of shortsighted military insanity governed by the laws of supply and demand. Quite simply, medics were in high demand in Vietnam in 1969 and the supply of trained medics coming in from the states wasn't enough to replace the wounded, dead or those medics rotating home after completing their Tour(s) of Duty.

We were the number two target on the "VC and NVA Hit List," second only to the radioman. We were being killed off or wounded faster than Fort Sam Houston (The US Army Medical Training Center) could supply replacements! The deadly logic behind it was that if you killed a medic, you would decrease effective troop strength by increasing the number of wounded who would die without immediate medical care but of more significance, it would reduce the fighting effectiveness of a man with minor wounds and injuries. The enemy strategy to kill off the medics was well thought out and extremely effective.

In desperation, our new Battalion Surgeon, Dr. Rist, brought in men from other MOS (Military Occupational Specialties) including mechanics, infantrymen, cooks, etc and we were asked to train them "On the Job," as medics. It was a difficult and time consuming task. Most times we didn't have the bandwidth to spend teaching them, because we were always either in the field or in the compound treating men.

Fellow medic JC and I struggled to keep the two hundred men in camp healthy. Our work days were long…eighteen to twenty hours in most cases, but we loved our jobs and more than that, we loved sending men home alive and healthy. Losing a man to wounds or injury was an experience more painful than being injured ourselves.

JC and I alternated going to worksites or on patrols. On any given day there were as many as three groups of men working or patrolling outside the confines of camp. Providing immediate medical coverage for everyone outside the compound was impossible for just one medic. When it was my time to work in the field, I either went with the men who were working furthest from camp or I joined a long or short range patrol. When working at fixed locations, if help was needed elsewhere, a radio call would be sent asking me to come ASAP. A jeep would then transport me to that site. If I was on patrol, there would be no medical care for men at fixed work sites.

It was a pathetic compromise in health care based on available medical resources but it usually sufficed … until "Operation Mid-Way"!

Operation Mid-Way was pure insanity from its inception. Conceived in the mind of a moron second lieutenant trying to impress our commanding officer, it was a plan that almost cost me my life.

On paper, Operation Mid-Way was in fact, a simple mathematical formula that just didn't work. It called for a medic (in this case me), to be dropped off at a point outside the camp, mid way between the closest and farthest group of men. The logic behind it was to place medical assistance at a point equidistant to the men at either end of the distance scale from camp. It was a flawed plan from the get go.

Had I known about the plan and how dangerous it was the night before its inception, I would have shot the mother fucker who conceived it and taken my chances with a Courts Marshall.

At 5 AM the next morning, I was briefed on the plan. After hearing it, I was speechless! It was a child like attempt to address a problem that's only solution was more medics.

"You idiots," I wanted so desperately to say, "are you crazy, what a stupid ass plan," but in true military fashion, I said "Yes Sir," and walked away.

By 5:30 AM, the jeep that I was riding in stopped along the roadside in the middle of nowhere. Our camp was about fifteen miles away. Operation Mid-Way had begun!

I hopped out of the jeep and asked the officer sitting in the passenger's seat for a radio to keep in contact with camp. "Sorry Doc, none to spare," was his reply.

"Excuse me sir but what do I do if I get in trouble?" A shrug of his shoulders was his answer as the jeep pulled away in a cloud of dust.

"Stay near the road so we can find you if we need you," the officer yelled out as the jeep disappeared into the distance. "You mother fucker," I mumbled under my breath. I was alone, in the middle of nowhere, with no means to call for help, should I need it. "Shit!"

I did a quick survey of the area around me. Along one side of the dirt road was a grassy space that extended more than one hundred yards and ended in a thickly forested area. My orders were to wait by the roadside until someone came for me. Were they out of their fucking minds? Staying here would be a death sentence for me!

Fuck the orders! I picked up my gear and moved about thirty yards into the six foot high dry grass then, like an animal making a nest, trampled down the grass and made a clearing about five feet in diameter. I hoped that by going into the tall grass, I would conceal myself from prying eyes.

Lowering my aid bag and ammo to the ground, I sat down, placed my carbine across my lap and prepared for a long day in the furnace like conditions. The temperature had to be close to one hundred degrees and the hottest part of the day was yet to come. Within minutes, my jungle fatigues were completely saturated with salt laden sweat. Chewing, biting and stinging insects of every flavor descended upon me from the tall grass and began feeding, turning my body into a free lunch counter.

What a fucking day!

So as not to give away my position, I quietly crushed the bugs dining on me with my hands rather than slapping them to death. The three canteens of water that I brought with me had to last all day so I tried to ration it carefully. Considering the already brutal heat, that would be a real challenge. I had no means to refill them since there was no stream or river nearby.

I had one and only one mission for today, to survive!

For the next eight hours, I sat quietly, sipping warm water, listening, sweating, crushing bugs and cursing under my breath. There were no farms or villages in the area, so I figured the chances that anyone would come through this field of grass were slim. I was wrong!

In the distance, I suddenly heard voices, Vietnamese Voices. "Shit!"

They slowly grew louder and louder...they were coming in my direction! Were they, friend or foe? I had no way of knowing. Hoping to avoid a confrontation, I quietly picked up my gear and moved slowly, quietly, backwards, deeper into the grassy field and farther away from the road and safety.

The voices followed me like metal drawn to a magnet.

"This far and no farther. I was already too deep into the sea of grass. Any deeper would be a certain death sentence for me."

I backed up another thirty or forty yards, then realizing that I was distancing myself too far from the road, I stopped, turned and faced the oncoming threat. Quietly laying down my aid bag onto the dry grass beneath my feet, I went down onto one knee, switched the safety on my carbine "Off," pushed the fire selector switch forward to "Auto" and waited.

My visibility in the tall grass was near zero. Raising my rifle to my shoulder, I pushed the barrel into the grass in front of me. My heart was pounding like a Bull Elephant running uphill. Sweat continued to pour into my eyes but I dared not move to wipe it away and possibly give away my position.

Maybe they were just local villagers or farmers moving through the high grass to some unknown destination…maybe. I prayed that this would be true but in my heart, knew that it wasn't.

Suddenly the grass around me came to life as bullets passed over my head and around me, kicking up dirt clods at my feet and cutting off shards of grass. The issue of friend or foe was now rendered academic. My response was immediate and I hoped deadly. Aiming waist high or lower, I fired three, ten round bursts in quick succession into the grass, trying to hit the unseen enemy in the torso or legs. I quickly reversed the thirty round magazine, shoved in a fresh one and continued to fire ten round bursts. It was a waste of ammunition against an unseen enemy but I wanted to put out as much firepower as I could to discourage them from coming forward and getting me or surrounding me and finishing me off.

More rounds started coming my way so I fired an extended burst of twenty rounds then finished off with a burst of ten. Realizing that my supply of five hundred rounds of ammunition would soon run out at this pace, leaving me with only a handgun, a survival knife, three grenades and a prayer, I switched to Plan B, which I had just formulated.

I grabbed one of my fragmentation grenades, pulled the pin, released the handle and threw it as far as I could in the direction I thought the fire was coming from. A few seconds later, a large explosion erupted. I grabbed my second and last fragmentation grenade and repeated the process. Another explosion shook the ground.

I was probably outnumbered and knew that if I stayed there much longer, they would probably surround and kill me. Fear turned to anger and with my adrenalin pumping like water through a fire hose, I decided that I wouldn't die here, in the grass. If I had to die, I would do so by the roadside, where I hoped, somebody might, at least, find my body!

I grabbed my aid bag and retraced the matted grass trail that I left, firing five and ten round bursts in a semi-circle in front of me. There was no return fire. Suddenly, the tall grass parted as I stepped out into a large open area that had been cleared by my grenades. What grass remained was charred black from the explosions. To my left and on the ground were splashes of bright red blood that extended back into the weeds in a different direction than my original path into this area.

Should I follow it and try to finish them off? Doing so might lead me straight into a trap so I retraced my steps and pushed on towards the road and my hope of relative safety. I withheld further firing, choosing to save ammo. After what seemed like an eternity of walking, sweating and praying, I emerged onto the road and did a quick look around. I saw no one, so I crossed the road and positioned myself in a depression just off the edge. I lay down flat on my stomach. A quick glance behind me revealed a large area devoid of undergrowth. It would be easy to spot anyone coming up on me from behind so I decided to remain here until help arrived or the enemy returned. I would retreat no further.

For the next two hours I concentrated my attention on the high grass just across the road, listening for any sounds that would indicate movement in my direction. Occasionally, I would glance behind me to see if anyone was approaching, however my main threat was still from the weeds in front of me and not from behind.

Suddenly, to my right, in the weeds…a rustling sound. Was it my imagination? Was I hearing a phantom sound brought on by my heightened sense of hearing? Was it the adrenalin pumping through my body that was causing me to hear things or was this the real deal? I repositioned my body to the right and towards the sound. Pointing my carbine in that direction, I placed my finger on the trigger and began to apply a slight rearwards pressure on it…not enough to trigger the firing sequence but just about.

I fixed my attention on the grassy area in question and watched with the intensity of a hawk zeroing in on its prey. I waited, watched and listened for additional sounds or evidence of movement. Sweat poured down my face and into my eyes. I wanted so desperately to wipe away the burning, stinging liquid but I dare not. One blink of the eyes, one wiping of the sweat from my eyes might cost me the edge that I needed to stay alive today.

Seconds later…another noise from my targeted area. Shit, that was enough for me! There was no time to wait…no time for indecision. I pulled back the trigger and sent a ten round burst at knee level into the grass. Two ten round bursts followed, one to the left of my initial aiming point and the next to the right. I quickly rolled over onto my left side, ejected the empty magazine, reversed it, chambered a round, and then fired a sustained burst of thirty into the weeds in a semi circular pattern.

As the last round exited the barrel I swapped in a fresh magazine then took a quick look into my claymore bag and saw that I had only two piggy back magazines left. That meant one hundred twenty rounds in my claymore bag and sixty in my carbine. When that was gone, I was down to my 45 ACP Pistol. If the enemy was right on top of me, the 45 would be a great weapon to use but any target beyond twenty feet would be wasted unless I was an expert shot and I wasn't.

"An example of a White Phosphorus grenade just after detonation"

In all of the confusion in the firefight, I had forgotten about my Willie Pete, my white phosphorus grenade attached to my gun belt. It was so damn heavy that I couldn't throw it very far but my targeted area was close by. I removed it from my pistol belt, pulled the pin then made a conscious decision to get to my knees to throw it since I had very little leverage throwing it from a prone position.

I lay down my carbine, quickly rose to a one knee, kneeling position, released the handle and threw it into the weeds. Quickly laying back down I started to crawl backwards to distance myself from the burning white phosphorus metal that would be ejected by this grenade. I had no idea how far the phosphorus would be thrown but I knew that I had no more than three to four seconds before it went off. I crawled backwards maybe five to seven feet, then, knowing my time was up, buried my face in the ground, covered my head with my hands and waited for the inevitable. The detonation shook the ground around me.

I quickly looked up to see if any white phosphorus might be coming my way. Some of the burning metal was arcing high into the air and coming in my direction so I grabbed my weapon and claymore bag and ran backwards about thirty yards then turned again to face the roadway. The white burning clouds of metal looked like a surreal fireworks display. As it settled to the ground I quickly ran back to the road and fired thirty rounds into the detonation area and the weeds that surrounded it. I was now down to one hundred fifty rounds!

I decided not to cross the road and go back into the weeds to confirm whether I was shooting at the enemy, an animal or my imagination. If the enemy were out there and wanted me, they would have to come out of the weeds and do a face to face fight, so I moved back to my original position across the road, turned, raised my rifle, pointed it towards the weeds and waited.

There would be no more hiding! I was exhausted and almost out of ammo. Any further confrontations would be a stand up fight! I flipped the selector switch on my carbine back to the semi-auto position. I could no longer afford to fire at full auto. Every shot from now on had to be a single, well placed shot.

A quick glance at my watch revealed it was almost 3 PM. "Shit," I mumbled under my breath. My best guess was that I could expect no help for at least another two hours. I had been left in this Hell Hole for more than nine hours. Time seemed to stand still as I watched the weeds and waited for help to arrive. Two and a half nerve racking hours later a jeep approached in the distance. As it neared me, the wild man driving it locked the brakes and skidded about twenty feet past me on the road. In the passenger's seat was the smiling second lieutenant who had left me here.

As I approached the jeep, I flipped the selective fire switch on my M2 Carbine from the semi-auto to the full auto position. The adrenalin that had coursed through my body this day and helped save my life now turned my body into a weapon of rage against the son-of-a-bitch who left me to fend for myself this morning.

Staring straight into the eyes of the Lieutenant, I screamed at him, "You almost got me killed out here with your stupid ass plan you dumb mother fucker! Do you see the still smoking ground behind you? That's from the Willie Pete that I had to use. About thirty yards into the weeds are craters from the two frags that I threw to keep the enemy from surrounding and killing me." I also fired more than three hundred fifty rounds of ammunition at them.

"I was attacked in the high grass and had to fight for my life. If I didn't have all this ammo and a few grenades, I'd be dead. I should kill you where you sit you sorry mother fucker!"

I just wanted to blow him the fuck away. Nobody would blame me for it. It was payback time!

His face turned pale. "I'm sorry Doc. I never knew that this would happen...I'm sorry."

"I told you that I would be helpless out here without a radio," I screamed out at him, "and you just shrugged your fucking shoulders and sped away. This bullshit ends now or you won't make it back to the compound. Got It?"

"Sorry doc, I got it, the plan is cancelled."

I jumped into the back of the jeep, still steaming mad. Back at camp, I told my friends what had happened and they commented, "Did you kill the mother fucker?"

"No," I responded, "but I should have!"

"Deeper into the field"

CHAPTER 19
CATS AND RATS

Drawn to food and garbage, our neighbors carried leptospirosis, plague, typhus, rabies, tularemia, trichinosis, leishmaniasis, spirilary rat bite fever, spirochetal jaundice and 26 others diseases. Scientists refer to them by their taxonomic designations... *Rattus rattus or Rattus norvegicus...we just called them rats.*

They were everywhere! We lived, ate and slept with them. Our four legged neighbors tunneled under our bunkers and tents and set up residence. We tried eliminating them with Rat Poison but found that it's only effect was to enhance the sheen in their already brilliant gray coats. Standard spring loaded traps caught a few of the less intelligent ones but most either avoided the traps or learned how to remove the bait without tripping them. The stories that I was told as a child about rats being stupid creatures was totally disproven in the outpost camps in Vietnam. They were in fact quite intelligent, cunning and learned very quickly.

Anyone scratched or bitten by a rat was subject to a mandatory series of twelve painful rabies shots, spread out over a two week period. My assumption was that "all rats" carried rabies even though I knew that statement not to be true. I figured, better safe than sorry with a man's life.

My first encounter with them was at base camp, early in the year. I had just completed my day's work assignments at the medical tent and was returning from chow. It was my very first night sleeping in a tent in Vietnam. As I sat on my cot listening to the conversations around me, I heard strange noises coming from somewhere within the tent but I couldn't figure out from where. It would start; continue for a few seconds, stop, and then start again a few minutes later in a different location.

No one seemed to take notice of it except me. After a half hour or so, my curiosity got the best of me. "Does anyone hear that?" I asked. All conversations in the tent immediately ceased while my roomies listened intently.

One of them then smiled and said, "Oh, that's just the rats."

"Rats, what do you mean rats, what rats, where," I said in a raised voice?

"It's OK Doc; don't get excited, we have rats in the tent. They live in the pallets and in burrows under our bunks."

"You gotta be shittin me," I replied in an ever-increasing voice.

"No man, they share the tent with us. They're our neighbors. In the evening they mess around in the pallets. They're just havin fun. That's the noise you hear."

"Do you guys know how dangerous those little bastards are?" I retorted. "One bite, one scratch and you might get Rabies. That means a series of twelve shots that I wouldn't wish on my worst enemy."

"OK doc, calm down, it's ok, there's no reason to get excited, the rats are cool. No one's been bitten yet and besides there's no way to get rid of them."

"What do you mean no way to get rid of them," I said, "what about poison?"

"Nah, they just get fat on it."

"What about moving the pallets?"

"If you get rid of the pallets they just burrow holes in the ground under the bunks. If you move the pallets, they just follow wherever we move them to and settle in again. It's ok Doc, relax, don't mean nuthin!"

I couldn't believe I had to share my tent with rats. When I was a kid, I use to go to the dump and shoot at them with my twenty two caliber rifle. Now they're my neighbors! Shit!

That night everyone in the tent slept contently except for me and my newly found neighbors. The men snored, the rats played and I listened. I couldn't believe that everyone was oblivious to the sounds and unconcerned of the dangers.

The following evening, my new neighbors became increasingly bold. Their playful antics were no longer confined to the pallets, now they emerged from their wooden enclosures and scurried among the bunks and cots, playing like kids in a schoolyard playground. At the far end of the tent, two of them emerged from the pallets, jumped onto the nearest bunk then hopped from bunk to bunk, chasing each other, playing tag as they traversed the length of the tent. Men sitting or laying in cots and beds in their path leaped off, allowing them unimpeded access. I however, sat on my cot, propped up on my elbows, my legs fully extended, mesmerized by the approaching pair.

The lead rat jumped from the adjacent bunk onto the edge of mine, scurried across my legs to the other side then onto the next bunk. He was closely followed by his buddy who repeated the process. They continued to the end of the tent where they vaulted to the ground and disappeared into the pallets. While the rest of the men returned to their bunks, I sat there, motionless, contemplating what had just happened.

Never had I witnessed such daring, speed, courage and skill from a creature that I always considered dumb, stupid and cowardly. To my great surprise, I slept like a baby that night. I shouldn't have, especially after this night's activities. Maybe I was just exhausted from not having slept the night before or maybe I was just getting use to the idea of sharing a tent with the rats. Whatever the reason, I was thankful for the needed sleep.

Two mornings later, I opened my eyes and immediately knew that something wasn't quite right. A voice deep inside me told me to lie perfectly still, so I lay there motionless, waiting, listening and watching. After a few minutes, I realized that my right calf felt warmer than my left and there was pressure against it.

Lodged up against it was a dark gray mass about the size of a small cat. I could see no identifying features and couldn't imagine what it could be. Suddenly, there was movement and a flicker of a long pointed tail. "Shit, it's a rat."

I froze! My heart started pounding wildly. The only thought running through my mind was how to get away from my sleeping partner without getting bitten. Any movement on my part might awaken and anger it, however, if I waited too long, it might awaken or be frightened awake by someone in the tent and bite or scratch me. Shit!

Somehow, I had to jump out of bed and distance myself from the sleeping rat before it awoke.

I estimated my chances at success to be no better than 50/50, not very good when you consider the consequences of failure. Taking a deep breath, I sprang off the cot with the speed of a man shot out of a cannon.

I was at the far end of the tent, unscratched and unbitten, before my sleeping partner awoke and jumped off the cot. Some of the men, awakened by the sudden commotion, raised their heads and looked at me in amazement, wondering what had just happened. After telling them the story, they just smiled and went back to sleep.

That evening all hell broke loose in the tent. Within the pallets, the rats were fighting and making the most God awful screeching noises I'd ever heard. As I sat on my cot, listening to the battle royal taking place beneath us, I noticed a soldier sitting five bunks away from me, frozen in bed with his knees drawn in almost to his chest and the soles of his boots resting flat on the blanket. Both arms were wrapped around his bent legs and clasped in front, locking them in place. His face was contorted with anger as he stared catatonically into the pallets. If looks could kill, the rats would have died a thousand deaths that night.

Suddenly, his hands began to tremble and he jumped off his bunk, grabbed his rifle, locked a twenty round magazine into the receiver, chambered a round, took aim at the closest pallet and started firing.

"I'll get you, you mother fuckers," he screamed at the top of his lungs, firing round after round into the wooden pallets, targeting them in no particular order. It was almost as if he could see the rats through the wooden planks.

Men dove for cover but there was no cover. Some tried hiding behind wooden footlockers, cots, beds or duffel bags but there was no protection from the steel jacketed 7.62 mm military bullets. These would penetrate multiple layers of anything that we could hide behind. A couple of men dove out of the tent entrance into the darkness beyond as the shooting began. Those of us not hiding, played hopscotch, running and hopping from bunk to bunk or pallet to pallet. Wherever he wasn't shooting at the moment, we ran to. As I jumped from pallet to pallet, I prayed for a miracle. I didn't want to be sent home in a body bag because someone freaked out and accidentally killed me while shooting at rats.

For the few brief moments that it took him to empty the eighteen rounds into the pallets, chaos reigned in the tent. I had brief thoughts of trying to make a dash for the tent entrance but quickly decided against it. He was standing next to it and I might get caught in his line of fire. No one was foolish enough to try to disarm him.

Finally it was over. His ammunition expended, he stood there, frozen like a statue. Smoke poured out the barrel of his weapon. Slowly, he sat down on his bunk, lay down his rifle and put his head into his hands. Men began to arise from behind footlockers and bunks. Those of us who had been playing hopscotch approached his bunk and one soldier took his weapon. By the grace of God, no one had been injured.

Outside, sirens were screaming and the sound of men moving everywhere could be heard. The camp was on full alert, one initiated by the shooting within our tent. The gun fire was interpreted as an "enemy within the compound condition."

The entire complement of men in camp searched for enemy infiltrators, infiltrators who did not exist. Within minutes, an officer came running into our tent, 45-caliber pistol in hand yelling, "What the fuck is going on?" The smell of burned gunpowder still hung heavy in the air. After telling him our account of the chaotic shooting spree, the soldier, still in shock, was led away by the officer and two sergeants. We never heard from or saw him again.

His shooting spree was for naught. Not a rat was killed. Exhausted from the melee, I soon fell into a deep sleep, oblivious of my neighbors below.

Back at Camp Swampy, we tried everything short of explosives to eliminate the rats, but nothing worked. To add insult to injury, we noticed that they were breeding at an alarming rate. In our quest for the high tech solution to reducing the rat population, we forgot the simplest solution of all, a natural predator, a cat...how simple, yet how elegant. But where to find a cat in a country that considered them an evening meal delicacy?

"The cat exercises a strategic withdrawal"

We began our feline search, scouring other camps and bases, local villages and towns, each time coming up empty until one day we struck gold. A truck from our camp, carrying our newly found predator, entered the compound. We gathered around it like kids surrounding an ice cream truck. The driver got out, walked to the back of the truck and quickly put on a pair of elbow length leather gloves.

Why such long gloves, I wondered, until he reached into a makeshift chicken wire cage and pulled out a large, nasty, unhappy, scar laden gray cat. Never had I seen a cat in such a foul mood. It hissed, screeched and struggled desperately to get free. We all smiled, knowing that we had not only found a perfect predator but a mean, pissed off one that was just looking for a fight. A cat with an attitude...the rats didn't stand a chance!

The first area of operation for the cat would be the Mess Tent, where massive wooden pallets were used as flooring. These pallets had large openings between the top and bottom slats which provided the rat's easy access. It was a great place for them to live and play and it also provided enough clearance for the cat to get in and maneuver easily.

The plan was simple, set the cat loose into the openings between the pallets, where it would find, kill and dine on the rats. Success was guaranteed!

We released the cat into the pallets where it quickly disappeared. Waiting in anticipation, we, listened, hoped and prayed. Suddenly... screaming, hissing and noises such as I'd never heard before started somewhere beneath our feet. Each of us standing nearby looked at each other and broke out in large, genuine smiles. The cat had finally met his targets and was dispatching them to Saint Peter.

The noise and commotion continued for a few minutes when suddenly, the cat emerged from the pallets with its ears pinned back flat against its neck and its tail curled beneath its butt. It was crouched down low to the ground and running faster than any cat had the right to. Emerging close behind it were three huge rats whose size equaled that of the cat. The quartet passed us at supersonic speed, making a straight line run for the main gate some seventy five yards away. For the first twenty five yards, the rats were gaining on the cat but realizing that they would soon be upon him; the cat put on a massive burst of speed and started to pull away. The foursome ran under the main gate and disappeared.

We guessed that the cat found the rats, attacked, was quickly outnumbered and started to fight for his life. Deciding that he was strategically outnumbered and was about to lose the fight, he executed a strategic military withdrawal. We never saw the cat again. The rats remained!

Only one solution remained… disassemble the mess tent, remove all of its equipment, leaving only the pallets, then encircle the pallets with as many men as we could find, giving each man a two by four or other implement to dispatch the rats to Saint Peter. Someone would then pick up the pallets one by one. As the rats scrambled for cover, they would have to run through the circle of men who would hopefully beat them to death.

I gave the plan a minimal chance for success but what the heck, there was no other plan and we somehow, desperately needed to reduce their population.

It was a risky endeavor. The rats could have easily bitten or scratched men in their panic to avoid being beaten to death. In addition, we had not anticipated the speed at which a frightened rat could run and how easily it could avoid our attempts to kill it.

The first pallet was lifted and a swarm of rats emerged. Running at top speeds, they ran between our legs, over our boots, up our pants legs and jumped to the outside of the circle and freedom. From a distance, our killing efforts looked like a tribal ritual. If it were not for the seriousness of the matter, it would have been amusing.

After an hour of flailing and beating, it was over. The last pallet had been raised and the last rat escaped or killed. The results were surprising, three hundred rats KIA…most however, escaped to play another day.

Late that year, we adopted a stray dog. He was a mix breed with one ear that laid flat against his head while the other stood straight up. He was a friendly dog and everyone loved him. To our surprise and amazement, he hated rats. Not only did he hate them, but he had a unique ability to locate and kill them. Each morning we would find dead rats strewn throughout the compound, all courtesy of our friend. We would be playing with him and call out to him and say "Rat." He would freeze in his tracks, his eyes darting from side to side, looking for his prey.

He was loyal, dedicated and the best rat killer we'd ever seen. He significantly reduced the rat population in the compound. Often we would see him lying motionless close by an opening to a rats tunnel, waiting patiently for a potential victim. His patience was always rewarded.

In the end, however, the rats always prevailed!

CHAPTER 20
THE ETERNAL ENEMY

"Looking for a place to sleep"

They were everywhere! Layer upon layer of razor sharp Barb and Concertina Wire could not stop them. Bunkers, protected by Claymore Mines, reinforced with 8 inch square timbers and covered with tons of dirt and sandbags proved no obstacle to their innate ability to penetrate our defenses.

They basked in the tropical heat and humidity of the coastal plains, thrived in the elevated, hot highlands and rejoiced in the cool triple canopy of the mountains. Neither heat, nor dust, nor drought of the dry season nor rain, mud and mold of the wet season could deter their unyielding attacks upon us. Relentless, determined and in ever-increasing numbers, they assaulted us at every opportunity. Far more dangerous than an ambush and equally lethal to a booby trap, a Rocket Propelled Grenade or a Russian made sub-machine gun, they swarmed, slithered, crawled and walked into our lives. Long after we were gone, our eternal enemy would remain!

Born with stingers, pinchers, suckers, fangs and teeth… contaminated with Rabies, E-Coli, Salmonella and Chlamydia, the mosquitoes, ants, flies, leeches, lice, snakes, slugs, spiders, centipedes, bats, rats, monkeys and tigers contested us for every yard of Vietnamese Earth. We had no defense against them!

Insects and rodents with two legs, ten legs and hundreds of legs found the Vietnamese Countryside and especially our camps, ideal nesting areas. They hid in wooden crates and cardboard boxes, under beds, on the inside walls of tents, inside ammunition containers, between the slats of wooden pallets, inside the pockets, arms and legs of jungle pants and jackets and any other imaginable place. They chewed through boxes containing dry foodstuffs, ate the contents then raised families inside. They were ingenious, adaptive and above all persistent in their efforts to find food and residences. Those whose dietary requirements could not be satisfied with foodstuffs, garbage or carrion, fed off us.

Poisonous and non-poisonous snakes ranging in length from six inches to six feet, slithered across the coastal plains, highlands and mountains, swam the rivers and swamps and *climbed* the trees and bushes. Their natural camouflage made them almost impossible to see until we literally stepped on or ran into them face to face. The most feared was a small, green, tree-climbing variety. Its proper name was Bamboo Viper… we just called it the "Two Step." They were famous for hanging from tree branches or brush at eye level. Rumor has it that once bitten on the face; the neurotoxin was transmitted directly to the brain, killing the unlucky recipient in the time it took him to take two steps.

Medics always considered a snakebite to be poisonous since, in most cases, we couldn't tell a poisonous snake from a non-poisonous one, even if we saw it. The preferred treatment was the immediate administration of an anti-venom injection by a medic but not all men in the field had immediate access to a medic and most medics had no access to the snakebite anti-venom kits. These were rarely issued to field medics. They were instead, reserved for field hospitals, where, from a life saving point of view, they would do the least amount of good. Without a snakebite kit and a nearby medic, a soldier's only hope for survival was a tourniquet, a Medivac and a prayer.

At the top of the animal food chain were the Bengal Tigers. Drawn to the mountains and highlands by the rotting corpses from the decades of war with the French, Japanese and British, they roamed unhindered. To these large carnivores, Vietnam was a "Free Food Counter." Having acquired a taste for human flesh, they often pounced upon unsuspecting GI's at night. There was little that an individual soldier could do against a four hundred pound ravenous cat, bent on a meal. Most night encounters were fatal, fatal for the human. During daylight hours, they were much less of a threat, the exception being a tigress defending her cubs. On occasion at night, I would hear the loud moaning of the big cats as they cleared their throats and declared their dominance of the Vietnamese Highlands.

Jungle boots, taken off at night, provided safe and secluded sleeping quarters for creatures like centipedes, spiders, scorpions, rats and the occasional snake. They crawled in and set up residence, usually in the toe area of the boots. A bite or sting on the foot meant a guaranteed painful episode or a one-way ticket home in a gray metal casket.

Morning "Boot Banging" was a process everyone quickly learned. It involved grabbing a boot, orienting it such that the heel was down and the toe pointed upwards, then forcefully banging the heel on the ground or any other hard surface three or four times. This usually dislodged any squatters from the toe area, causing them to fall to the heel where you promptly shook them out then beat them to death with the boot. Unfortunately, boot banging was never a 100% guaranteed process. Diehard boot inhabitants often held onto their residence in the toes of boots with death like grips. We always assumed boot banging to be unsuccessful until the final, scariest step, hand checking the boots.

I hated this part. It involved slowly pushing my hand into the boot and hopefully touching the toe of the boot before encountering any furry, slimy or multi-leg life form. A couple of close encounters, once with a scorpion and the second time with a centipede forced me into another boot banging and toe checking process. I was fortunate never to have been bitten or stung.

Creature infestation turned simple jobs into dangerous tasks and forced us to be more aware of our surroundings. For the combat engineer working on a piece of machinery, the unwritten rule was, "never stick an exposed hand into an area you couldn't see." Sticks were used as probes into these areas. Gloves, where available, provided protection for mechanics or engineers but many refused to wear them because it reduced their sensitivity to "Feel."

On one occasion at base camp, a soldier walked into the medical tent gripping what appeared to be an inflated, red rubber glove. As he walked closer, I realized it wasn't a rubber glove but his hand, swollen to three times normal size, red and inflamed. While working on the underside of a vehicle without gloves, something bit him. Within minutes, the swelling began.

I ran to the mess tent and asked the mess sergeant for a supply of ice for my patient. Returning with a large chunk, I chopped it into smaller pieces with my survival knife then added it to a large stainless steel bowl filled with water and immediately immersed his hand in it, hoping to reduce the swelling and the spread of toxins. A small single puncture mark was visible on his thumb. Because there was only one puncture mark, I concluded that it was not a snakebite but most probably a bite from a giant centipede or a scorpion sting. Scorpions however, rarely set up shop on the underside of trucks because of the difficulty in moving and climbing across the oily, greasy, metal surfaces. Centipedes, however, climbed everything and went everywhere. The battalion surgeon looked at the hand and the puncture and agreed with me that it was a centipede bite. Such bites on the torso, arms or legs were not usually fatal but they were extremely painful.

I gave him a codeine based painkiller and Benadryl to counteract any possible allergic reactions. For the next forty-eight hours, I kept him in the medical tent, all the time icing his hand. It took three days for the swelling to go down completely and another week before his hand was fully functional. He was lucky. The price to pay for carelessness in Vietnam was often quite high.

None of our training for Vietnam covered the dangers posed by the indigenous creatures. This, we learned through practical experience only. For some, the experience came too late to be useful. Today, forty years later, I still "Bang Out" my boots. Old habits are hard to break.

CHAPTER 21
MIND OVER MATTER

"Time had no meaning to us in Vietnam. Every day was the
same as the next. It was just another day trying to stay alive"
Jack Manick

Surrounded by a large cloud of dust, the weekly supply truck pulled up in front of the Command Bunker and came to a brake squealing halt. The passenger door opened and an enormous, hulking man, dressed in bright green jungle fatigues, carefully stepped down from the elevated cab onto the ground below. He looked more like a Sumo Wrestler than a soldier. Turns out, he was our new assistant cook. Holy shit, I thought to myself, how is this guy going to survive here, he won't last a month!

His weight surely must have tipped the scales at close to three hundred pounds. By any standards, he was grossly overweight; by Vietnam standards he was lethally overweight! The Army should never have sent him here. Only a desperate need for ever more troops forced such a callous, life threatening decision. It was insanity!

Our new assistant cook sweated like a pig. His clothes were constantly wringing wet. Oft times, while serving chow in the mess tent, I would watch as sweat poured from his brow and fell directly into the prepared food containers or a food tray held in the outstretched hand of a GI. The first time it happened to me, I stared in disbelief as he slopped some form of food onto my stainless steel tray then added a quantity of fresh salt and bacteria laden sweat.

"Hey man," I said to him, "you're sweating into the food."

Without so much as an eye blink, he slowly raised his head, starred at me briefly then in a nasty tone said "Move on Doc!"

"Mother fucker," I mumbled to myself. I had eaten far worse than this, but I didn't feel like any of the men should get sick because of his sloppy health habits. I spoke to the Mess Sergeant about it and shortly thereafter, the assistant cook started serving food with a bandana made of a cut up GI towel tied around his head.

"An incoming B-40 round detonates"

Every step that he took seemed to require an enormous effort.

On one oppressively hot evening, I was walking towards the Medical Bunker with my rifle in hand when, in the distance I heard that familiar sound that always stopped me dead in my tracks. It was a B-40 rocket leaving its launch tube.

I screamed out at the top of my lungs, "Incoming, Incoming."

I had heard the sound many times before and knew that I had only a few seconds at best before it hit, but where would it hit? It was a Crap Shoot. The targeted area could be anywhere. There was no cover for 30 yards in any direction and no time for me to make it to safety before the rocket hit, so I decided to just stand in place, wait for the inevitable and pray. It was a stupid move!!! I should have started running for cover but split second decisions are often governed by gut feelings rather than good judgment!

I crouched down as low as I could without actually laying on the ground. If it didn't hit me, I wanted to be able to start a full run for safety immediately after it detonated.

A tremendous concussion wave shook my body. It was immediately followed by a deafening noise.

Adrenalin took over my body as I stood up and started a full run for the command bunker and safety. I was in excellent physical shape and was running as fast as my one hundred fifty five pound frame and legs would permit when I streaked by the wooden structure that housed the shower.

"Run past the mortar pit"

Suddenly, the door flew open and a large, butt naked body emerged running at what appeared to be "Light Speed." It was the assistant cook. I couldn't believe how fast he was running. It was as if he had been shot out of a cannon. Within a few strides he had caught up to and started to pass me as we ran past the mortar pit!

No one that heavy, had the right to run that fast! We ran in parallel paths across a field of baseball sized, jagged edged gravel that had been put down to reduce the mud in the rainy season. I was fully clothed and wearing my combat boots and could feel the uneven surfaces, dips and rises in the gravel as my boots touched down on them.

My running partner was barefoot!

With his tremendous weight load, he had to be tearing up his feet on the gravel as he ran but not once did I hear him scream in pain. He looked like a gazelle escaping ͬ ͟ɪɪ a lion, floating great distances in the air from one stride to the next. It was an awe inspiring sight.

Glancing over at him, I saw the layers of fat on his upper torso shifting harmonically from side to side and up and down. He looked like a bowl of Jello in motion. Our parallel running paths parted when he suddenly veered right and headed for the mess tent bunker while I continued straight ahead towards the Command/Medical Bunker. I should have followed him to the Mess Tent Bunker since it was a shorter distance to safety than my route but logic was not with me that night and my path to safety was already locked into my legs.

Out of the corner of my eye, I saw him reach the bunker and dive head first inside. I still had a few yards to go to reach safety.

"Jack outside shower bldg and next to mortar pit "

147

"The run began at the shower building on the right and proceeded past the mortar pit and 40 yards farther "

Five yards from the bunker entrance another B-40 hit somewhere close by, shaking the ground and sending pain into my adrenaline saturated body. One more stride and I was safely inside the sand bag protected bunker. I lay down my rifle and claymore bag filled with ammo on the litter and sat down. A quick survey showed that all of my moving parts seemed to be functional but there was blood oozing through my jungle fatigues.

Pulling down my pants, I saw a number of penetration wounds, some of which had fragments of rock still protruding from them. Other wounds had no visible signs of rock fragments and I guessed that these had either fallen out or had penetrated below the level of the skin. I grabbed a bottle of sterile water and poured it down my legs and over my arms and torso. My wounds seemed to be confined to the front part and right side of my body.

I removed the fragments that I could see and reach. Most were shards of rock with a few small slivers of metal. The rock fragments were the most difficult to remove because they had a tendency to break up into smaller pieces when I tried to pull them out with forceps. Some areas of penetration had to be forced open and irrigated with water or saline to insure that no small fragments remained. Antibiotic cream was applied to the wounds then bandaged. I was lucky.

Twenty minutes later the last incoming round hit and soon thereafter, my overweight running partner hobbled into the medical bunker, propped up by two men, one under each arm. His feet were bandaged and wrapped with white T-shirts that were now a reddish brown color from the massive amount of clotted blood that had infused into it. His clothing wrapped feet reminded me of drawings of soldiers at Valley Forge.

I sat him down and carefully unwound the T-shirts. The clotted blood had almost glued them to his feet. It took many liters of sterile saline and water to free them. His feet were a mess. Deep cuts and lacerations were everywhere. Embedded in them were slivers of rock. Those that I could see I pulled out. I then washed his feet as best I could. The cuts and gouges were so extensive and deep that I determined a surgeon needed to evaluate and suture them so I asked that a Medivac be called in to take him to a field or base hospital. I never saw him again.

In his run for safety, our cook's mind convinced his body that the pain of crossing the gravel field did not matter. It was truly "Mind over Matter."

CHAPTER 22
DEATH IN THE PASS

"Television brought the brutality of war into the comfort of the living room. Vietnam was lost in the living rooms of America--not on the battlefields of Vietnam."

--Marshall McLuhan, 1975

"Vigilance is life" Jack Manick 1969

"Vehicles lined up for convoy to Cam Ranh Bay"

The last convoy that we sent through the Tran Duc Pass was ambushed. The survivors told us that the NVA had come out of hiding from the tall grass next to the roadway and surprised them. No one had expected it and there was no time to react. My turn at the Tran Duc Pass was fast approaching!

Our convoy consisted of twenty vehicles, four jeeps, four or five low bed trailers, and a mixture of dump trucks, deuce-and-a-halves and five tons. Each jeep was armed with a pedestal mounted M-60 machine gun. Convoy personnel carried a mixture of M-16s, M-14s or M-79 Grenade Launchers. By most standards, our convoy was lightly armed.

I rode shotgun in a five ton cab that was towing a low bed trailer. My driver was a middle aged gentleman from the Vermont National Guard named Pidge. I was twenty two years old and Pidge was a bit over forty. To me, he was an old man. Pidge was a great guy with a wonderful personality and a kind heart. During our two hundred fifty mile convoy we became fast friends.

I brought a bag of tropical chocolate bars with me to give away to any kids that we passed by on the roadside. The Army referred to them as tropical chocolate because they never melted, even in the blistering heat of Vietnam. My first bite into one, months earlier, almost made me puke. It tasted like the bittersweet chocolate laxative that my grandmother always gave me. Most guys refused to eat them unless they were starving. We tried trading them for goods with the Vietnamese but they hated them too. I once threw a handful to some children who were playing by the roadside. They picked them up and threw them back at me. So much for good will!

I jumped up into the cab of our truck, threw my equipment, aid bag and additional medical supplies down onto the floor and watched it quickly disappear from sight. "What the fuck," I said to myself, where did my equipment go? A closer look at the floorboards inside the cab on my side of the vehicle revealed no floor boards. They were gone and my equipment was resting on the ground beneath our truck. Shit!

I crawled under the truck and retrieved my equipment, all the while muttering obscenities.

"Hey Pidge," I yelled up to him, "where are the damn floorboards… how are we going to drive this rig to Cam Ranh Bay with half of the floor missing?" I quickly walked to the convoy commander's jeep and asked him if we could trade this cab in for another…one with floorboards.

His response was short and terse, "None available Doc, you'll have to make due."

"Yes Sir," I replied, in a proper military manner as I walked back to my ride.

Shit…that was easy for him to say, he didn't have to eat road debris for the next 250 miles.

I climbed into the elevated cab. Pidge pushed the starter button and the massive five ton diesel engine roared to life with a loud metallic sound and a large thick cloud of black diesel smoke. The truck in front of us pulled out and we followed. Almost immediately, small pieces of dirt and rock, kicked up by our front tires, started coming up through the opening in the floor boards and into the cab. After a few miles of being pelted with road debris, I removed my flak jacket and threw it over the missing floorboards, hoping to reduce the flow of material into the cab. Pidge then removed his flak jacket and I put his on top of mine on the floor. It didn't prevent the dirt and dust from coming through but it did spare us from being hit by the gravel and rocks.

With our flak jackets on the floor of the truck, however, we had no protection from shrapnel hits should we be attacked. Pidge and I figured the tradeoff was worth it…after all…no one lives forever!

Three hours into the trip, the trucks in front of us slowed and then pulled off to the side of the road just at the outskirts of a small village. This was a rest and piss stop. Children rushed up to our trucks, trying to sell us cold canned or bottled sodas. A cold soda was a buck…a worthwhile tradeoff after sucking down tons of road dust and drinking warm canteen water.

"Pidge (Cleon Pidgeon) giving candy to kids at rest stop. Pidge was undoubtedly the nicest , kindest, most caring soldier and man who I ever met. He treated the Vietnamese children as though they were his own. It was truly inspirational to have served with him if only for a short period of time"

Just before our convoy departed camp that morning we were once again warned about buying soda from the locals. The VC and NVA were adding ground glass and acids to soda bottles and cans and then giving them to the children to sell to us. This was old news. We were all told about these and others dangers during our in-country lectures months earlier at our ports of arrival. I found it hard to believe that children would willingly sell us such deadly drinks.

Ground glass was the medium of choice for bottled soda. It was a simple process to remove a bottle cap, pour in a quantity of ground glass then immediately close it again. If it were done properly and quickly, very little carbonation would be lost, thus keeping the soda as fresh and tamper free looking as possible.

Adding acid to a can of soda was somewhat more difficult and very hard to detect. Nineteen Sixty Vintage Soda cans were made of metal and had to be soldered together. The soldered seams were the weakest point in the can and the easiest portal of entry for the acid. The tools needed to introduce the acid were fairly easy to scrounge up: a glass syringe with a stainless steel needle, acid and a soldering gun. The acid was drawn into the glass syringe then a soldering gun's red hot tip placed against a spot on the soldered seam where the two metal surfaces met. The point of the needle was then placed next to the soldering iron tip and a moderate amount of downward pressure exerted on it. When the solder reached melting point and started to flow, the tip of the needle penetrated the solder and went straight into the can. The acid was then injected into the soda and the needle quickly removed. The hot liquid solder then flowed back into the puncture, sealing it. The soldering iron was then removed and the solder quickly solidified...voila, one can of poisoned soda.

Detecting acid laced soda cans was difficult at best. Our only means to detect an acid laced can was to pour a small amount of the soda onto a metal surface and look for evidence of the metal being eaten away. Usually, the bubbles that are released when an acid is eating away a metal are a dead giveaway but how would we distinguish between the bubbles being released from the carbonation in the soda versus the bubbles from the acid reacting to a metal surface?

What if you had no metal handy...what if you were too thirsty to wait? There were no foolproof means of detection. The rule was, when in doubt, don't drink it.

I was dying for a cold drink, so I decided to go for it. I handed a young girl a red, one dollar MPC(Military Payment Certificate alias funny money) and smiling back at me, she handed me a cold can of coke. She then moved on to another truck in the convoy trying to sell the remainder of the soda that she was carrying. I opened the can and poured a little on a flat portion of one of the fenders on our truck. I waited a few minutes until the bubbles from the carbonation dissipated. What I saw next shocked and pissed me off. The OD Green painted metal surface was changing color and eroding. Shit, I never thought I'd encounter a can of "tampered soda." I threw it to the ground and grabbed my canteen of warm water. Pidge bought a can of non-tampered soda and shared it with me.

"The beginnings of the Pass"

A few minutes later, we departed and two hours later, we were at the beginnings of the Tran Duc Pass. This 5-mile section of the road connected the Central Highlands Plateau to the coastal plain below. It twisted and turned as it threaded its way downwards. There were no guardrails and few places to pull off. It was a driving nightmare for the careless or inattentive driver and a death sentence for those not prepared for an attack.

To our left the ground sloped upwards at a 45-degree angle. To our right, it dropped off sharply for at least five hundred to one thousand feet. On both sides of the road, there was sufficient chest high dried grass, scrub brush and small trees for anyone to hide in. I had an uneasy feeling about this section of the road.

Because of the ambush last week, I was especially cautious. I kept my carbine in my hand with my finger on the safety.

"Hanging over the edge. A careless mistake and a helping hand from a higher spirit allowed the two occupants of this truck to live today"

About a half mile into the pass, I noticed the truck in front of us driving much too fast for the road conditions. What an idiot, I thought. Were his brakes not working?

The distance between us began to grow ever larger. We could have matched his speed through the tight hairpin turns but that would have been too dangerous. Just before going into a sharp left hand turn, he locked up his rear brakes in an obvious attempt to slow down but it was too little too late...not enough braking power and not enough road remaining.

He made a desperation move and cut the wheels hard left throwing the truck into a counterclockwise spin. The rear of the truck headed for the embankment and the steep drop off just beyond the edge of the road.

In a cloud of dust, the rear end started going over the drop off and all I could think of was "Shit, these guys are dead," then suddenly the truck stopped. It hung over the cliff like a teeter totter for a few brief seconds but the weight of the rear end hanging over the embankment started to slowly pull it backwards and downwards. Just before what I thought would be the last few seconds in the driver and passenger's lives, the front wheels that were turned fully left, caught on the lip in the road and brought the truck to an abrupt halt.

Pidge slammed on the brakes of our truck and we came to a screeching halt about twenty yards from them. I jumped out and ran towards them yelling "get the fuck out, get the fuck out of the truck!" They both jumped out of the windows and onto the steep downward slope. For a few brief seconds, the truck just sat there, motionless, almost as if it was deciding what to do, then with a loud groan, rolled over the lip in the road and started its downward death plunge.

"The Death plunge"

Picking up speed at an alarming rate it then flipped over and started doing cartwheels down the ever steepening slope until it came to rest about a quarter mile down.

The truck carried nothing of value but because of its location, it was lost forever. It was unsalvageable! The driver of the truck blamed brake failure as the cause but Pidge and I knew better.

The men inside had made it out unharmed and that's all that mattered. It was only a truck.

"The final resting place of the truck"

The convoy started up again and we proceeded to thread our way downwards. I kept my eyes on the roadside to my right and the grass covered slope that ran right up to the edge. After traveling another three quarters of a mile, a sudden explosion shook our truck. Fragments of either shrapnel or rock pelted the driver's side of our cab.

"We travel deeper into the pass"

"Just fucking great, I said to myself, our flak jackets are on the floor and no time to get them!" I tried to look out over Pidge's shoulder and up the slope to see where the explosions were hitting but the angle of the window would allow me to see only about twenty feet up the slope. Shit!

Another explosion, then another and with each detonation, our truck was being hit with shrapnel, rock fragments or both. Each new explosion was closer to us than the one before it. It seemed as though they had singled out our truck as an aiming point. Just our luck!

It was probably a diversion, I thought, they're probably going to hit us from the roadside! I changed my focus from the explosions on the hillside and refocused it onto grassy down slope to my right. I flipped the safety on my carbine to the off position and then moved my body to provide a face to face firing position into the chest high grass.

Out of the corner of my eye, I detected movement. The sound of AK-47 firing suddenly added to the explosions on the hillside close by us. Steel jacketed rounds began punching holes in the door around my feet and by the grace of God, none hit me or Pidge.

The truck in front of us slowed, forcing us to do the same. Were they fucking crazy? Stopping now was suicide! It was just what the NVA wanted us to do! Was the lead truck hit or damaged? I had no way of knowing. We were now barely moving.

In the blink of an eye, three NVA emerged from the tall grass directly in front of me and were within hand shaking distance in a second or two. Their weapons were pointing directly at our cab…but they didn't fire.

"Why didn't they open up…what were they waiting for," I thought. In the split second of their indecision, time froze. They were terrified. I could see it in their faces. So was I.

I pulled the trigger and loosed a sustained burst of thirty rounds into them, emptying the magazine. I could see the pain in their eyes as the 30 caliber lead bullets ripped through their bodies. They collapsed to the ground. I will never understand why, in that moment of time, Pidge and I were selected to live and they to die.

I reloaded. There was no way to tell how many NVA were waiting in the high grass, waiting for their moment to attack, so I pointed my M-2 Carbine at the grassy area near the roadside and emptied the thirty round magazine. There was firing from vehicles in front of and behind us. There was no way to tell how extensive the attack was. If the NVA disabled the lead vehicle and blocked the road with it, then we were all dead men. Retreat was impossible because in most areas, the road was too narrow to turn our large vehicles around.

Suddenly, a deafening blast and concussion wave shook our vehicle. I leaned out of the passenger window and looked behind us. The vehicle immediately following us was hit and was burning. "They're hit," I yelled out at Pidge. "I gotta go and help, you keep going."

"Are you crazy" he yelled out, "they'll kill you too."

"I can't leave them. Keep going! Once you guys get to a safe area, send back help." With that, I grabbed my aid bag, rifle and ammo, opened the door and jumped off the truck.

The damaged truck was about thirty yards from me and burning. Flames and thick black clouds of smoke were pouring from it. I crouched down and started to run to the truck. About half way there I saw two NVA in the grass to my left. Both were covered with blood and were severely injured. I couldn't take a chance that they could shoot back so I fired two bursts into each of them and continued back towards the truck.

The passenger's side of the truck was crumpled from the explosion so I approached from the driver's side.

Reaching the driver's door, I saw that the convoy had come to a complete stop. Shit…were they fucking crazy? That's just what the NVA wanted; stop the whole convoy for one truck. I motioned at the truck immediately behind me to come forward. As he came up next to me I yelled out, "keep it moving or we all die here. I'm staying to help the wounded, send back help when you can and motioned for him to move on. As the next truck approached I waved it on and yelled out, "keep going, send back help when you can."

I had probably just signed my death sentence!

I ran to the truck, stepped up to the driver's door and looked in. There was blood everywhere. I had never seen so much blood in a confined area. The passenger was blown near in half and the driver was unconscious but still breathing. I tried to open the door but it was stuck. The explosion had probably buckled it. I pulled and pulled until my arms grew numb. Reaching in through the open window, I grabbed the driver under his arm pits and slowly pulled him out of the door. I was precariously balanced on the running board and as I pulled him out of the cab, we both fell to the pavement, he on top of me.

I rolled him off me and dragged him away from the burning truck, lest it explode. Men in trucks passing by me yelled out, "want me to stop, want help?" I just waved them on yelling "get the fuck out of here."

As the last truck in the convoy approached, two men jumped off and ran up to me. "Get the fuck outta here I yelled. If you stay here, you will die with the two of us."

"It's OK Doc, we're not leaving you. If we die, we die together! No one is leaving you here alone!"

"Thanks guys," I said as I turned my attention back to the injured man. I ripped open his shirt and saw some small puncture wounds but they were in the area of his shoulder blades…nothing serious. There were also some shrapnel wound in his legs but nothing life threatening. I pulled back his eyelids and looked at his pupils. Both seemed to react equally, which meant no brain damage.

All went quiet as the last truck disappeared into the distance. Now we waited, waited for either help to come or for the NVA to return. At best, I gave us a ten percent chance of survival.

I dragged my patient across the road and up against the steep embankment that rose upwards from the edge. At least here, with our backs against the embankment, the NVA couldn't approach us from behind. If they came, it would be a face to face fight.

I looked at my watch…it was a little after 1 PM. I continued to check the vital signs of the injured man. His pulse was strong but he was still unconscious. In between checking him, I kept watch on the grass across the road. My two friends had moved a few yards down the road to my right and left to cover those areas of approach.

"Gooks, Gooks coming in," I heard from the man on my left. Looking left, I saw two NVA coming out of the grass and running in our direction. The man to my left fired a long burst at them dropping them immediately. Just then I heard screaming coming from the grassy area directly in front of me. Three NVA emerged firing their AK-47's. I was in a kneeling position on the roadside. I took quick aim at their chests then let loose a half magazine into them. Luckily for me, they were bunched close together…a fatal mistake on their part. My sustained burst didn't have to be all that accurate to take them out.

I realized that my original idea of putting our backs against the upslope prevented us from being hit from behind but it also gave us little or no reaction time to any NVA emerging at the roads edge from the grass.

I heard firing from my right but dared not take my attention from the grass directly in front of me.

"Let's move forward," I yelled out at my buddies. I crouched down and moved towards the grassy area and the beginning of the down slope then peering down, saw three or four NVA about thirty yards down the hillside coming our way. I carefully aimed and fired three, three round bursts. One NVA fell but the other three continued.

My magazine was out! I reached down into my claymore bag and grabbed a fresh magazine while screaming, "I'm out, three Gooks coming up the slope." I heard more firing from my buddies. "Got em Doc!"

I pulled a grenade from my pistol belt, pulled the pin then threw it down the slope. "Grenade out," I yelled. A few second later it went off. "If you have any grenades," I screamed, use them now!" Four more explosions followed in quick succession. I had one grenade left; a white phosphorus. I pulled it from my claymore bag, pulled the pin and threw it as far as I could. "Willy Pete Out," I yelled. A few seconds later an explosion and a fireworks like display of burning white phosphorus filled the air.

Reaching into my Claymore Bag, I found only four magazines left. After that was expended, my remaining defense was my 45 pistol.

"How are you guys doing on ammo?"

"Four mags Doc...Three mags Doc!" Shit, I said to myself. We didn't have enough rounds to take the offensive at the edge of the road.

"Let's move back to the wall, I yelled out...we are too short on ammo to use auto fire." We back peddled to the wall, all the while never taking our eyes off the tall grass. Here, we would live or die. I had heard stories about the torture we would face as prisoners so I looked at my two friends and in a calm voice said, "Don't let them take you alive!"

They both looked at me and after a second or two quietly said, "OK Doc."

"If I have to," I said, I'll take out my patient and force them to kill me!"

We waited and waited and waited for the inevitable, for a final push by the enemy. Time seemed to stand still as we looked and waited and prayed for a miracle. Suddenly I heard the familiar sound of a diesel engine, just as a truck, loaded with heavily armed men, rounded the bend about fifty yards from us. Immediately behind it was another truck, loaded with armed men. They lay down an incredible amount of firepower on the down slope.

The trucks were from our convoy...they had returned for us!

As the lead truck approached, an officer jumped out and ran up to us. "What the hell are you doing here sir," I exclaimed?

"You didn't think we were gonna leave you here Doc, did you," he said. The convoy is a few miles down the road, in a relatively safe area. I had to make sure that the convoy was safe before we came back for you. It took us a few minutes to get the men together and turn around the trucks. Every man volunteered to come back!

Men piled off the trucks and formed a perimeter around us and the destroyed truck.

"They came back for us sir, the NVA. We took out five here along the roadside and at least three down the hillside. Thanks for coming back sir, we figured our time was just about up. Our ammo was low and we made a pact not to be taken alive sir."

"No need for that Doc, we are all in this together!"

Men were screaming, "get in the truck Doc." A litter was brought over to us and we loaded the injured man on it.

"What about the other man," the lieutenant asked?

"Gone sir! Not much left after the explosion and fire. We need to get someone up here to bring back what's left of his body."

"Choppers are on the way," he said. "They will recover the body. We gotta di di(get out of here). It's too hot here!"

I jumped up onto the truck bed with my patient in the back and we headed for our final destination, Cam Ranh Bay.

"After the ambush nearing Cam Ranh Bay"

Chapter 23
Hey Soldier

Five hours later, our truck followed the long line of olive drab vehicles through the heavily fortified main gate of the Cam Ranh Bay Base and into relative safety. It seemed like ages ago that I had last been here, but in reality it was barely seven months. Our injured man was met at the gate by a medical team and transported to the hospital. I later found out that he lived and was sent home.

As we drove deeper into the base, I realized that this wasn't the same place that I remembered when I first came into country. It had dramatically changed!

"In the 8 months since I'd been here, Cam Ranh Bay had transformed itself into a paradise...however, the modern barracks and the resort like facilities of Cam Ranh Bay gave everyone a false sense of security for outside the gates and layers of Barb wire lay an enemy determined not to lose the war"

The city of tents that once covered the huge expanse of sand was replaced with permanent buildings made of wood and corrugated metal. The barron, sandy landscape that once dominated Cam Ranh Bay was now seeded with grass and planted with shrubbery. Roads that were once dirt or gravel had been transformed into blacktop. My jaw dropped as we passed by tennis and volleyball courts, Enlisted Men's and USO Clubs, reading rooms and libraries. It was a virtual paradise. I couldn't believe such dramatic changes could be made in such a short period of time!

I soon found out that all weapons in Cam Ranh Bay were kept under lock and key in Arms Rooms…an insane and incredibly stupid decision that could cost men their lives. If attackers penetrated the outer defense perimeter, they could easily slaughter the unarmed troops inside before they ever had a chance to get to their "Locked UP" weapons and ammunition. Did the officers in charge of the base feel so secure in their abilities to repulse an initial ground attack with only those on guard duty that they denied others easy access to their weapons?

The "New" Cam Ranh Bay had all the conveniences of home… volleyball and tennis courts, weight rooms, movies, PX's, and swimming at the beach…complete with life guards. If you ignored the guard bunkers, barb wire, rocket attacks and weapons, you would swear that you were at a stateside military base.

While the changes made during the past seven months were progressive from a facilities and convenience perspective, I didn't like them. It gave those living within the confines of the base a false sense of security, for in reality, a few feet outside the mass of barb and concertina wire, lurked an enemy, determined not to lose the war.

We passed by men lounging in beach chairs, just "catching some rays." It looked more like a college campus than a military base in a war zone!

"Clean sheets...Wow!"

We stopped in front of a large wood framed, metal roofed building. It was our barracks for the night. Inside were scores of bunk beds, all containing clean white cotton sheets and pillowcases the likes of which I hadn't seen in months.

I dumped my flak jacket on a bed and made a b-line for the Post Exchange (PX). It was close by and I was dying for a cold soda, one without ground glass or battery acid. We were all filthy, dirty, tired and recovering from the loss of a fellow comrade in the pass. I removed my boonie hat from my head and hung it from the lanyard of my pistol. In my right hand, I carried my Carbine. I had un-chambered the round from the firing chamber but left the magazine in the receiver housing.

Nearing the entrance to the PX, I noticed a second lieutenant just in from the states. He was a sight...wearing heavily starched bright green jungle fatigues, new spit shined jungle boots and a boonie hat with a second Lieutenant bar sewn to the front. He looked like a poster boy for a recruitment campaign.

He walked straight at me, hoping that I would move out of his way. I didn't! I was too tired to stray from my direct path to the PX entrance so I forced him to move around me and my friends. As he passed me by, I did not salute. Military protocol and saluting was the farthest thing from my mind at that moment, besides, saluting an officer in Nam was just like issuing the recipient a death sentence. If you wanted to get an officer killed while stationed in the bush or in an outpost camp, just salute him and point him out to any VC or NVA sniper in the area.

After we passed, I heard someone yell out in a loud, forceful voice, "Hey soldier."

I kept walking.

"Hey soldier, I'm talking to you…you without a hat."

I kept walking and didn't turn around. He quickly ran up and positioned himself no more than a foot in front of my face. He must have thought he was my drill instructor from basic training.

He was short, thin and looked like he had just gotten out of high school. "Where's your hat mister? Don't you know how to salute an officer? Why is there a magazine in that weapon? Why didn't you salute me? What kind of weapon are you carrying? That's an unauthorized weapon! You are filthy and your boots need polish! You are a disgrace to the army."

I could see some of the other guys from my convoy standing behind him, making faces at me, trying to make me laugh.

"Don't you have anything to say soldier? What's your name?" If I wasn't so tired, pissed and thirsty, I might have thought the situation amusing…but I was tired and pissed and thirsty.

I did a quick scan of him from head to toe then looked him straight in the eye and said, "Get the fuck out of my way."

"What did you say soldier," he quickly replied.

"You heard me the first time, get the fuck out of my way," I said, as I slowly raised my carbine and chambered a round. Looking as if he'd seen his life passing before him, he stepped aside and let me pass. He never spoke another word to me.

Arriving at the PX, I drank five or six cold cokes, made my purchases then went back to the barracks for a welcomed hot shower, a clean bed and a semi-protected night's sleep.

Camp Swampy - Late 1969 - D9 Dozer with medic Jack Manick in the driver seat

"A Caterpiller D-9. It was the biggest, yellowist dozer I'd ever seen"

"On our way back to the Central Highlands"

The next morning our truck was loaded with the largest, yellowist, yellow bulldozer I'd ever seen. Painted on its side was the model number… D9D. It was a great advertisement for Caterpillar but was also something else; it was a great aiming point for any NVA wanting to shoot at us. It would be a difficult target to miss.

We left Cam Ranh Bay about mid morning… not a good sign. There wouldn't be nearly enough time to make it back to camp before dark even if it was an incident free trip and it wasn't.

Because of the weight of the dozer, our convoy was forced to drive at a snail's pace over the pot hole ridden roads. When we hit the upward slope of the Tran Duc Pass, we crawled. The weight of the D-9 forced Pidge to use low, low gears in order to get the most pulling power. We were going so slow that people walking on the road were passing us.

It took most of the remaining daylight hours to make it to the top of the pass, then, suddenly, everything went wrong. One of the right rear axles on our trailer broke due to the tremendous weight of the dozer, bringing our convoy to a grinding halt.

The broken axle and the tires attached to it were pulled upwards, away from the road surface and chained there, allowing us to continue our drive. Minutes later, as fate would have it; the remaining axel on the same side of the trailer broke. With two axels gone, the truck could not be driven with the dozer on the back.

Our options were limited…we had no means to repair the truck where it sat in the few hours of daylight that remained and we needed to find a place of relative safety for the convoy to stay for the night. Pulling out his map, the convoy commander found a joint US/Korean Compound about five miles away.

We had no choice but to offload the dozer and drive it to the compound. Daylight was quickly disappearing so I jumped on the dozer with Pidge and we started the slow five mile trek to our "Motel for the Night." With the weight of the dozer no longer weighing down the trailer, it was slowly driven to the camp. Working through the night, a semi-permanent repair was put into place allowing the convoy to pull out early in the morning.

We made it back to Camp Swampy without any further incidents. Our convoy to Cam Ranh Bay was a tragic reminder of how fragile life is and how no one promises us tomorrow.

CHAPTER 24
OUR OWN WORST ENEMY

"The Bunker by Day"

"The Bunker by Night"

In spite of our best intentions, we are often our own worst enemy. The sun had just dropped below the horizon and a wisp of residual light still lingered in the western sky. I was in the medical bunker, removing layers of dust from scores of prescription drug bottles when a large concussion shook the bunker. It was immediately followed by an ear shattering explosion. I instinctively ducked down into a crouching position, forgetting that I was protected from the razor sharp shrapnel by the tons of timber and dirt that surrounded me. I reached down for my pistol belt, strapped it on, grabbed my rifle, ammo bag, aid bag and waited for the inevitable screams for "Medic!"

Another explosion and concussion wave followed close behind the first, shaking the bunker and causing wisps of dirt to fall from between the wooden ceiling joists. Although a great source of protection from rocket or mortar fire, this or any other bunker could easily become our coffins should the enemy penetrate the wire and gain entrance into the compound. I hoped this wouldn't be a repeat of Lac Thien!

I positioned myself close to the entrance of the Medical Bunker when suddenly a man burst in and almost knocked me over. Breathing heavily, he told me that a soldier was down by guard tower number six. Crouching low, I followed him outside. The light from the stars that night were as beautiful as I'd ever seen in Vietnam and they provided me with all the light that I needed to get to the injured man.

Thirty or forty strides later, I saw three beams of light focused on the ground. As I drew closer, I realized that they were focused on the injured man. His leg was terribly deformed. A bone was protruding through the muscle just above the knee. In addition, both bones were broken in his lower leg. I asked him what happened and he said that he had jumped from the top level of the guard tower to the lower level when the first rocket came in, breaking his leg. The lower level of the guard tower was more heavily fortified and would have provided him with better protection from shrapnel, he said, so he made the decision to jump down rather than climb down the ladder. It was a poor decision!

I was surprised that there wasn't more blood loss. I bandaged the area and immobilized the leg with wire mesh material, lightly taping the mesh to the uninjured parts of the leg above and below the break. I could not set the leg; that would have to be done at a hospital. I asked one of the men standing nearby to go back to the medical bunker and bring back a litter. We carefully picked him off the ground a few inches (while supporting the broken leg) and placed him onto the litter. I was fearful that we might puncture an artery with the broken bones if we were not extremely careful.

Once inside the medical bunker I asked Paul Skerritt, my good friend and one of the Radio Operators, to call for a Medivac. I packed pillows around and under the leg, trying to cushion it from any jarring he might encounter in the chopper or our transporting him to it. He was in pain but not enough to warrant administering Morphine. I always preferred pain and a clear head rather than morphine which, while reducing pain, slowed bodily functions and masked the underlying causes of the pain.

Thirty minutes later a Medivac called in and said he was inbound and was five minutes out. We grabbed the litter and carried him outside towards a prearranged area within the compound where the helicopter would land.

One of the lieutenants in our company and two other men accompanied us. About half way to the landing area I caught a whiff of something I never expected to smell in Vietnam, Tear Gas. The last time I smelled it was at the gas chamber at Fort Dix in January 1968, during my basic training.

"Shit, they're gassing us," I yelled out. My eyes immediately started to tear uncontrollably...then the burning began.

We had no gas masks. Although they were issued to us, we never expected to use them in Vietnam so we just threw them away. "If the gooks attack us now," I yelled out, "We're screwed!" Trying to defend yourself while being gassed is like trying to drive a car with your eyes closed.

The burning however wasn't as bad as I remembered. That indicated to me that the source of the gas was a distance away and the wind was probably helping to dissipate it.

Suddenly, I heard the familiar whop, whop, whop staccato like noise of the approaching "Huey." We stopped close to the area where the bird was to come in, put down the litter and waited. Someone popped red smoke to indicate the wind direction to the helicopter pilot while at the same time, a number of trucks pointed their headlights at the Landing Zone. The chopper, now on its final approach, turned on a spotlight to survey its touchdown point.

Twenty feet off the ground, he turned 180 degrees and slowly started settling to earth. The smell of tear gas still permeated the air. As it touched down, we picked up the litter and ran towards the Medivac. A first lieutenant in our battalion who accompanied us to the LZ was being waved at by the chopper pilot. He ran up and there was a very brief discussion between the two. It was about the Tear Gas. The pilot was a real trooper and agreed to stay for the pickup regardless of the gas.

We put the litter on the chopper and I gave the medic on board a quick description of the injuries. I had to yell directly into his ear in order to be heard over the roar of the engines. Exiting the bird, the engines revved up and the chopper lifted off the ground and disappeared into the blackness of the night.

We later found out that the gassing was not hostile, but friendly. In his haste to illuminate the Landing Zone with a parachute flare, a sergeant grabbed a CS Tear gas rocket canister instead and fired it. It landed in the wire upwind of our location and with the wind blowing in, we gassed ourselves.

On that evening we were our own worst enemy.

CHAPTER 25
DONUT DOLLIES

They didn't come for money because there was none. They didn't come for the climate because it was either oppressively hot, humid and dusty or depressingly hot, wet and moldy year round. Their benefits were zero, their vacation time non-existent, the food they ate disgusting, the living conditions deplorable and their prospects for early retirement very high. They came because of the audience, they came because of us.

They weren't performers or comedians or instructors or professors although in reality, they may have been. They were the woman or the girl next door, your best friend's sister, someone's daughter, granddaughter, wife or even mother. They earned no college credits and were given no awards for their service, although they should have. No one promised them good jobs or any jobs when they got back to the states. No one promised them anything. They came to Vietnam to be with the troops, to be with us. They were affectionately known as "Donut Dollies" but we thought of them as angels.

They served food in the large mess halls in Saigon, Cam Ranh Bay and Ben Hoa where the food was tolerable and the eating conditions good and in the sweaty, bug infested, mess tents and bunkers that were scattered throughout the country. The only payback that they ever asked from us was a smile.

It was a little after 5 PM on another hot, dusty, dirty day in late 1969, in the Central Highlands. I don't remember the exact date because time and dates had no meaning in combat areas. The only thing that mattered was surviving until tomorrow.

I had just returned from a short range patrol and was tired, dirty and hungry. I dropped my equipment off in the medical bunker and headed straight for the mess tent. Entering the tent, I was stopped dead in my tracks by a sight that would have turned Medusa into Mary Poppins. It was a she, a woman, a "Donut Dollie." I couldn't believe it!!!

Wearing a brown dress, she stood behind the serving line with a stainless steel spoon in her hand, dishing out food onto our metal mess trays. I grabbed a tray and moved into the serving line in front of her and just stared. I didn't know what else to do. I wanted to say hello but couldn't form those words or any words in my mouth. Was she real? Did I imagine her? Was I suffering from heat exposure?

"What can I get for you she said?" My lips were numb. It was as if I'd been bitten on the face by a Bamboo Viper and the neurotoxins had made its way to my lips, numbing them. "What can I get for you" she repeated again?

Still unable to speak, I just pointed at something; I'm not sure what it was…for all that I knew, I might have been pointing at a pot of boiling water. I just wanted to stand there and look at her…I didn't care about the food. She put something on my tray. I have no idea what it was. She was beautiful in a way I could not explain. I moved off to a table where I found a nearby seat and positioned it so I could continue to look at her.

Everyone was looking at her and just shoveling food into their mouths, regardless of what it was. It was the most attentive audience in the world. She continued to serve food to a packed house, a virtually silent audience. After eating, men refused to leave, they just sat there. I never thought the presence of a woman from back home could render us totally helpless, but she did.

No gift could ever prove to be as important and as well received as her presence with us. She risked so much to be with us and we appreciated it more than words could ever express. She stayed the night in the command bunker and was gone the next morning, gone to another camp to mesmerize yet another group of GIs.

A Better Kind Of War Game

Nancy Smoyer was a **Donut Dollie** during the war in Vietnam. She brought fun and games to our men in the field when they needed it the most.

Her **remembrances** are reprinted here in Jack Manick's column **Insights Of A Veteran**.

"Nancy Smoyer – Donut Dolly"

Almost ten years ago, I wrote the following article about Donut Dollies for www.inthegardenstate.com. The article follows.

Jack Manick

Insights Of A
Veteran

"My Byline when I was writing for Comcast and wrote the Donut Dolly Article"

Honoring Donut Dollies from the Vietnam War

What's a Donut Dollie? No, it's not someone who works at the local donut shop or the person who buys donuts for your office every morning and certainly not the fast food trucks that stop by your place of business every morning. They are a group of women who tirelessly gave of themselves to make the horrors of war more bearable for those who fought it. These women were employed by the American Red Cross, and volunteered to go to South East Asia (Vietnam) for their own "Tour's of Duty."

We called them Donut Dollies, although I don't know how that name really started. If they handed out donuts to the troops, that was certainly a very small part of what they did and what they were about. They worked at big bases like Cam Ranh Bay and Long Binh as well as outposts that had no name and could not be found on any military map. Their goal was to get out to where the troops were, spend some time with them and bring a little bit of home and love and kindness to a place that had little of that.

My first experience with a Donut Dollie was earthshaking. I had been out all day with a crew of men trying to replace a bridge that was blown by the NVA months earlier during the Tet 68 Offensive with a Bailey Bridge. We came into camp after 5 PM and went directly to the mess tent (appropriately named). I grabbed a stainless steel food tray (those funky trays with the little food compartments - like the ones you give to your two year old to eat with) and walked up to the serving line to get my portion of the culinary delights. My eyes darted across the selections of food available. I stuck out my tray in the direction of the person serving the mess, raised my eyes from the food to a sight that almost did to me what the NVA and VC had been trying to do for the past 7 months, "Kill Me."

It was a smiling face of a woman, holding a portion of a food like substance in a large serving spoon. I couldn't move, I just stared at her in disbelief, my mind trying to process the signals that my eyes and ears were sending me. She said something to me and I said nothing, my mouth and tongue had forgotten how to form words. Wow…she was an American!

Again she spoke and it seemed like an eternity before I was able to only nod yes. She placed the portion of food onto my tray. Who was she, what was she doing out in the boonies serving us food? Could she really be an American Woman? I moved down the chow line to the next server. Once again another beautiful, smiling face, another American Woman greeted me. Was this some kind of VC trick, maybe I was dreaming this or could this really be true?

It was real enough. We took our food to the tables, sat down and ate not a bite. Our attention was focused on these lovely women. Our stares were returned with smiles. After serving chow, the 2 women sat with groups of guys and talked, trying to mingle with as many men as possible within the short time that they were allocated in our camp. I hadn't seen an American Woman for more than 7 months, actually I rarely saw any women of any ethnic origin at our isolated location.

I don't remember if I ever spoke to the either of the two women that day, but their presence with us was a gift more precious than any wealth that could have been bestowed upon us. It was the first time that I had seen groups of men smiling for what seemed like hours.

Two months later, the American Red Cross allowed 2 Donut Dollies to visit us again. They came in the late morning and were to leave late that afternoon but insisted on staying longer and eventually lost their window for departure. They were forced to spend the night in the compound. They used the time to talk to men in their bunkers or sat with us on the Berm well into the wee hours of the morning.

They risked life and limb every day to give back to us a little of what we had lost. Donut Dollies were not motivated by financial gain, certainly these jobs did not qualify as high paying jobs. At best, their living accommodations were little better than ours. Their concern for personal safety was overridden by their desire to be where they could do the most good, with the troops. They were not drafted, they could have stayed home and watched the events of war unfold on CBS or NBC or ABC News. They chose not to. Theirs was a higher calling!

Amongst the fear and terror and carnage and sickness and loneliness of my tour in Vietnam, the Donut Dollie visits were the fondest and most meaningful of my memories. We called them Donut Dollies but I believe they were Angels in disguise.

If any Donut Dollies read this book, please know that we, the troops love you and we will never forget what you have done for us.

CHAPTER 26
PACKAGES FROM HOME

*"Packages and letters from home were as important to us as
the weapons of war that we carried to defend ourselves!"*

Jack Manick

**"The Purple Letter. Gail loved colorful writing paper and envelopes.
I loved receiving them."**

Packages from home never belonged to the person to whom they were sent; they belonged instead to everyone else in camp who knew that you received it. A package from home was a gift from God. Most times it contained food because GI's always wrote home for food. GIs were blessed with sixth senses and knew when even a single parcel containing food arrived in camp.

Once the recipient was identified, the fight was over. The only remaining question was how much of the food in the package would be shared with the other men in camp. In most cases, if you were able to consume and enjoy ten percent of what you received, you were lucky.

During my Tour of Duty, my best friend's girlfriend, Juliana was going to nursing school in Allentown Pennsylvania. Juliana asked her roommate and friend from Nursing School, Gail Girtch to write to me and become a pen pal. Mail from home was always precious and having Gail as a pen pal and a friend brightened even my darkest days. Her letters were always written on pretty colored stationary and her handwriting was beautiful.

Although my father and grandparents sent me packages, none could surpass those sent by Gail. The most memorable one contained a humongous jar of peanut butter and jelly. It was an all-in-one jar of peanut butter and jelly the likes of which I had never seen before but the most amazing thing in the package was a loaf of bread. I couldn't believe that she sent me a loaf of bread. I now had all of the ingredients needed to make a peanut butter and jelly sandwich.

Unfortunately, the six week transit time from home for the package rendered the bread to a rock hard consistency. It was also covered with various shades of green and yellow bread mold. Bread mold was not an unusual occurrence for the bread baked in Saigon and sent to the outpost camps. We usually just scraped the green mold off with our knives before eating it.

Having no bread to enjoy with my Peanut Butter and Jelly, I made a beeline for the mess tent and asked for some. Scraping off the green mold, I made and immediately engulfed three PBJ Sandwiches. I also shared it with my fellow medics and the guys in the radio bunker. It was heaven! I thought of Gail as I ate the sandwiches and of her kindness in sending me such wonderful gifts.

Throughout my tour of duty, Gail sent me cookies, candy, dried sausage and the best of all, canned bacon. I loved bacon and cooked it over a fire fueled by burning C-4 plastic explosives. The smell of cooking bacon was a heavenly smell that filled up the entire bunker. I was in seventh heaven and still thinking about Gail.

My stepmother, Marge makes the best chocolate chip cakes in the world. I remember, when visiting Marge and my Dad on Sundays how much I looked forward to having it for dessert after the Sunday dinner. She baked it in a Bundt pan. It was so light and fluffy and seemed to be a mile high. I wrote and asked if she would make me one and send it. She did. Packing the unfrosted cake in a box, she mailed it to me. Upon receiving it, I opened it to find three pounds of multicolored crumbs. Once again the six week transit time from the East Coast of the United States to our Camp gave the cake sufficient time to dry to a rock like consistency. The rough handling conditions during transit pulverized the cake into crumbs.

JC and I grabbed a couple of spoons and proceeded to consume the entire box of dried cake crumbs. It was delicious. Within minutes we reduced it to nothing. To this day, it is the best cake I'd ever eaten.

Many of the men in camp were married or had girlfriends. I had neither and was envious of them and the love letters they exchanged. Although I never told her in writing, I considered Gail to be my girlfriend. I so desperately wanted to call her my girlfriend and have her call me sweetheart or darling in a letter but in this aspect of my life I was too shy and afraid of rejection to ask. Even after returning home, I was afraid to meet her…a mistake that I regret to this day.

If I could find her now, I would correct this and tell her how much she meant to me in a time of my life when life and death were as certain as a coin flip.

CHAPTER 27
FRIENDLY FIRE

Friendly fire is not friendly! There is nothing more terrifying, more frightening, more confusing and more wasteful of human life than being targeted and fired upon by your own side. When a soldier is killed in action, it matters not to him whether the bullet or explosive came from a friendly or non-friendly source; the end result is the same.

If you are at home, working in an office and you make a mistake while working on a word processor or a spreadsheet, you simply go back and make the correction or hit the "Undo Function." When you make a mistake while painting a room in your home or apartment you simply paint over your mistake. When you make a mistake and you fire an explosive round onto the wrong map coordinates, there is no corrective action, there is no take back...no undo function. Once it leaves the tube or the barrel or the bomb bay, it's too late to call it back...the deed is done!

A bad map coordinate, a plotter too tired to hear the coordinates properly, someone who is hung over, stupid or is on drugs, you pick a reason, any reason will do, it doesn't matter. As we would say in the bush, "excuses are like ass holes...everybody has one!" The end result is always the same.

Such was our dilemma one evening when I was in the compound. I was about forty yards from the command bunker when I heard a whistling noise, the likes of which I'd never heard before and it was growing louder. It wasn't the sound of an incoming enemy B-40 rocket or an enemy mortar or an enemy recoilless rifle, it was something different but what was it?

The sound came from the north but to the best of my knowledge, there was nothing north of us.

Kaboom, the first round and explosion hit about fifty yards outside the outer most layer of wire that surrounded our compound. I could see the dirt and debris being thrown up into the air as it impacted. I didn't wait for round number two, I started running for cover. By the time I reached the medical bunker entrance, round two hit. The explosion was louder and the time between the explosion and the concussion less than the first round indicating that the explosive rounds were being walked into us. Kaboom, round three hit. Someone in the bunker started yelling "Incoming, Incoming, Friendly Fire, Friendly Fire!"

How did he know it was friendly fire? To the best of my knowledge, there were no artillery units in that direction. We had patrolled that area two days ago and found nothing but our patrol carried us only ten kilometers out then we swept back in a long arc towards camp. Whoever or whatever was out there had either set up shop in the last two days or was farther out than our deepest penetration into the bush.

Paul Skerritt immediately placed an emergency call into base camp and asked about any Artillery Units recently moved into our area.

"Jack and Paul Skerritt"

To our surprise, we were told that an Infantry Unit had set up a Firebase north of us, about 15 clicks (Kilometers), with 105 mm Howitzers. Our compound was well within the effective firing range of their guns but why were they shooting at us?

Our Commanding Officer ran into the radio shack and told the operator to get that arty base on the horn.

Quickly checking his codebook, Paul keyed his microphone then shouted into it "Bravo two six xray, this is 70 charlie pappa, over." Receiving no response he repeated, "Bravo two six xray, this is 70 charlie pappa, over."

"70 charlie pappa, this is Bravo two six xray , over." Paul handed the mike to the Commanding Officer.

"Roger two six xray this is 70 charlie pappa six, please be advised that we are taking 105 Mike Mike fire from our north, over. Are you firing on us, over?"

"Negative 70 charlie pappa six, we are firing support for an ARVN platoon under fire ten clicks from you, over." Explosion followed explosion as the rounds started to enter the compound.

"This is 70 charlie pappa six, you are firing on our coordinates and the rounds are now inside my perimeter you asshole…check your fire…check your fire!!! You have the wrong coordinates you fucking idiot…cease fire… cease fire, you are killing friendlies here!"

Keying his microphone and holding it in the air above his head the CO waited for the next explosions to go off then yelled into the mike, do you hear that you fucking idiot, that's your shit dropping on us, cease fire cease-fire. Boom, Boom, boom, 3 more in succession then all went quiet.

"Sorry, 70 charlie pappa six, wrong coordinates," was the last word from the firebase. They were three meaningless words, "Sorry…Wrong Coordinates." Grabbing my aid bad and rifle, I ran outside the bunker to treat the wounded. By the grace of God, there were none.

Long triangular twisted pieces of shrapnel from the 105's were everywhere. Any piece hitting a man would have cut him in two.

A number of massive five and ten ton trucks were reduced to rubble and a few tents were shredded. The term Friendly fire would forever have a special meaning to me. Friendly fire is never friendly!

CHAPTER 28
NAM PEI

I sucked in a mouthful of the vile liquid through the long bamboo straw and immediately felt the urge to vomit. The muscles in my diaphragm started to contract violently. It was as if they were trying to expel my guts through my mouth, but I hadn't yet swallowed it.

The smell reminded me of road kill which had cooked in the hot summer sun for a day or two and liquefied into an amorphous puddle of rotting fat and protein. In Vietnamese, this stuff was called Nam Pei or Rice Wine. I called it liquid vomit!

With the contractions in my gut growing ever more severe and painful, I had but fractions of a second to make a decision before my body made one for me. My host, the Montgnard Village Chief, was standing but a few meters in front of me. Protocol dictated that spitting it out was not an option and vomiting would be even worse!

In the back of my mind I kept saying to myself, "you can do this... you can do this, it's not as bad as being shot at." In reality, I'd rather be shot at than drink this swill but to keep up good relations with our allies, I swallowed.

Keeping it down was as much a nightmare as swallowing it. The contractions and pain that I felt when it was still in my mouth was nothing compared to the wild animal that I'd loosed in my stomach. My episodes of food poisoning earlier in the year were mild compared to the feelings I was now experiencing. Staring at the Chief, I tried to smile but could only grimace. My buddy, standing close beside me, leaned over and in a soft voice said "keep it down!"

I closed my eyes and said a silent prayer, praying for the strength to hold it down. After what appeared to be an eternity, I opened my eyes and saw the chief staring straight at me and smiling. I mustered a half smile in return, content in the knowledge that I'd fulfilled my obligations until I was asked to take a second mouthful!

With the taste of the first swallow still lingering in my mouth I sucked down another. Moments later I felt a warm feeling engulfing my body. It

185

was a feeling such as I'd never experienced before. This was after all, only the second alcoholic beverage that I'd ever consumed…in my life. It was a real eye opener!

Within a few moments, I downed two additional full cups of Nam Pei that was slated for my two buddies. Coming down from his elevated bamboo chair, the chief walked up to me and with a big grin on his face patted me on the back. He then presented me with a hand carved wooden cross bow. Our Vietnamese translator told me that this was a great honor.

I guess I had gone from nothing to drunk in seconds. It was a strange and rather pleasant feeling. Everything around me seemed bright and happy regardless of whether it was or wasn't. Nam Pei, being a home brewed product was fermented in four foot high earthen ware jugs. It was a prize drink for the Montgnard. After coming down off my alcoholic high, the remainder of the day was productive and personally satisfying. I was in the village as part of the Medcap Program, a military/civilian program that involved medics from camps and bases visiting local Montgnard Villages and treating the sick and injured with what medical supplies that we had excess of.

Among the pharmaceuticals that I stuffed into my aid bag for the Medcap was APC's(an aspirin based pain pill), antifungal/antibacterial creams, Tetracycline, V-Cillin K (Penicillin), eye drops, antacid tablets, laxatives, topical astringents like mercurychrome, bandages, bandaids, rubbing alcohol, peroxide, suturing kits, etc. With these supplies, I and my fellow medics were able to treat many common ailments and some injuries.

I treated the neediest first. Unfortunately there was never enough medicine to treat everyone who was sick. It was very frustrating and troubled me greatly. I always took extra medication with me even if it meant going short on supplies for the men in camp. Our new battalion surgeon, Dr. Rist, always understood my desire to treat the Montgnard, even if it depleted our supplies. He always replaced what I dispensed.

My first patient that day was an elderly lady who was probably in her fifties. She was crippled by arthritis, walked hunched over and was in obvious pain when she moved. The only relief that I could provide her was a bottle of APC's to ease her pain. Through a translator I told her how frequently to take them, then handed her a full bottle of one hundred tablets. She smiled at me then reached up and kissed me on the cheek. I felt bad that I couldn't do more to help her and realized that the APCs would run out within a month. I hoped that I could come back within a couple of months to give her additional medication but there were no guarantees that I would ever return.

Next was another elderly woman with an infection of her outer ear canal. It was covered with a rash that was red and crusty. When I looked into her ear canal with my otoscope, I saw that the rash extended the length of the ear canal up to her ear drum. It looked like a bacterial infection so I applied an antibacterial cream to the ear canal with a cotton tipped applicator. I squeezed some additional cream into a small, sterile vile and capped it. I then gave her the vial and some additional applicators, instructing her to have someone apply the cream twice a day until the cream was gone. I also gave her a seven day supply of penicillin tablets and told her to take them three times a day. The combination of the topical cream and the penicillin should knock out the problem. What I didn't know and had no way of knowing was if she was allergic to penicillin. I asked her to take one pill now and hoped that if she had a reaction it would occur while we were still there.

JC, my fellow medic and companion on this trip, and I treated women, men, children and babies as best we could. Some had broken blood vessels in their eyes, others abdominal pain or chest pain. Some symptoms were too complex for us to diagnose so we just gave them some APCs.

The Montgnard were grateful for any help that we could provide them and weren't offended when we ran out of medication.

I soon became friends with the chief and in subsequent visits to the village didn't have to partake of the rice wine ritual, thank God. Even though I couldn't understand his language, nor he mine, we communicated in a homemade sign language. The Montgnard were a good and kind and just people and I respected them greatly.

My dealings with them were among the most satisfying experiences in my Tour of Duty. I swore, never again to partake of the Nam Pei!

"Montgnard Chief being taken back to village after being sutured
from a head injury"

CHAPTER 29
THE MAD MINUTE, FREEFIRE AND SAPPERS

The sound of rifle and machinegun fire shattered the silence of an otherwise peaceful evening. Explosions from 81 millimeter High Explosive (HE) Mortar and 40 millimeter grenade rounds joined with the rifle and machine gun fire to create a deafening symphony of sound, color and death to all who wandered into its destructive path.

A tap on the shoulder from my buddy was my "go ahead" to join in with the massive exhibition of outgoing firepower that surrounded me. I took aim at a clump of banana trees located two hundred meters or so from the west wall of our compound then pulled back on the trigger and held it. In the blink of an eye, thirty rounds of steel jacketed, armor piercing fifty caliber bullets disappeared into the fading light of the Vietnamese Evening, tearing apart everything in its path. The noise from the "fifty" was deafening.

Every fourth or fifth round exiting the barrels of the machine guns were a phosphorescent tracer. My red tracer rounds joined in with those from the dozen or so M60 Machine Guns that resided in guard towers and bunkers along the outer earthen walls (Berm) that surrounded camp and like so many lightening bugs on a warm summer's eve, lit up the sky in a deadly dance of manmade firepower.

The sound of exploding mortar and grenade rounds added to the machinegun and small arms fire, reminding me of a 4'th of July Fireworks show back home. Sixty seconds after it started, a single illumination flare was launched high up into the night sky and suddenly, quiet returned to camp and the surrounding grounds. It was over...sixty seconds of madness...sixty seconds of throat clearing military bravado...sixty seconds to test fire our weapons and demonstrate to any enemy hiding nearby, the level of firepower that we could put out in the event of a ground or rocket attack.

Appropriately, we called it the "Mad Minute" for reasons obvious to anyone who participated in it. Prior to the start of this "Once a week" exercise, radio calls went out to any friendly forces in the area, warning them to keep a safe distance from the lethal killing zone that was about to form. We usually recommended everyone to keep back five or more kilometers due to the extreme killing range of the fifty Caliber machine guns and the mortar rounds.

Our "Mad Minute" was scheduled to start at 7:30 PM; one half hour after the main gate to camp was shut. After 7 PM, anything outside the Berm and wire was considered to be hostile. We called it a "FreeFire Zone."

Freefire is a word like "Friendly Fire." You won't find either in a dictionary, yet each has a terribly lethal connotation to it. To this day, the mention of either word sends shivers down my spine.

The NVA and VC in our area rarely attacked camps during the day. In reality, a daylight attack would have been the best time to hit us because most men were out of camp and those in guard towers formed a skeleton staff at best. We however believed it was because they were too chickenshit for a stand up, face to face fight. Nothing could be farther from the truth!

All incursions and attacks against our camps were night time rocket or mortar attacks or sapper infiltrations.

Skilled and determined sappers were difficult to stop. Trained to crawl through our perimeter defenses undetected, place explosive charges at key locations in the compound and escape undetected before the explosives detonated, the sapper was as deadly a force against us as was an all out ground attack. Most sappers are killed on the "way out" of a compound, having already set their explosive charges.

In most cases, getting through the layers of wire, circumventing the trip flares and appearing invisible in the bright flood lights that illuminated the wire was relatively easy for an experienced sapper. They knew the hours when our guards were at their most vulnerable, when they were the sleepiest and not as attentive as they could be. The deadly hours were usually from 2 AM to 4 AM.

Despite their training and determination, sappers were told that their missions were "One Way Trips."

The Madness of the Mad Minute, the determination of the sappers and the no man's land just outside the boundaries of our wire made each day in Vietnam a challenge and an exercise in survival.

CHAPTER 30
INDIAN COUNTRY

Our three truck convoy left for base camp a little after 5 AM. We always traveled in twos or threes in order to protect each other on the long drive through "Indian Country." An attack on a single, unescorted vehicle in Indian Country was effectively a death sentence for those foolish enough to tempt the fates. A mechanical breakdown of a lone vehicle traveling through hostile territory was equally lethal.

The purpose of this trip to base camp was to replenish medical supplies. Our drive to base camp was quiet and uneventful…the return trip would not be so. Because of mechanical problems with our truck, our three vehicle convoy could not leave Base Camp until 5:00 PM… a dangerously late start for a drive of that distance. Normally, it would take us an hour and 45 minutes for this trip barring unforeseen conditions. I figured that with a little luck, we could make it back to camp before the gates closed at 7 PM.

Exiting the main gate we entered the pot hole ridden, depression laden, dirt and gravel road that ran from Camp Jerome towards our turnoff point onto QL21 near Ban Me Thuout…almost 4 kilometers away. Initially, we were the only vehicles on the road but that quickly changed as we approached the city and our turn off point.

"Lambrettas waiting for passengers"

"A Lambretta jammed to the gills with people"

Within moments, it went from no traffic to a full fledge, "stop and go", "bumper to bumper", "Traffic Jam."

A quick glance at my Timex revealed that we were behind schedule and losing time quickly. Our slim margin of safety was just about gone. Forward progress was now measured in inches per minute rather than miles per hour. Bicyclists and those on foot passed us with ease as we sat behind vehicles pouring out clouds of diesel or two stroke exhaust. There were no alternate roads and no way to circumvent the traffic. We were at the mercy of the vehicles in front of us and we were stuck!

Forty five frustrating minutes later we reached our turnoff point onto QL21 south. I honked my horn and waved at the other two trucks to pull over so we could discuss our options.

"We are about twenty five minutes behind schedule," I said to the six members of our party as we stood by the roadside ..."we need to make a go or no go decision. This part of the trip shouldn't have taken us more than twenty minutes."

"We have an hour and fifteen minutes left to make it back to camp before the 7 PM deadline. What do you want to do?"

"It's up to you Doc," was the reply.

If we drive fast, I thought, we might make it. In a spur of the moment decision based on a gut feeling, I said "OK, let's go for it."

With that we all ran back to our vehicles and with three large clouds of dust trailing behind us, we started our drag race back to camp. I was driving a two and a half ton transport truck. Our driving speeds averaged between forty and forty five mph. That was ten to fifteen mph faster than our normal driving speed on this road. Road conditions and reports of enemy activity along our routes of travel usually dictated driving speeds. It was a double edged sword...poor road conditions usually dictated slower driving speeds and increased enemy activity dictated faster driving speeds.

It was a "No Win" situation!

We were screwed on two counts...the road conditions on QL 21 were poor and the entire route from here to camp was in "Indian Territory!"

We had no choice but to drive at forty to forty five mph, but even at our increased rate of speed, by the time we had driven for fifty minutes, we were still thirty five minutes out.

"The R- :e back to camp and safety"

We were in deep shit! At our present rate of speed, we were fifteen to twenty minutes short of our destination and this would force us to spend the night on the road, in Indian Country with no radio. That would be suicide!

Without hesitating, I knew that our only option was an "all out run for camp." We had to push our trucks to the max and beyond.

I looked over to my passenger and yelled out, "If we don't make it back to camp before seven, we're fucking dead out here...no time to stop...I'm just gonna push the truck in front of me to go faster."

"OK Doc," was his response.

I stomped on the accelerator pedal and drove it almost onto the metal floorboard. The engine let out a loud scream as we lurched forward.

"Wave at the truck behind us to keep up," I screamed out to my buddy. With no radio communication between vehicles he leaned out the open window and motioned at the truck behind us to keep up. Within seconds, he had closed the distance behind me to within a few feet.

I lay my right hand on the horn and kept a steady blast going, pulling within inches of the rear bumper of the jeep in front of me. I then gave him a slight bumper bang. The jeep driver looked at his side view mirror to see what was going on and I repeated the bang, this time harder as I started to literally push him. Having gotten his attention, I motioned with my left hand for him to pick up his speed. I kept motioning and banging his rear bumper until he finally understood. He stomped on his accelerator pedal and started to pull away from me. I followed suit and was right behind him.

The jeep in front of me bounced wildly in and out of the pot hole filled road like a child on a pogo stick. My "deuce" started bouncing in and out of potholes and depressions but because of its weight and its momentum, I was constantly on the verge of losing control of it. Each time we bounced into, then out of a large hole or depression I would lose partial or complete steering control for a second or two. With each gut wrenching episode, I struggled with the massive steering wheel, utilizing all of the strength in my arms to regain control. It was a fight between my will power and strength and the forces of nature and physics. In the end, I would not permit nature to win. My will to live was stronger than natures desire to kill me!

My arms were glued to the massive steering wheel as it twisted left then right after emerging from yet another depression or massive pothole in the road. Using the brakes was never a consideration!

A quick glance at the speedometer showed that I was doing almost sixty mph. Once again, I slammed my right hand onto the horn pad located in the center of the steering wheel and motioned at the truck in front of me to go faster while simultaneously yelling at the top of my lungs "Move it."

A quick look at my watch sent a shiver down my spine. It was a couple of minutes before seven. Shit!

My passenger yelled to me. "We're not gonna make it Doc!"

"I hear ya," I replied.

Camp was still three to four miles out. "We gotta go for it," I yelled out as I turned on my headlights and blew my horn again at the jeep in front and motioned at them to just keep going. We were too close not to go for it.

Driving like a man possessed, I heard my buddy shout out, "It's seven." I just ignored him. If our camp defenses are gonna shoot us, so be it, I said to myself. I started praying that the guys in the guard towers would have enough sense not to blow us away but you never know what a man with an itchy trigger finger will do.

A half mile to go! Shit…one more left hand bend in the road and the camp would be visible. Exiting the rubber plantation, I saw the camp in the distance. I was waiting for the red tracers to start coming my way but nothing happened. Why weren't they firing? I waited and waited and waited. Nothing happened!

Maybe they were waiting for us to get closer. All I could think of was death by friendly fire. Shit!

Fifty yards from the main gate, I realized that at my current 60 plus mph speed, I would blow right past the main gate if I didn't immediately start to slow down. The jeep in front of me suddenly locked his brakes and went into a skid as he tried to burn off his speed. I followed suit and slammed on the brakes. I immediately went into a rear end skid with the rear end skidding to the right.

I couldn't wreck the vehicle so I released the brakes, allowing the rear end to once again realign with the front then slammed the brakes down again. Once again I went into a right rear end skid. This time I kept the brakes locked. Within a few seconds, I had come to rest in front of the open gate with the front end of my truck facing it.

I never found out why the guards didn't open fire on us. Despite my bad decision to "go for it" and the impossible driving conditions, we made it safely back to camp. It is my belief that luck had nothing to do with it… rather it was the call of a higher power, who had future plans for us.

CHAPTER 31
PAYBACK IS A BITCH

"The Rubber Plantation. It was a beautiful plantation with thousands of trees planted with the precision of a dress parade...until Payback Time"

It looked like an immense Orange Grove. Thousands of acres of lush, green trees were planted in perfectly parallel rows, each tree equidistant from the next. Collectively, they formed a perfect checkerboard pattern. Not one tree, however, carried an orange or tangerine; instead, they bore the fruit of 20'Th century's greatest technology product deep within their veins. It was the lifeblood of an industry, a technology and a way of life that modern man counted and depended on. The white, viscous liquid that coursed through its veins was not the sugary syrup from the Maple Trees of Vermont...but rather rubber.

Because of its immense financial importance, we were ordered never to damage even one tree with gunfire. We were ordered to "never fire into the rubber plantation …no matter what!" It was an order that was a godsend to the NVA and VC and would send many to the hospital.

The rubber plantation was about two hundred meters from the outermost layer of trip wire that formed the eastern border of our compound. It stretched the entire length of the camp and continued on for an additional ¼ mile. No one knew who owned the plantation but it had to be one of the "Big Three Names in Tires and Rubber"… Harvey Firestone, Charles Goodyear or Andre Michelin.

The orders not to fire was a financial decision, not a military one. The long arm of big business stretched its hand from the corporate headquarters of Goodyear in Akron or Firestone in Nashville or Michelin in Paris to the highlands of Vietnam and clamped a protective cover over their financial assets, validating the old saying that "Money talks."

We received the orders "Not to fire into the plantation" by radio transmission in a top secret crypto code. The authority to decode these special transmissions was held by a select few within the Command Bunker. The NVA translated it almost immediately and within a week, the "Incoming" rockets started!

We could see the flashes from the B-40 Rockets as they left their launchers. Once an attack started, our only options were to run for cover, pray that it wasn't our time and wait for them to just run out of rockets. Camp Swampy became one, big shooting gallery.

We protested to the company commander and the senior NCO's but they felt as we did," not one American life was worth all of the rubber plantations in Vietnam," but orders were orders.

Day after day and week after week, we took incoming fire from the plantation. Most times we were lucky, no KIAs but men were injured. Even with mounting casualties, we did nothing…nothing that is, until our commanding officer decided that enough was enough.

He radioed the battalion commander informing him that he was overriding his orders not to return fire and if fired upon, we would reciprocate with "Deadly Force." We admired him for this act of common sense and his desire to save lives, our lives!

The orders quickly went out to every man in camp…"Any Incoming from the Rubber Plantation would be returned with a massive response." Men, who were not on guard duty that night gathered on the berm facing the plantation. We knew that an attack was coming…we welcomed it!

Everyone was loaded down with a massive amount of ammunition. It was payback time!

Shortly after 7 PM the attack came. The flash of a B-40 Rocket leaving its launching tube provided us with an initial aiming point for our response but within moments, the entire plantation was targeted.

Gun fire erupted on the berm such as I have never seen before or since. It was like the fourth of July. Red tracers from machineguns and M-16s traversed the 200 meter open area between the berm and the plantation and disappeared into the trees beyond. Eighty one millimeter mortars went into action, dropping round after round of high explosives into the plantation, causing massive explosions and eye blinding flashes in the pitch black night.

"Hanging an 81 millimeter White Phosphorus Round into the plantation"

Thousands of rounds per second of steel jacketed bullets tore away at the delicate rubber bearing trees. The price to pay for the months of incoming fire was the utter destruction of a major portion of the plantation. Nothing was spared!

The show continued for 15 minutes, and then it was over. Except for the first rocket launched that night, we received no further incoming from the plantation again…ever.

The next morning, we sent a patrol into the rubber plantation to look for bodies. None were found.

That night, the rubber giants paid a high price for their "Dollars above life policy." Had they allowed us to fire selectively into the plantation when the initial rocketing started months before, the mass destruction would not have been necessary.

Payback is a bitch.

CHAPTER 32
OUT THE DOOR

"Man down, Man down, Hey Doc, we got a man down with snakebite, follow me."

I grabbed my aid bag and ran in the direction of the river. Next to the bank was a man, in a semi sitting position on the ground with his pant leg pulled up above his knee. He was dripping wet from head to toe, looking so much like a man who'd just come from a swim.

He was breathing heavily and had a terrified look on his face. "What happened," I yelled to him as I kneeled down.

"Went swimming, Doc. It was hot and I wanted to cool off."

"You dumb mother fucker," I screamed at him. "Don't you know there are snakes in the river and they're all poisonous? How fucking stupid are you?"

I was pissed because I was concerned, and knew that this was not good! He showed me the two puncture wounds on his calf, just below the knee. The area around the marks was already turning red.

No one saw the snake and even if they did, no one could tell a poisonous snake from a non-poisonous one, not even me. I made the assumption that it was poisonous and since I had no Anti Venom Kit, my only treatment was to tourniquet his leg and call for a Medivac.

I applied the tourniquet just above the knee and asked one of the guys to run to the command jeep and call for a Medivac. Once the tourniquet was applied, I couldn't release it for fear that the toxins would spread throughout his body. I had about thirty to forty five minutes before the effects of the tourniquet would start to destroy his leg muscle.

Fifteen minutes later I heard the familiar whoop, whoop, whoop of the Huey Helicopter. That was quick, I thought. I'd never seen a Medivac come in that quickly unless it was already nearby. It landed about forty yards away. I and another soldier carried him to the waiting chopper. As we approached, I noticed that the Red Cross that is usually painted on its nose or side was missing. Instead I saw a door gunner with a machine gun. Shit, it was a gunship!

A gunship meant only one thing, no medic on board. A lieutenant in our unit approached me and yelled as loud as he could in my left ear that all Medivacs were committed to other areas and that the only available transport was this gun ship. Knowing that time was running out, I decided that he had to go on this bird. The door gunner and another soldier lifted him into the chopper and placed him on a seat then the co-pilot motioned for me to get in. I jumped on board and left behind my jungle shirt and boonies hat.

I knelt next to him and put my aid bag on the floor. While holding onto the tourniquet, I watched him for any signs of labored breathing.

My right hand tightly gripped the tourniquet that was wrapped around his left leg. My left hand held onto a stainless steel cylindrical metal post that ran from the floor to ceiling. I jammed my right foot up against the floor brace for the seat, insuring that when we took off, I would be in a steady, safe position. I was wrong!

I yelled up at my patient "How ya doin?" He nodded that he was ok.

The noise level and pitch of the engines suddenly increased and the rear of the helicopter lifted while the front seemed to remain in place. I was pitched slightly forward, towards the cockpit but my grip on the bar and my solid foothold held me stationary. We started moving forward then quickly rose about thirty feet into the air. I felt like I was in a fast moving elevator going up. Suddenly and without warning, it banked sharply right and I felt myself falling downwards towards the open door. Only my handhold on the bar and a foot wedged against the metal seat frame prevented me from exiting the chopper, but my grip was quickly loosening and so was my foot hold.

I tried to force my foot back onto the metal bracing that anchored the seats to the deck but it was too late. My body started to pendulum downwards towards the open door. Whether by act of God or just by chance, as my handhold on the bar was about to release a shoelace in my right boot caught in a metal obstruction on the almost vertical floor and my motion out the door stopped immediately. I could clearly see the ground forty or more feet below me. Suddenly, the helicopter banked left, leveled itself out and I was thrown to the floor.

As I looked back towards the door gunner then forward towards the pilot and copilot, I saw them all laughing hysterically. They had planned this. This was a joke but I wasn't laughing. I wanted to be angry but was too frightened to be. It was a joke that almost cost me my life.

The remainder of the ride was uneventful. Within fifteen minutes we were landing at Camp Coryell, a compound with an underground hospital. I recognized it as we landed since I had been there many times by truck. It was about six miles from Camp Jerome, our base camp. As we neared touchdown, two nurses and two orderlies with a litter approached. I helped the patient off the chopper and onto the litter and followed him into the hospital.

We walked down a long dirt road that was pitched downwards to the hospital entrance located some fifteen feet below ground level. I gave the specifics of what had happened to the patient and what treatment I had used, to the nurses accompanying us.

They examined him and immediately administered a snake anti venom shot. One of the nurses told me that I could go back to my unit.

Go back to my unit…now how in the fuck do I do that, I thought? I was flown here on a gunship. Did they expect the gunship to take me back? I had no way of communicating with base camp or Camp Swampy. I'm sure that the guys back at the river reported my absence to the commanding officer, but how would I get back there?

I asked one of the nurses what arrangements they could make to get me back to camp. She told me I was "On My Own."

That's fucking great, I thought, what would I do now? It was late afternoon. I could start walking but the only place to walk to would be base camp, some six miles away but in which direction? I didn't know which roads to take.

I walked out to the main gate and looked for any trucks passing by that might be from my unit. God must have been watching out for me… a few minutes later a deuce and a half approached the gate to the hospital compound. The unit designation on the front bumper read "70 Engr B Co." I couldn't believe my luck. It was a truck from my company. I ran out in front of it waving my arms.

The truck stopped and I walked around to the driver's side. Recognizing me, the driver said, "Shit Doc, what the fuck are you doing here?" No sweeter words had ever been spoken.

I yelled up, "You won't believe it, I'll tell ya later but I need a ride back to camp."

"Hop in," he responded.

He had just picked up supplies and was on his way back to B Company. He told me that "I was one lucky mother fucker because he came here for supplies only once a week. Indeed I was lucky. I later found out later that my patient had survived. After being stabilized, he was sent to Japan then home.

My "Out the door" experience was one that I would always remember!

**"The river was infested with poisonous snakes.
I was eliminating one of them"**

"A gunship landing"

"Turning on its Side"

CHAPTER 33
THE GREAT CORN CAPER

It stretched from the road to the Montgnard Village, almost one hundred yards away. For months, we watched the stalks with their distinctive leaves stretch ever upwards until the first ears began to appear. Tiny at first, then almost overnight, they grew into, "Meal Size" ears. By late 1969, the field had grown to a height of more than six feet, high enough to hide a man walking through it!

It was a terrible temptation, almost an irresistible one…picking just a few ears and enjoying that sweet, delicious taste. And so, the "Great Corn Caper" was born!

Fellow medic JC and I borrowed a jeep and drove it to a point on the road just out of sight of the village and parked. Upon entering the field, I dropped down on all fours and started to crawl. JC followed me. It was a terribly stupid move for no one could ever have seen us.

"Hey John," I said in a low tone, "why are we crawling?"

"Don't know," he replied. "You started crawling and I followed you." With that, we both stood upright and started pulling off the fullest looking ears from the stalks.

In our haste to plan and pull off the Great Corn Caper, we forgot to bring something to carry the corn in. We couldn't carry more than a dozen or so ears each so we started stuffing them in our shirts and the cargo pockets of our jungle pants. In less than two minutes, we had all that we could carry and we literally ran out of the field, back to the jeep, dropping an occasional ear here and there.

We hid the corn in the back of the jeep and stole back to camp where we unloaded our precious cargo. Inside the medical bunker, we tallied up our stolen booty… thirty eight ears. We kept the caper as quiet as possible, letting only the guys in the radio room, adjacent to us, to know about it.

I could have taken the ears to the mess hall and asked the cooks to boil it for us, but they would have ruined it by turning it into creamed corn. In addition, it would have been an open invitation for all to partake and on that day, sharing was not our intention...but how to cook it?

"Paul Skerritt and the famous Ritz Cracker Can"

We had no stove, no pots nor any practical means of cooking it. In desperation I devised a plan that only a GI could come up with. In place of a real pot, I would use two empty Ritz Cracker Cans from packages that were sent to me from home. The heat source would be a couple of bricks of C-4 that I had in my bunker from a recent demolition job. Breaking off a piece about the size of a golf ball, I put it on a metal plate. Before lighting it, I had to get past my next dilemma, how to suspend the Ritz Can, now filled 2/3 of the way with water, over burning C-4?

Plan A called for me to find three pieces of baseball-sized gravel, each piece having two relatively flat surfaces opposite each other then place them around the C-4. This would act as a platform to set the can onto. It was a crude means of suspending the can safely above the C-4 but it should work.

I lit the C-4 with a match and watched as it burned with a hot blue flame. After carefully placing the can onto the gravel that surrounded the C-4, we started to husk the corn. I grabbed one and started to strip it. As I pulled off the outer covering I noticed something strange, it was colored, like a rainbow. Fully exposing the ear, I realized that we had robbed a field of Indian Corn. Shit!

John looked at me and said, "Can we eat this stuff?"

"Don't know," I replied as I continued to strip the corn. At home, we used Indian Corn for house decorations during the Thanksgiving Holidays but I'd never heard of anyone eating it. Maybe the Indians did!

Looking at my partner in crime, I said, "Hey man, we went through too much trouble to get this stuff so let's give it a try." He nodded his head in agreement. Just about then, I heard a sizzling noise coming from the can and saw water leaking out from the bottom. The intense heat from the C-4 had apparently softened the soldered seams on the can, allowing water to leak out. I quickly grabbed some gauze and removed the can of hot water from the flame.

I grabbed my second and last Ritz Can and added water to it. Since I couldn't use the burning C-4 as a heat source, I had to extinguish it…but how. I tried dousing it with water with no effect. I could just wait it out and let it burn itself out but I was too impatient.

I wrapped some cotton gauze around my hand and carefully grabbed the hot metal plate with the burning C-4 on it and carried it outside. Gently placing it on the ground, I covered it with dirt. That appeared to extinguish it.

Staring at it for a few minutes, I wondered if it really went out. Not wanting to leave and take a chance that someone might step on it and possibly detonate it, I carefully removed the dirt. The fire was out and the C-4 cold to the touch. It was once again safe to handle. I balled it up in my hand and shoved it into one of my cargo pockets.

Inside the bunker, the question was still the same… how to boil the water.

Our only other source of combustion was an alcohol burner, which I used to disinfect instruments, but the flame from this crude source of heat was relatively cold. All other options being expended, I fired it up and placed it under the can.

The Ritz Can was relatively small. It limited to two, the number of ears of corn that would fit into it at a time. With such a cold flame, I guessed that it would take at least two hours for the water to come to a boil and another ten to fifteen minutes to cook the corn.

We took shifts watching and refilling the alcohol lamp with isopropyl alcohol. Two and a half hours later, the first two ears were done. I carefully pulled one out of the can and took a bite. Surprisingly, it tasted good. It tasted like corn. While not as sweet as the Jersey corn back home, it was still surprisingly tasty. The theft, anticipation and waiting were all worth it.

After taking the first bite, I passed the ear around to the five or six of us in the bunker. We all agreed that it was good. Seven more hours of covert cooking and eating and we'd had our fill. Eighteen ears remained, which I took to the mess sergeant and asked that he cook them for the men. Eighteen wasn't much to pass among one hundred men. The cooked corn was broken into three sections per ear then given to the first fifty who entered the Mess Tent.

The great corn caper was never to be repeated. The planning, execution, cooking and improvisation were magnificent examples of GI Ingenuity and what a desire for an ear of corn will do.

CHAPTER 34
AMBUSH

"One of the problems with an ambush is not to get ambushed yourself."

Jack Manick

The first few moments of an ambush are the most chaotic, critical and deadly for both the ambusher and the ambushed. The best laid ambushes often fall apart in the first few, heart stopping seconds of firing, pain and death.

It's almost impossible to prevent being caught up in an ambush. Being alert and conscious of your surroundings, being ready at a moment's notice to engage in a close in firefight are factors that increase a person's "Survivability Quotient" but in reality…when your time's up…its up!

We set up our ambush about ten clicks from camp, in an area where intelligence believed the NVA and VC regularly passed through. Most intelligence reports that we'd received in the past weren't worth the paper that they were printed on…they were just plain wrong. Tonight would be different.

Green, inexperienced ambush teams are as much a danger to themselves as they are to the enemy. An ambush set by a green team is as likely to lose an equal number of dead and wounded as the enemy.

Over the many days and evenings that I spent on patrols, we had flushed out the misfits from our ranks…men who were careless, noisy, clumsy or snored. By my sixth month in country, our patrol consisted of tested, hardened veterans.

We learned early on, that our biggest enemy to setting up and executing a successful ambush was a simple bar of soap.

Most soap manufacturers put fragrance into it to encourage sales. Chemical fragrances, however, remain on a person's body for one to two days after showering. Even the most desensitized nose of an NVA or VC could smell the soap fragrance on a man hundreds of feet away, giving them an opportunity to alter their route of travel, bypass us or reverse ambush us.

To avoid this problem, the answer was as simple as not showering or bathing or washing anything on our bodies or our jungle fatigues for at least two days prior to setting up an ambush. The sweat and body odor that we generated in those two days seemed to aid in neutralizing the fragrance of the soap. The down side was a drastic reduction in the number of friends who came near us. We were like Lepers!

Our mission on this trip out was a night ambush… the worst of all types. I hated night ambushes!

I have always been a morning person…up at 5 AM and asleep by 11 PM! Night ambushes were hell for me. My adrenalin would keep me awake until about 3 AM, after that, it was pure willpower.

The march out to the ambush site was a long, hot, sweltering eight hours. This was to be an "in and out" ambush…in during the day, spring the ambush that night, home the next day. We carried just enough food, water and ammo for two days.

We carried light loads on our backs, probably no more than thirty pounds. Ammunition and water accounted for most of the weight. I carried about ten pounds more because I wanted a double quantity of medical supplies as well as the five hundred rounds of ammunition for my carbine and five grenades.

Intelligence told us that we had a better than an eighty percent chance of engaging the enemy that night, but what did they know, they're track record was anything but stellar. All logic told me that this ambush would be another waste of time but I had a real sick feeling in the pit of my stomach…telling me otherwise.

We paired off into two man teams. Half of the teams went on one side of the trail, the remainder on the other. I found a spot behind a group of small trees. These, I hoped, would provide me with some cover and some protection but in reality, AK47 and SKS steel jacketed rounds used by our counterparts would penetrate the small trees like hot knives through butter. It was at best, a false sense of security.

Under most conditions, one member of a two man team would sleep for an hour while the other stayed awake. This allowed both men the luxury of a couple hours sleep during the night, assuming there was no enemy contact.

It was unusually warm that evening, even for the Central Highlands. Based on the amount of sweat pouring off my face, I guessed that the temperature was near 90 degrees.

As the sun dropped below the horizon, the infamous "Fuck You Lizards" started their night long chanting…"Fuck u…fuck u." When I first arrived in the Central Highlands and was told about them, I thought it was a joke until I heard them singing that night. Each night, they sang their sweet love songs to us…"Fuck You, Fuck You."

I wondered if they knew something that we didn't.

We set out trip flares thirty yards in front of us and then placed Claymore Mines five yards inside the flares. We packed dirt and rock behind the Claymores to force most of the blast forward, towards the oncoming enemy…then we waited.

With us, we carried one M-60 machine gun, one M-79 Grenade Launcher, an assortment of M-16 rifles, hand grenades and a few side arms.

One of the biggest dangers on any night ambush was the possibility of ambushing the leading elements of a vastly superior enemy force. There was no way of telling how many, if any, of the enemy would walk into an ambush. We could get lucky and get all of them or it could be another "Little Big Horn" for us.

The first few hours were quiet. The insects were especially hungry that night…biting and stinging every inch of my exposed skin. The moon that night was full and provided crystal clear visibility for as far as I could see into the dense overgrowth. The stars above us were as beautiful as any that I had ever seen at home. My mind started to wander… to thoughts of home and friends and times and places gone…times that were happy and safe. The memories brought a smile to my face. Realizing that I was slipping into a dangerous mindset, I snapped myself back to the reality of watching and listening for anything outside the ordinary.

It was almost 2 AM and I was starting to feel sleepy. My partner was right next to me and was fast asleep. Despite wearing eyeglasses, I was highly adept at picking up movement in the bush. In basic training and much to the surprise of my drill instructors, I scored highest in my target detection class. If my eyes were keen then my ears were even more acute. Over the many months that I'd been "In Country," I had trained myself to awaken at the slightest hint of an unusual noise. Luckily, after awakening and checking out the noise, I was usually able to quickly go back to sleep.

Suddenly, as if on cue by the wand of an orchestra leader, all went quiet, dead quiet. The sounds of the jungle were gone!

A sense of foreboding ran through my body as the muscles in my back, legs and arms tensed up like the tightly wound strings on a fine violin. In my peripheral vision, I detected a hint of movement to my right, about thirty yards away and off the trail. Shifting my attention to that area, I continued to watch, look and wait. My breathing grew shallower and the pounding of my heart more pronounced as I stared across the moonlit undergrowth. I forced my eyes not to blink, knowing that a blink might cost me my life!

There it was again…movement! "I got you now, you mother fuckers," I said to myself! Something or somebody was out there and was coming this way, but why hadn't they tripped one of our flares? They were certainly in the area where flares were set out.

Maybe it was an animal…a bird or a monkey or maybe it was just the reflection of the moonlight off a branch or leaf…maybe. Thoughts and images of what might be out there raced through my mind.

Movement again…this time no more than twenty yards away. I looked down at my buddy, placed my hand over his mouth then gave him a quick shaking. He awoke instantly and looked up at me. I placed my index finger over my mouth indicating I wanted him to be silent then pointed outwards towards where I saw movement.

He slowly rose to a kneeling position. As he did so I leaned over and whispered to him, "Gooks coming in… we gotta open up now. They are past our trip flares."

He signaled me with a thumbs up then we both pointed ours weapons in the direction I saw the movement. I flipped off the safety on my carbine, took aim about waist high then fired a sustained burst of 30 rounds.

In the darkness, the automatic fire from my weapon shot out a two foot long continuous flame of death. As I opened fire, so did my buddy. Within seconds the rest of the ambush patrol joined in.

Trip flares started to go off in various locations in front of us. Illuminated in the bright burning phosphorescent flares were shapes and figures. Within seconds, the trees, behind which I sought cover and concealment, were vaporized by incoming fire. I quickly reloaded and started to fire at targets made visible by the flares and the full moon.

Suddenly, a figure sprung to his feet about twenty yards in front of me and started shooting but it seemed like his rounds were directed everywhere but at me. I shifted my fire direction, pointed the muzzle at his chest and fired a continuous burst of at least fifteen rounds into him. It was really a waste of rounds. One or two could have just as easily done the job but as close as he was to me, I wasn't taking any chances. The burst stopped him in his tracks.

"Somebody blow the Claymores, I yelled out! Blow the fucking Claymores!"

Seconds later the sounds of the ball bearing containing mines exploding echoed out in the night and joined in with the rifle and machine gun fire. It was now a contest of who would live and who would die.

The exchange of fire continued for what seemed like an eternity until suddenly, as suddenly as it had started, it was over. For a few precious moments, we watched and waited and prayed. "Any wounded," I yelled out. There was no answer. Could we be so lucky? Everybody started to move forward and search for bodies. "Anyone hit," I yelled out again. There was no response.

The NVA who I'd shot remained face down in the grass but I noticed that his left foot and leg was twitching sporadically. He was either dead and this was an after death reaction or he was not yet dead. I fired two more rounds into him. The twitching stopped.

By military standards, the ambush was successful. Zero casualties and wounded on our side…a miracle considering the amount of firepower that was exchanged by both sides.

We found nine enemy bodies. My guess was that the total number of enemy that we had engaged was somewhat over twenty. Twelve of us versus twenty of them… considering that surprise was on our side, it was an even odds fight. We removed their weapons and searched the bodies for any written documents that might be of use to intelligence.

We waited for first light before packing up our equipment and heading back to camp. The firefight had drained all of us both physically and mentally. The eight hour walk back to camp seemed like it would never end. Sometime around 3 or 4 PM we exited the bush about a mile from camp on QL21. It was good to be near camp, safety, a hot meal, a shower and a good night's sleep.

For those who were non-believers, "we cheated Death for yet another day." For believers, "It wasn't yet our time."

CHAPTER 35
DOC IS DOWN

"Jack inside medical bunker"

"Doc at entrance to Medical Bunker"

The bunker shook violently. Within seconds, the lights went out, leaving me in the pitch black. I reached into my pocket, pulled out my Zippo Lighter, flipped open the lid, rolled the spark wheel with my thumb and turned darkness into light. I lit the candles scattered about the medical bunker and then lit the Coleman Lamp.

One explosion followed another in a seemingly endless display of firepower.

"Man Down...Man Down!" I heard the screaming from outside. Bursting in was a man almost completely out of breath.

"We got a man down Doc...follow me." Exiting the bunker into the darkness beyond, we were both running at full speed. In all of the excitement, I never asked him where the man was down.

In the darkness, I quickly lost sight of him. There was no way to tell if I was a half step behind him, if he had turned and gone in a different direction or if he just outdistanced me in the race to the injured man.

The sounds of ear piercing explosions drowned out everything so I couldn't even yell out to ask him where he was.

I hadn't gone more than thirty or forty paces when a body numbing explosion tossed me upwards into the black night. I felt no pain as my body flew through the air. It was a wonderful and peaceful feeling. Maybe I was dying, maybe I was dead. If so, it wasn't so bad. I don't remember hitting the ground.

At some point I must have passed out. I awoke to the sounds of ever more explosions. I couldn't see a thing! I tried focusing my eyes to improve my vision but it was no use. Reaching up to my face to adjust my eyeglasses, I found nothing but face. Without the eyeglasses, I was helpless and for all practical purposes, blind!

I propped myself up into a sitting position then felt around on the gravel first with my right hand then my left. Nothing...then I realized that I had also lost my rifle!

Without warning, the incoming suddenly stopped and all went eerily quiet. Blind and without my rifle, I sat there, trying to clear my head.

Would this "Incoming" be followed up by a ground attack? Would the next living body to come across me be an NVA, VC or would I be lucky and it be a friend? In my nearly blind state, I couldn't distinguish friend from foe.

I had no intention of calling out into the darkness for help, so I just sat there. Reaching down, I removed my pistol from its holster, chambered a round then waited, waited for someone to find me. I hoped it would be the right person!

Minutes seemed like hours until I heard movement in front of me. My heart started pounding wildly as I pointed my handgun in the direction of the noise. I released the safety, said a silent prayer then waited for the inevitable.

"Hey Doc, where are you?"

"Over here," I yelled out as I lowered my weapon. I saw the beam of a flashlight approaching.

"Hey Doc, you OK?"

"Don't know," I said.

"Doc is down, Doc is down," he started yelling. Two men helped me to my feet then propped me up. "My glasses" I said, "I can't see shit without them, and I lost my weapon."

"OK doc we'll find them, we gotta get you back to the medical bunker."

My head was spinning like a top. I tried walking without their assistance but try as I might, my legs wouldn't support my body weight. I refused their offer of a litter or to be carried. No matter how unsteady I was, I was determined to try to walk into the medical bunker.

As they half dragged and half carried me, I felt some control of my legs returning. Nearing the bunker, I was able to take a few, shaky steps. It felt good to be able to walk again, even though they were like baby steps at first.

Inside the bunker I could recognize some objects but barely. "OK Doc, sit down."

"Where," I replied," I can't see shit. "In the top right drawer, I have a pair of spare glasses, please give them to me."

Putting them on, I once again returned to the land of the living.

"Shit doc, you're bleeding like a stuck pig," my friend said.

"Give me that mirror" I said pointing to a mirror on a metal chest. Blood covered most of my face and appeared to be flowing freely from my scalp. I asked one of the guys in the bunker to fill a stainless steel bowl with water. I also needed for someone to tell me how bad the wound on my head was. The only way to do that was to wash off the mass of blood in my scalp then look for the free flowing stream. As my buddy poured the water over the top of my head I tried to shampoo it throughout my hair to get as much blood off as possible.

I immediately grabbed a towel, patted my face and scalp to remove as much water and blood as possible then took a look in the mirror. The source of blood was a gash high on my right temple.

I grabbed a towel, folded it into a roughly square shape then applied it directly to the gash, hoping that the pressure on the wound would stop the flow of blood. I asked one of the men who had helped me into the bunker to go and get JC and ask him to check out the injured man. For the next fifteen minutes I sat on the cot and held pressure on the towel.

My head was still spinning like a top.

Ten minutes later, an injured man was brought into the bunker. His leg was severely injured and there was little that we could do besides patch him up, stabilize him and call for a Medivac. The Medivac came about an hour later and took him away.

Considering how much ordnance was thrown at us that night, we were very lucky that no one was killed.

My wound stopped bleeding with pressure although in reality, it probably should have been sutured. Within 24 hours, my body turned into a massive black and blue landscape. I could barely move off the cot for days as my body tried to heal itself. Food was brought to me in the bunker but it was a bitch when I had to go out to the shitter or to urinate. I hobbled around like a ninety year old man with advanced arthritis but like everything else in life, the pain and stiffness and soreness went away. At twenty two years of age, most things healed quickly.

Of all of my encounters with death in Vietnam, this was the closest that I came to visiting Saint Peter in my Tour of Duty.

CHAPTER 36
MONSOON

I thought nothing could be worse than the incessant, lung choking dust and unyielding heat of the dry season, until the Monsoon hit. For half of my tour of duty, mud, mold, dampness and rain clamped a choke hold on South East Asia and all of its inhabitants. Torrents of rain turned peaceful streams and creeks into raging brown rivers. Streams that we had walked through on patrol during the dry season were now impassable. Waterfalls appeared where none had been before. Bridge bypasses that had conducted two to three feet of water through its corrugated metal tubes during the dry season were now buried beneath fifteen feet of uncontrolled brown water.

Within the first few hours of the onset of Monsoon, the Vietnamese Soil was transformed into a thick brown mass of unforgiving Goo that more closely resembled quicksand or rubber glue than mud.

Mud in camp ranged from ankle to knee deep. The only places that a man could walk and not sink in were those areas where baseball sized gravel had been spread out in the dry season in preparation for this. In the dry season, the gravel was a nightmare to traverse, in the wet season, it was a Godsend. Where gravel was laid, there was no mud. Had it not been for the ingenuity and forethought of the Engineers of the Vermont National Guard, Camp Swampy would have been a large, impassable mud pit.

The deeper pools of mud in the compound were very unforgiving of those careless enough to wander into them. Once stuck in the mud, extricating yourself was a difficult and embarrassing process. The deeper you sank, the stronger the vacuum effect was when you tried to pull your leg out.

Camp Swampy - mid 1969 - Laundry Service
Entrance to Command Bunker in background

"The maid's day out forces Doc to do his own clothes"

During the dry season, I washed my clothes in a two gallon pail with a bar of Lux Soap then hung them to dry on the barb wire apron outside our sleeping bunker. In the intense heat of the dry season, clothes usually dried within minutes. The down side of drying jungle fatigues on the Barb Wire was the mass of pencil point sized punctures caused by the razor sharp wire.

Following closely on the heels of the first rainfall came a new life form...one that I can't remember seeing back home..."Mold." In the wet season, washing clothes was almost impossible...they never seemed to dry, no matter where they were hung...instead they molded into a pretty shade of green or brown. Leather goods were especially prone and molded overnight.

Some days the rain was so intense that virtually everything came to a standstill. Even the NVA and VC took a break during Monsoon.

Monsoon was a living, breathing entity and presented its own dangers. After a couple of months of not seeing the sun, being beat down on by the rain and attacked by the mold, depression set in among many of the men. Keeping their spirits upbeat was tough and one of the most difficult parts of my job but before I could raise their spirits, I had to elevate mine. I always smiled and joked with the guys even though I might not have wanted to or didn't feel like it.

In Monsoon, combat boots usually rotted out in less than 4 weeks. Drinking water that was slightly muddy in the dry season turned into a deep chocolate brown color during Monsoon. Before drinking any water, we had to let it stand for a minute or so to allow the majority of the mud to settle to the bottom of a cup or canteen. Only the top third of any water container could be drunk, the rest was usually discarded.

In the Mess Tent, water was mixed with Cherry Kool Aid to try to hide the mud but that was pointless. Even in a cup of dark cherry Kool Aid, the mud on the bottom was clearly visible.

Monsoon seemed to breed a bigger version of bug than we normally were exposed to in the dry season. I don't know why. Giant slugs and enormous centipedes were everywhere and luckily for us so were our eternal friends, the bats. Without them, the population of insects and other undesirable creatures would have been significantly higher.

Being constantly damp or wet is a terrible feeling. Wet Jungle fatigues rubbing against skin acted like sandpaper, removing layers of protective skin and causing all kinds of skin disorders. Being wet all the time is OK if you're a fish but humans can't deal with it for prolonged periods of time.

Morale during Monsoon was non-existent. Men snapped at each other...boots and clothes rotted out in front of our eyes. The feeling of always being wet or damp for a few days in a row is an inconvenience, for a few weeks in a row it's annoying and for months on end, it is horrible.

Survival in the Monsoon Season became a matter of will power, mind over rain and mind over mud! The only good thing about Monsoon was that it limited the NVA and VC Operational Plans and efforts. Still, I longed for the return of the lung choking dust of the Dry Season, complete with its blistering heat and its ability to bleach our green jungle uniforms into red, yellow or brown color.

Civilian foot traffic across newly built bypassr
QL 21 – 1969 – B Company

"Civilians making their way across a river bed of poured gravel in the dry season. This was due to the VC blowing up all of the bridges a year earlier during their Tet 1968 Offensive"

CHAPTER 37
PLAYING WITH DYNAMITE

Children play with firecrackers, adults play with dynamite... it's a saying that applies to an incident in early 1969 at the Camp Swampy Quarry, involving lots of dynamite.

Rock was the key ingredient to all of the work being done by the engineers who called Camp Swampy home. Used in its native form and crushed to a proper size, it was used to build gravel roads, to lay river and stream crossings and combined with cement and sand to make concrete.

The engineers at Camp Swampy were assigned to "Quarry" the rock then crush it to a size appropriate for the work projects. Quarrying meant removing it from the solid rock deposit that it resided in by means of drilling and the liberal use of explosives. Dynamite was the explosive of choice. Invented in 1866 by Alfred Bernhard Nobel, it was relatively stable (unless it was leaking) and easy to use. Miners and quarry workers had used it since its invention.

To Quarry the rock, holes were drilled into it, to a specific depth and a measured number of dynamite sticks dropped in. Detonators were then attached and the explosives triggered electronically. The idea was to blow away a certain amount of rock from the rock face and transport it to a crushing machine for further processing. The size of the pieces blown away from the face had to be small enough to fit into the jaws of the first stage of the rock crusher without jamming it. That size was usually no more than two basketballs.

Mathematical formulas were used to determine drilling patterns, drilling depths and the amount of dynamite to use. The idea was to use just enough to blow a portion of a rock face off, no more.

Holes were drilled using large semi-automated pneumatic drills. These monsters looked like giant mosquitoes bent over a victim, sucking out its blood. They were powered by compressed air from large diesel powered air compressors. When operating, the drills made the devils own noise. It was a deafening, ear shattering noise caused by the air pressure pounding and twisting the drill bits into the rock. Columns of gray rock dust rose from each drill as the material was pulverized beneath the super hard surface of the bit. The pounding action of the drills caused the rock and the surrounding area to vibrate.

After a drill had reached its prescribed drilling depth, it was moved by a drill operator (an engineer) to the next location then started again. It required constant monitoring and relocation of the drills. The job was dirty, hot and dangerous. The noise level (even with hearing protectors) damaged ears. The constant vibrations of the rock caused legs and arms to tingle long after the work day was over and the rock dust emanating from the drill heads choked lungs and permeated nasal passages and membranes. Men coughed up or blew out large black masses from their lungs and noses constantly. Rock chips flew off the drill heads, cutting into flesh, bruising and injuring the engineers. It was a lousy, dangerous, thankless job.

During one such effort, the engineers drilled holes, dropped in the dynamite and set the detonators. The quarry area was cleared of all personnel. We were all warned earlier in the day that the detonation would take place today. A warning siren would be set off ten minutes before the blast then again thirty seconds before the blast to give anyone a chance to vacate the area. I heard the first siren while I was inside the medical bunker and decided to go outside to observe the event.

We were standing about one hundred yards from the point of detonation. My first indication that something had happened was a large black mass rising from the quarry then an ear shattering explosion and concussion. I watched the black cloud rise ever higher into the sky. It was accompanied by a number of solid objects. The dust cloud and the objects began climbing at different rates with the solid objects now far ahead of the cloud. A portion of them started to come towards the camp in a high arc.

The closer the objects came, the larger they appeared. These weren't basketball sized pieces of rock, dislodged by the explosion, they were chunks the size of motorcycles. Men in the open, made mad dashes for the nearest cover. Some dove under trucks, others into bunkers. I was closest to the command bunker so I ran inside. After reaching the safety of the bunker I heard the sounds of rocks crashing into metal and sandbags. Less than a minute later the noise stopped. I grabbed my medical bag and ran out looking for any injured. There were a few scrapes and scratches from those diving under equipment but none due to hits from rock. We were lucky.

A damage assessment to the compound revealed a number of vehicles and equipment that were hit by large rocks. Something had gone terribly wrong!

A post mortem on it revealed that the engineers had miscalculated the drilling patterns and depths and amount of dynamite. Too many holes were drilled and too much dynamite was used…ten times too much dynamite!

Apparently, someone had just gotten the formula wrong!

Subsequent explosions were smaller and controlled and did what they were supposed to. The engineers learned but Oh what a blast it was!!!

CHAPTER 38
POINT MAN DOWN

"A Short Range Patrol Jack and Stubby(in hut) looking for weapons cache"

It was the third day of our six day patrol and we were tired, low on water and running out of food. The late afternoon sun was relentless, beating down on us with the force of a thousand blast furnaces, sapping away our energy and saturating our jungle fatigues with sweat. Nine months ago I wondered how any man, any human could survive such terrible conditions of heat and humidity yet here I was, surviving and tolerating it. The sun had long since transformed my milky white skin to a deep chocolate brown color. I could have passed as a poster boy for Coppertone.

I was the fourth man in the column…just behind the machine gunner and about fifty yards back from the point man. We always staggered our walking intervals between ten to fifteen yards so as not to give the enemy, targets at predictable distances. This, we hoped, would make it more difficult for them to take out more than one man with a burst of automatic fire.

We stopped for a fifteen minute, in place break. I walked back to the lieutenant in charge of the patrol and told him that we needed to find water soon. Most of us were down to about a half canteen each, which at best could be stretched for another ½ day in this blistering heat.

He pulled out his map and doing a quick search, found a river two clicks west of our current position. When we left camp, we knew that there would be no food or water resupply. We had to make do with what we carried; besides a helicopter resupply would alert every gook within ten clicks of our location.

Our "Point Man" was called back from his forward position and redirected towards the river. I grabbed canteen number four from my pistol belt, unscrewed the cap and downed a large mouthful of hot water. It wasn't refreshing but it helped to replace the water that I'd sweated out. That brought me down to ¼ canteen of water. Some of the men were out so we all shared what little water we had with those who had none.

Minutes seemed like seconds as our break ended and the Lieutenant motioned for us to get up and start moving. No words were spoken. Everything was done with hand signals. I was having problems readjusting my pack and claymore bag and didn't want to allow the stagger in the men's position in the column to change because they were waiting for me so I motioned the man behind me to move up and take my place. Finally, my equipment adjusted, I slipped back into the column.

We hadn't gone more than two hundred yards in a westerly direction when the sound of automatic weapons shattered the silence. I instinctively dove for the ground, landing chest first with a thud onto my claymore bag. It almost knocked the wind out of me.

"Fuck me," I uttered to myself. "We walked right into an ambush!"

Gasping for breath, I quickly looked to my left, then my right, in hopes of catching a glimpse of the enemy but I saw nothing!

I crawled to my left and the cover of some two foot high dry grass. Before getting there, I heard the words that every medic dreads, "Man down"!

"Where," I yelled out… needing to know whether to head forward in the column or back to the rear.

"Point man is down," rang out!

"Shit," I said to myself, knowing that this was a worst case scenario! He was probably forty to fifty yards in front of me…a huge distance to travel under fire. I turned on my left side and wiggled out of the right shoulder strap of my rucksack then extracted my left arm from the left rucksack strap. I reached over… grabbed my aid bag, weapon and ammo and crawled up to the man directly in front of me. The noise from the weapons fire around me was deafening. Men were shooting at invisible targets. It was a waste of ammo but we had to return fire even if we couldn't see them. There was always a chance that we would hit someone but without a clear target it was just a matter of luck.

I tried to get the man in front of me's attention by screaming into his ear but his concentration was elsewhere. I grabbed him by the shoulder and shook him. He shifted his gaze to me. I yelled into his right ear" Point is down, I'm going after him…don't shoot in my direction. If I make it back …cover me. "

"OK Doc" he screamed back…"good luck."

I would need more than luck now.

As I crawled forward to the next two men in the patrol, I repeated my instructions. Just then someone from behind me yelled out, "Doc is going out, redirect fire away from that area."

I started my crawl forward. Steel jacketed rounds dug holes and furrows in the dirt all around me. Twenty yards forward I caught a hint of movement to my left. Rising up to my knees, I turned left quickly and saw an NVA almost on top of me. He was crunched down low and running quickly. I started to elevate the barrel of my Carbine but there was no time for aiming so I just pointed and fired about ten or fifteen rounds in his direction. The first rounds caught him in the shin and left thigh. As the barrel moved ever higher, the remaining rounds tore into his torso. He dropped to the ground.

I did a quick scan to the right and seeing no one, decided to foolishly jump up and make a mad dash forward. As I rose to my feet another NVA jumped up about twenty yards in front of me and slightly to my left.

"Shit, I mumbled to myself, they are all over the fucking place."

I took quick aim at the meaty part of his body and emptied the remaining rounds in my magazine into him. He fell into the weeds. I knelt, ejected the magazine, turned it over and inserted its sister magazine into the receiver housing. Charging a round into the firing chamber, I stood up and started my run again. I was running strictly on adrenalin now!

To my right, I heard, "Doc, Doc." I turned and saw my point man on the ground. His jungle fatigue pants were covered with blood from the waist down. I took a quick look around and seeing no one knelt and yelled out to him, "Where are you hit?"

"In the legs Doc!"

The sound of gun fire was all around me but I paid no attention to it. I had to stop the bleeding, stabilize him as best I could then get him back to the patrol.

I removed my survival knife from its sheath and cut his pants in the area where I noticed the largest flow of blood. There were two holes in his right thigh and one in his left calf. The blood loss from the right leg was substantial. I worried that he might go into shock if I didn't quickly get the bleeding under control.

The blood flow was steady and not pulsating…a good sign indicating his femoral artery was unharmed. I pulled a tourniquet from my bag, applied it just below the groin and tightened it just enough to reduce the flow of blood yet not so tight as to cut off the flow of arterial blood. It was a tricky balance of pressure that I was trying to achieve.

Just then I heard him scream out …"Doc" …as he raised his head and looked straight behind me.

Instinctively I reached down for my carbine, turned in the direction he was looking and saw two men running straight for us. I tried to bring my carbine into firing position but I was nowhere near getting a bead on them.

They just kept running. A split second later, I reached firing position, pulled the trigger and held it down, emptying 30 rounds. Both men hit the ground and didn't move. I reloaded. The firing around me continued unabated.

I turned my attention back to the point man and bandaged his left calf. There was no time for an IV. I had to patch him, grab him and make a run for safety. I asked him how he was feeling. He said OK but I could see that he was weak from blood loss and probably on the edge of shock.

"We gotta get out of here" I yelled at him. I knew that he probably couldn't walk but I had to give it a try. I unhooked his pack, grabbed him by the shirt and pulled him to a sitting position. He was a big man, outweighing me by more than fifty pounds.

It knew that it would be a struggle to get such a big man back to the relative safety of the patrol, a distance of fifty yards or more. I handed him my carbine pulled him to his feet with a massive tug and shouted lets go. He tried to walk but his feet wouldn't work. I grabbed him under his waist, propped up his two hundred pound plus body with my skinny but muscular one hundred fifty pound frame and started to drag him as best I could. Five or ten strides later I felt an intense burning in my left calf and went down to the ground like a ton of bricks with my patient falling on top of me. I pushed him off me then realized that I couldn't see anything clearly. Everything was a blur! Shit, my eyeglasses were gone, again!

Blind and helpless, I started searching for my glasses by crawling and feeling. "Ronnie, I lost my glasses. Do you see them? Look around, I can't see shit."

"OK doc hang on let me look."

"If we don't find them soon, we're dead."

"Got em doc," he yelled out.

Putting them on, I once again returned to a smiling face lying on the ground.

I looked down at my left calf and saw oozing blood. I ripped open my pant leg and saw a clean bullet wound through the outer part of the leg. Grabbing a large bandage from my aid bag, I tied it over the wound. The wound wasn't bad but hurt like hell.

"We gotta go now Ronnie," I screamed! I tried standing up only to fall back down with waves of pain emanating from my leg. "Shit!"

"What's the matter doc?"

"Took a round in the leg…can't stand", I yelled back.

"We gonna die here, huh Doc?"

His words hit me like a freight train. I had no intention of either of us dying in this fucking field of grass in the middle of nowhere.

"No fucking way," I yelled out.

I knew that I didn't have the strength to drag him back to the patrol so I decided to try a fireman's carry on a leg that wouldn't even support my own weight. It was an insane idea but it was either that or die. I pulled myself to one knee with a grimace, grabbed Ronnie by the shirt with both hands and pulled him to a sitting position.

Leaning over, I brought my face close to his and yelled "ya gotta help me Ronnie, ya gotta help me, ya gotta stand or we die here" I screamed at him!

I knew that he didn't want to die here, in this miserable bush, any more than I did. Digging deep inside himself, he pushed himself to a standing position.

I handed him my carbine and yelled out "you shoot any fucking thing that comes on us from behind!"

I pulled out my 45 pistol and cocked the hammer. I grabbed Ronnie by the seat of his pants and lifted him straight up onto my shoulder in a modified fireman's carry.

"You Ok?" I yelled at him."

"OK Doc."

I started to run as best I could. Every time I placed my left foot down, waves of pain shot up my leg and into my torso. I needed to somehow take my mind off the pain so as I ran, I screamed at the top of my lungs "you mother fuckers...you mother fuckers." It seemed to help!

It felt as if I was running in slow motion. Suddenly, I heard a burst of carbine fire go off behind me.

"Shit...they must be coming at us from behind now!"

An NVA suddenly burst out of the bush directly in front of me. I raised my 45 slightly, fired twice and missed both times. I continued to fire, not hitting a dam thing when suddenly, he grabbed his chest and fell to the ground. I wasn't sure what had happened. I certainly had not shot him! Maybe we were close to the patrol and one of our guys got him. Whatever the reason, I was grateful since I certainly would not have been able to bring him down.

Ten more painful strides and we reached the patrol. I dropped to one knee and off loaded my passenger to the ground with a thump and a loud groan. The firing seemed to be all around us. I was certain that we were surrounded!

While laying flat on my stomach, I checked the bandages that I had so quickly applied to Ronnie only moments before. They seemed to be working. I added one more pressure dressing. Just then, the lieutenant crawled up to me and asked how Ronnie and I were doing.

"We need to Medivac him ASAP, Sir," I replied.

"What about you Doc" he asked. "Leg wound" I replied, "but it's not bad."

"These fucking Gooks are everywhere LT," I yelled out. "We need gunships in here to waste these mother fuckers."

"They're on the way Doc! I'm gonna close the patrol into a small area then mark our position with smoke. The gunships will waste everything around us."

Amidst the continued gunfire, I heard the radioman scream out "gunships two minutes out LT."

"Pass the word," LT barked out, "close in the patrol."

"Purple Smoke Out"

With that, men began crawling back in towards each other, forming a circular area about twenty feet in diameter. Moments later LT popped a purple smoke canister in the center of the group. Looking at the radioman, he gave orders to the gunships to waste everything thirty yards outside center of the smoke.

Seconds later the sounds of heavy machine gun and rocket fire erupted all around us. The noise was deafening as the steel jacketed rounds and exploding rockets chewed up and destroyed the trees, brush and grass around us. The firing continued unabated for at least ten minutes then all went quite except for the sound of the helicopters hovering around us.

We waited and silently prayed that the gunships had done their jobs and killed, wounded or driven off the enemy.

The radioman called out to LT," the gunships want a Sitrep (Situation report)."

"Tell them to wait one while I send out a couple of men to check."

It was a gutsy and dangerous move, sending out two men to check to see if the enemy had gone but we had no choice.

"Smith, Fedor, check to see if the enemy are gone."

"OK LT," was the response as each man rose to a crouching position and quickly disappeared into the shredded brush in directions opposite to each other.

Seconds turned to minutes as we waited, hoped and prayed. In the distance, over the roar of the Huey Engines, I heard "All clear LT, but there are bodies and body parts everywhere in there… same here LT," as both men returned now standing fully erect.

"LT," the radioman barked out, "the gunships and Medivac will pick us up in a clearing one hundred yards to the east."

"Helping an injured man"

"OK, everybody up, grab the wounded and let's move for an emergency Evac. Fedor, take point and head east…that's to your left…let's move folks," LT commanded. Four men grabbed Ronnie and carried him while I leaned on LT as we headed for the clearing.

Just then, the radioman yelled out, "LT, the gunships are going to clear out the LZ with machine gun and rocket fire, just in case Charlie is there."

"Roger that," LT replied.

With that another series of rocket and machine gun fire started.

"The gunships want us to hold position while they finish clearing the area."

"Roger that."

"Hold one," was the command. We all stopped and waited for the gunfire and explosions to stop. I couldn't imagine anything living through such a pounding! Minutes later the life saving bombardment stopped and we were ordered forward.

Approaching the clearing I heard the familiar engines of the Huey Helicopters. On the ground a Medivac was waiting. Forty or fifty yards from us was a ring of three gunships hovering at about one hundred feet. They were surrounding the clearing and protecting the Medivac on the ground. Ronnie was lifted into the Medivac and placed on a litter. LT helped me up into the Medivac where I sat in a seat directly opposite Ronnie.

Looking back at LT standing on the ground, he gave me the thumbs up sign which I returned. As the engines started to rev up and LT backed away from the chopper, I snapped a salute to him out of respect for his professionalism and common sense in handling this ambush so as to minimize our casualties. Even though we never saluted in the bush, he snapped back a crisp salute to me.

With that we lifted off and turned for the nearest hospital at Tuy Hoa.

Ronnie made it and was sent home. I returned back to camp a few days later. I could have gone home but felt that I could do the most good here rather than stateside.

CHAPTER 39
THE FINAL BATTLE...
DREAM OR PREMONITION?

I knew that they were only dreams but were they also premonitions of things to come for me in the final months of my tour of duty? Each night, the dreams became clearer and more frightening. I kept them to myself for fear that they might become a self-fulfilling prophesy.

********************* The Final Battle *************************

Everything was ominously peaceful and quiet. I was relaxing in the medical bunker when I heard a panic call come into the radio room. It was from our Long Range Patrol.

Lima Alpha 26 this is Quebec Romeo niner... Lima Alpha 26 this is Quebec Romeo niner...Over." Our radio operator Paul Skerritt answered, "Quebec Romeo niner this is Lima Alpha 26...Over."

There was a sense of urgency in the voice of the radio operator in the field.

"Lima Alpha 26, there is a massive force of November Victor Alpha coming your way." Then I heard small arms fire over the radio...lots of it. "They spotted us 26...they spotted us."

"Roger niner, I copy" Paul said..."large force of NVA heading our way... get out of there niner...get out of there," Paul screamed into the microphone.

"Roger 26" was the response. The intensity of the gunfire increased over the radio and I knew that the patrol was in deep trouble.

Just then, the commanding officer came running into the radio room and was informed. He grabbed the mike and called out, "Quebec Romeo niner this is Lima Alpha 26, this is 6, what's your status?"

"They're all over us sir. Most of the men are down! "

"Can you make it back to camp niner?"

"Don't know sir. Were gonna make a run for it sir…I'm dropping the radio, pray for us sir."

"Niner…come in niner…this is six." There was no response!

Just then, the Commanding Officer dropped the mike and yelled out…"red warning in the compound." Paul reached over and threw a switch on the wall…a switch that triggered the siren in the compound, a siren that indicated an attack was imminent.

I grabbed my web gear, rifle, ammo and aid bag and reached into a drawer in the medical cabinet and removed the three grenades that I had in there, attached them to my web belt and ran outside.

Men were scurrying everywhere. The door to the ammo bunker was open and men were running inside and coming out with handfuls of M-16 ammo bandoleers. I ran down to the ammo bunker and went inside. The supply sergeant asked me what I wanted.

"Give me four grenades and a couple of Laws Rockets."

"Are u crazy doc…what do u want with that stuff?"

"Just give it to me," I said at which time he went into the back, brought out two LAWs Rockets and four grenades and handed them to me.

"Good luck doc," he said as I was leaving.

Turning around, I paused for a moment and looked into his eyes. We both knew that this would probably be it for us both.

"You too," I yelled back…"you too."

As I exited the ammo bunker, I heard the sound of small arms fire everywhere.

Shit, I thought that we would have more time to prepare for this attack besides the five or ten minutes since the radio warning came in from our patrol.

I started running back towards the medical bunker. I didn't bother ducking or running zig zag to avoid getting hit. I had about fifty yards to run and since the shortest distance between two points is a straight line, I made a straight line dash.

Within seconds of getting inside the bunker I felt the first concussions of the exploding B-40 rockets. Luckily, I was in the relative safety of the command bunker.

Within seconds a man came running into the bunker yelling, "Man down bunker five." I knew that bunker five was on the rubber plantation side of the compound. I thought we had discouraged the NVA from shooting at us from that side when we blew the shit out of the plantation earlier in the year. Exiting the bunker, I heard our mortars leaving the tubes from the three pits in the compound.

The run to bunker five was like a run thru a minefield. This time I crouched down and ran in a minimal zig zag pattern. B-40's were dropping all over the place! One hit about twenty yards from me. I paid it no mind and just kept running. Reaching the bunker, I saw the injured man sitting on a sandbag. His shirt was bloody. Removing it, I saw an entry and exit wound in his upper arm. Blood was flowing but not spurting from the wound. I bandaged him and had another man take him back to the medical bunker.

The gunfire all along the berm was intense. Truck mounted 50 caliber machine guns were positioned at key spots along the berm where there were openings. I climbed to the top of bunker and peered over looking towards the rubber plantation. What I saw sent a cold shiver down my spine. Armed men, scores of them, dressed in khaki and green uniforms were crossing the two hundred meters of open space between the rubber plantation and the outer layers of our wire and heading straight for us.

I ran back to the ammo bunker and yelled in at the sergeant handing out ammo, "Gooks heading for the wire, lots of them…pass this shit out ASAP and get the fuck out, get to a safer place."

With that I turned and started my run back to the medical bunker. I arrived to a sight that I'd never expected to see. Wounded men were everywhere. I dropped my ordnance on the floor and started looking at them. By then JC was already treating them. There were chest wounds, abdominal wounds and wounds to the extremities. Some men were already dead and many more were in the throes of dying. We were swamped with injured and had to make decisions on who, if we treated them, might survive. For the rest, it was a heartbreaking decision but I let them die in the company of the men who they had lived and laughed with these many months.

I had the dead removed outside to make room for the wounded who were being brought in, in a steady stream.

Men were down along all of the perimeters of the compound…men who needed help…many of whom could not make it to the medical bunker. Unfortunately there were only three of us, three medics to treat the masses of wounded. I left JC and another medic to treat the men inside the bunker and went out to treat those along the berm.

"Enemy view of the wire from the outside looking in "

"View of wire from inside a bunker looking out"

The heaviest fire was still coming from the NVA and VC attacking along the rubber plantation perimeter so I headed back in that direction. It was pure chaos in the compound, men running to positions where other men had been lost, men running to the ammo bunker for more ammunition, runners running from the Command Post to the three perimeters of the compound gathering status from the officers and men in those areas and relaying orders back to the commanding officer.

I arrived at the berm, climbed to the top and peered over towards the rubber plantation. The NVA had reached the wire and were cutting their way through. As quickly as one was killed, another grabbed the cutters from his dying buddy and proceeded to cut further into the wire. Soon, they were no more than fifteen yards from our innermost layer of wire.

Just then, I heard claymore mines going off all along the perimeter. The claymores were our last fixed defense against an attacking force from entering the compound. Although effective against a ground force, detonating the claymores would also blow away what barb wire still remained between us and them. Once the wire was gone, the outcome would be determined by the side with the most men, most ammunition and most will to live.

NVA and VC were dropping like bowling pins as the claymores did their lethal job but it was too little, too late. Men streamed out of their bunkers all along the berm and climbed to the tops of the earthen walls and into the spaces between them to meet the enemy face on. I took aim at a group of NVA who were closest to me and sent a sustained burst of 30 rounds into them, dropping a number of them.

All around me men were doing the same, firing and killing the enemy but we were losing men at an alarming rate. Still, the enemy kept coming. They seemed to have an inexhaustible supply of men.

God help me, but there was no time, now, for me to attend to the wounded. It had turned into a white knuckle fight for survival. If I died then the scores of wounded who depended on me would surely die.

As our number along the berm dwindled, we began to slowly fall back towards the center of the compound. The enemy strength was just too much for us. Ammunition was running low and many men were forced to retreat in order to go back to the ammo bunker.

The mortars and rockets had ceased. Now it was a test of strength, willpower and the decision of a higher power as to whether we lived or died.

I fired another burst of thirty rounds into another group of enemy approaching my position. Realizing it was time to go; I dropped my empty magazine, loaded in another and backed down the twelve foot high earthen berm. Half way down, two NVA appeared at the top. Before they had a chance to lower their weapons I fired a burst into their chests and abdomens.

With my ammunition running out, I pulled back on the selective fire switch putting it in single fire mode. Now I would have to aim and shoot a round at a time rather than point and fire in auto mode. I did not feel comfortable doing this but I had no choice.

All around me, men were involved in individual firefights, fights to stay alive. I was moving backwards slowly and steadily passing bodies of men everywhere. Where a man was wounded, I would help him to his feet and push him back in the direction of the medical bunker. I heard men yelling at me, "get back here doc," get back here.

"The final stand position... "The Trench"
with rubber plantation in background"

A quick look behind me revealed a group of men who had established themselves in the drainage ditch that was about fifty yards long and ran directly to the ammo dump.

Surprisingly, the NVA had either ignored the ammo dump, never found it, or were too engaged in fights to care to blow it. I crossed over the drainage ditch and headed back to the medical bunker. The dead and dying inside were everywhere. The Commanding Officer was on the radio in the adjoining room requesting artillery support, but where would they fire, the NVA were already inside the compound and mixed in with us?

"Sir," I yelled out, they're inside the compound and approaching the drainage ditch. They haven't found the ammo bunker yet but it's only a matter of time. If we're lucky we have maybe ten or fifteen minutes before they completely overrun us. Call in "Puff" sir if he is in the area, have them waste the plantation side or have arty waste it but whatever you do Sir, do it now!"

Turning to the wounded and dying inside the medical bunker I said, "We need your help outside. If you can fire a weapon we need you outside now, before it's too late! We will most likely be overrun in the next few minutes but let's see if we can fuck them over before we go."

With that, the wounded started slowly moving from their resting places and painfully rose to their feet. They grabbed what weapons were available and staggered out to join their comrades in the drainage ditch.

I heard the Commanding Officer exclaim on the radio, "American Unit about to be overrun," I say again "American Unit about to be overrun" over.

"Roger 26, all available resources being sent to you, specify fire control coordinates, over."

"This is 26; waste everything just inside our perimeter and for 100 meters outside it ASAP." "Roger 26."

I went outside with the walking wounded and joined them in the drainage ditch with the remaining survivors. I brought my LAWS Rockets, and a few more grenades that I had found. For every Gook that we dropped, two took his place. I expended my two LAWS Rockets, taking out a number of the enemy to my right. In a matter of minutes I had expended my grenades and still they came. The NVA were everywhere and many men had already run out of ammunition. The ammo dump was a mere thirty yards away and accessible through the drainage ditch. I couldn't understand why they hadn't blown it.

With ammo almost out, I handed my carbine to the man next to me. There were maybe a hundred rounds left. "Use this single shot only…make every shot count. I'm going for the ammo dump to get more ammo."

"You're crazy Doc …you'll never make it. They'll kill you before you get ten yards!"

"Without the ammo we're all dead anyway…don't mean nuthin."

I reached down grabbed my 45 and pulled back on the hammer and released the safety. "Don't shoot me on the way back" I said as I jumped up and ran twenty yards down the drainage ditch then climbed to the top and started my run above ground to the ammo dump. Suddenly, an NVA came out of nowhere on my right. He was probably as surprised to see me at close range as I was to see him. I fired one round into his face and continued my run.

Just before entering the ammo bunker an NVA jumped down in front of me from above and knocked my 45 out of my hand. I grabbed the barrel of his AK47 with my left hand and forced it away from my body just as he fired a burst of rounds from it.

The barrel of his rifle was burning hot and I felt a searing wave of pain as the flesh in my hand that was in contact with the barrel sizzled like a hamburger on a grill. I grabbed him around the neck with my right hand and tried to force him to the ground where I hoped to take away his weapon and kill him with it. Although smaller than me, he was equally strong and determined. We fell to the ground and struggled, each trying to gain a strategic advantage. Whatever happened, I could not let go of the barrel of his weapon. He hit me three or four times in the jaw with his fist while I was hitting him repeatedly with my elbow hoping to daze him long enough to somehow kill him.

Then almost as if we were thinking the same thing he reached down for his bayonet as I reached for my survival knife. My first blind reach down was successful as I pulled it from the sheath and plunged it into his neck just as he plunged his into my left forearm. I pulled my knife out and hit him again, this time in the sternum. He stopped moving!

Dazed and exhausted but pumped with adrenaline, I left my knife in his chest, pulled his bayonet from my forearm and ran into the bunker. There I gathered as many bandoleers of M-16 ammo as I could carry, draped them over both shoulders, shoved grenades into the pockets in my shirt and pants, then grabbed for a nearby M-16. A closer look revealed it was being held by the ammo dump sergeant. He had been shot in the chest and head and was dead. There was no time for remorse or sorrow.

I grabbed two loose grenades lying on a nearby sandbag, pulled the pin on one and threw it just outside the entrance to the bunker. This, I hoped would kill anyone just outside the bunker. I hoped that none of our guys were out there but I had no choice. Six seconds later the detonation shook the bunker. I ran out, pulled the pin on the second grenade, turned and threw it deep into the ammo dump.

That should keep the NVA from using the ammo against us; I said to myself as I started a slow run back to the ditch. Laden down with ammo I felt like I was running in slow motion. I had no time to load the M-16 that I'd pried from the hands of the ammo dump sergeant.

To my left and right I could see the enemy closing in on me.

I jumped into the ditch and was quickly inundated by men who looked like the walking dead, grabbing bandoleers off my shoulders. Within seconds, waves of M-16 fire from the ditch cut down scores of enemy attackers as they charged in human waves.

Seconds later I felt an intense wave of heat on my body as the entire perimeter erupted in a fireball of jellied gasoline. We all ducked and tried to hug the ground as closely as we could, trying to avoid being caught in the napalm. A second napalm sortie was quickly followed by a third. The napalm knew neither friend nor foe in its effort to consume all living objects.

After a few brief moments, the third sortie of Napalm had done its initial burnoff. Looking out over the ditch, it looked like Hell. Everything was on fire, dirt, tents, bunkers and men. I could see men dancing and screaming in the flames. I knew not whether they were friend or foe. I grabbed my M-16 and for those being consumed by fire, I took careful aim and killed them. Burning alive was no fate for a soldier no matter what side he was on.

The assault inside continued but with the enemy replacements being consumed by the Napalm, the odds had shifted slightly in our favor. It had been almost two hours since the battle started when suddenly we heard masses of small arms fire coming from the road and approaching us. We were once again almost out of ammo and now almost out of hope.

The enemy attacking us suddenly turned and started firing to the rear but at whom? What were they firing at? Then I saw men dressed in Jungle fatigues. It was volunteers from base camp and from A Company, men who volunteered to come to our aid. With the enemy caught in a cross fire, it was over within minutes. The carnage and terror and loss of life were over. Now there was only the dead, dying and injured to deal with.

I climbed out of the ditch to greet and join my brothers. After a few brief handshakes, I hobbled back to the medical bunker to help treat the wounded. We had lost two thirds of the two hundred men in Camp. Those who remained were either wounded or in shock or both.

This was a dream, my dream; one that I hoped would never see the light of day!

CHAPTER 40
GOING HOME

I was going home and I was pissed! I had extended for an additional six months in Vietnam to be the medic in Medevac Helicopters and my extension was approved. I would have gone home for 30 days then return for six months, then back home again, for good. It all seemed perfectly sane at the time, my decision that is. I really needed the money to buy my British Sports Car and if I got killed while on my six month extension, so be it.

I knew in my heart that with my extension, I could make a difference between life and death for those whose safety I was responsible for. My medical skills were finely honed by my constant exposure to illness, injury and wounds. I was also in the best shape of my life physically, complete with six pack abs.

To this day, I wonder how many men I could I have saved had I been there, how many men might be here today, reading this book had I stayed for the extra time. That question haunts me today and I will carry it with me to my grave.

I was coming home with a bad attitude towards the army. This is not what I expected my ride home on the "Freedom Bird" to be like.

What would I do stateside… change oil in ambulances, drill the troops? As pissed as I was, there was nothing that I could do about it. The massive machinery of war, ground ever forward, defying all common sense and logic, but such was the nature of war!

I guess from some points of view, going home was a good thing. My Dad, Step Mom and grandparents would never have understood me extending in Vietnam for six additional months… after all; I had survived where others had not.

Men in our battalion with more than six months left in country would be transferred to other units; the rest would go home with me. The last month before leaving was extremely busy. Heavy construction equipment was trucked to Cam Ranh Bay where it was loaded onto ships and carried away…to somewhere. We never learned where that final destination was although I suspect that the vast majority of it was sent to the Philippines since it was fairly close by.

As the deadline for our departure drew ever closer and we realized that there wasn't enough time to have the remaining equipment trucked to Cam Ranh Bay, so we destroyed it using C-4. When C-4 ran out, huge pits were dug and the equipment buried. Millions of dollars of prime equipment was lost. It was a waste of monumental proportions!

We were told that our withdrawal from Vietnam would allow the Vietnamese Army to take over the bulk of the fighting. A bigger crock of shit, I never heard. The military, the politicians and the Vietnamese themselves knew that Vietnam and the Vietnamese Army was not prepared to successfully defend itself. It was quite simply another throat choking line of propaganda.

In the past year, our unit had accomplished much. We built up the road infrastructure, rebuilt bridges, helped the Montgnards and now, we were just leaving, deserting everything and everyone who had befriended us. What would happen to them after our pullout was complete? We suspected that it would be a death sentence for them. Time proved this to be correct.

To those members of B Company who were remaining and being relocated to other units, it was a brief, Vietnam Style hand shake from us and a wish for them to come home alive. Stateside addresses were exchanged…most would be lost forever in the confusion to leave and the pain to stay.

Leaving friends behind was tougher than I ever expected it to be. As our truck pulled out of Camp for the last time, I took one last backwards glance at those with whom I had shared so much pain and so many laughs. I knew that I would never see them again.

A short stay at base camp and we were off. The ride to the Ban Me Thuout Airport was short. As our truck pulled out of Camp Jerome for the last time I looked behind me and thought of my arrival on this same road a year ago. A lump formed in my throat.

Almost four hundred of us boarded C130 Cargo Planes. Within an hour, we were landing at our final destination, Cam Ranh Bay. Our temporary barracks in Cam Ranh was nothing like the rat hole tent I had stayed in there almost a year ago. The beds in these brand new, wooden structure barracks were made up with clean white sheets and pillows and unbelievably, fans to cool us off. Close by was the NCO Club and Red

Cross Center where cold soda and reading material was always available. It was heaven.

We turned in our rifles and pistols but I still had a problem, my M2 Carbine. I had no way to get it home thanks to an "Unmentioned" National Guard unit getting caught smuggling weapons out of the country. The culprits were not from the Vermont National Guard. The men from that unit were kind and respectful and honest to the N'th Degree. Weeks prior to our departure, the military was permitting us to carry home non issue "Captured Weapons." No one could prove that my M2 wasn't at some point in time used by the enemy. After the National Guard Unit was caught, all weapons designated as captured weapons of war were no longer permitted to be taken home.

Thanks a lot guys!!!

"Jack in Cam Ranh Bay on the way home "

In our barracks building, there were a few new guys mixed in with us. It was an instant replay of a year ago only this time, I was going home and they were coming in. I never would have guessed a year ago, when I first burned my hand on the metal handrail of the steps from the plane to the tarmac below, that I would want to stay in a war zone longer than I had to.

One of the new guys admired my M2 carbine and asked if I was interested in selling it. I was between a rock and a hard place…no way to get it home legally so I sold it to him for fifty bucks, giving up my closest protector and friend over the past year. I hoped that it would help preserve and save this new guy's life. As a bonus, I gave him my survival knife. That brought a great smile to his face.

"Boarding the "Freedom Bird" for our flight home "

Three days later the battalion boarded two C141 transports and we started the long flight home. Almost all troops leaving Vietnam were flown home on civilian jet liners with pretty stewardesses…except us. We were flown home in Air Force jets with Stewardesses with names like Bruno, Frank and Larry. What a bummer! It was yet another letdown in an ever growing list of letdowns from my employer.

As we waited in line to board the plane, I knew that a major part of my life was about to end, an important part. Before entering the plane I took one last glance around, took a deep breath and let it out. Regardless of the conditions under which I was leaving and the fact that I didn't want to leave, I had made it out alive, I had survived my tour of duty.

Our first stop was Yokota Air Force Base in Japan for refueling. In the base mess hall, stories began to spread about a woman who had killed a soldier returning from Vietnam, at Travis Air Force Base in California just as he exited the plane. She shot him because she was angry that her son had died in Vietnam. Word was that she figured if her son died there then so should everyone else's. Good thing that our final destination was not Travis but Fort Lewis in Washington State.

Three hours later we were airborne. This was now "Full Circle" for me. Nearing the coast of the US we were informed that bad weather prevented us from landing at Fort Lewis so we were diverting to Travis AFB. Shit! We were going to the Death Airport.

"Outside Mess Hall at Travis Air Force Base with friends "

Talking amongst ourselves, we decided that we would not exit the plane when we landed. One of the officers would have to exit first.

The plane came to a stop near the terminal and the front door opened. No one got up, no one even moved. We all just sat there. Orders from the Commanding Officer to get up and exit the plane were ignored. We all just sat there.

"What's the matter with you people," he yelled. Someone sitting near him explained our dilemma. We had no intention of making it all the way back home from Vietnam just to be killed by an irate civilian. He understood. As a gesture of good faith, the Commanding Officer exited the plane. Hearing no shots, we followed.

We were led to the mess hall by an Air Force sergeant. The building was monstrous. I was the first man into the building. At the entrance, sitting at a desk and checking ids was another Air Force sergeant. He looked up from his check list and stared at me for a moment then asked what I wanted. By that time a line of four hundred men had formed behind me. All of us were wearing faded Vietnam Jungle clothes and we all sported dark tans.

I told him that we were returning from Vietnam and had been diverted from Fort Lewis to here because of weather and we were hungry. By that time the mess sergeant had come over, took one look at me and said "welcome back guys. The mess hall is yours as he pointed to the beginning of the serving line."

I moved into the serving line, grabbed a stainless steel food tray and moved to the first server in line. It was then that we encountered our first problem. There were three or four main dishes and all kinds of desserts. I didn't know what to do so I asked the mess sergeant "What can I have?"

"Whatever you want and as much as you want," he replied.

"Holy shit," I said as I smiled and thanked him. I hadn't seen so much food since my grandmothers table back home. I filled my tray knowing I couldn't eat a quarter of what was on it. In Vietnam eating was not an experience that we looked forward to but found it as necessary as going to the bathroom.

Exiting the chow, line I looked for a table to sit at. Nearby was a table with three Air Force Women Officers. I hadn't seen a woman in many months and they were a beautiful sight, all of them. I stared at them for a while as did the other guys. They were dressed in crisp blue uniforms and they had the bodies of a goddess.

One of them invited me to sit with them. I was almost tongue tied as I picked up my tray and moved to their table. "Where are you from specialist," one of them asked.

"We're just in from Vietnam Mam," I replied. "There's about four hundred of us."

"What was your job?"

"Medic, "I replied. I couldn't remove my eyes from one of the women. She was a brunette with medium brown hair that was rolled into a bun and tucked under her hat. She was slim and had a beautiful soft voice. If love at first site is real, I was in love.

We talked for a couple of hours and during the whole time, I barely touched my food. After a while she said she had to get back to her duty station. I was heartbroken that she had to leave because I felt there was an attachment between us. I should have asked her for a mailing address but I didn't. It was the shortest love affair I ever had. I like to think she felt the same way.

By early evening we were Fort Lewis bound, arriving there just before midnight. We were told that soldiers returning from Vietnam were entitled steak dinners but when we arrived stateside the mess sergeant felt differently. He told us that it was too late to start cooking and that he and his crew were leaving. All four hundred of us disagreed.

Having no weapons to express the depth of our displeasure, we began picking up bricks that lined the sidewalks. The sight of four hundred men, each with a brick in his hand must have been a very sobering sight to the mess sergeant. We were soon dining on steaks. By the time I got into the mess hall, the only clean silverware that remained were spoons so I cut and ate the steak with two spoons. It was the best steak I'd ever eaten.

The following day we were taken to the supply depot to turn in our Vietnam Clothing issue and receive a standard clothing issue. Most of us came back only with the clothes on our backs. We were asked where the rest of our clothing was and most of us just told them that it was destroyed in rocket attacks.

We received orders for our next duty stations. Mine was Fort Riley, located in the center of Kansas, but first it was home for thirty days of rest and relaxation.

As I entered the Seattle/Tacoma airport, I saw anti war protestors everywhere. They were carrying placards with pictures of dead children. Others carried signs emblazoned with big bold letters that called us murderers and rapists. The crowd was yelling and screaming at us the likes of which I'd never seen before. Like Ahab's white whale, we were the source and target of their rage.

Back in Vietnam, we had heard that this was happening to troops as they went into airports but the actual experience of an enraged crowd with hate painted on their faces is something that I shall never forget.

Two years earlier, I too was a student but I was never one of them. I could never say and do to returning troops what they did to us and to me. After all the shit and suffering we had endured, this was our welcome back to America. I had more respect for the VC and NVA than these animals who called themselves Americans. God Bless America!

I said nothing as I walked the gauntlet of abuse, surrounded on both sides by protestors. None of us did anything, we just quietly walked towards the gates for our flights home until a few of the protestors jumped from behind the ropes holding them back and hit one of the guys in the battalion. While we would do nothing in response to the verbal abuse, being attacked was a different story. This we would not tolerate!

Within seconds, a fight ensued and within seconds, the Military Police showed up. It was Quid Pro Quo time!

As the MP's quickly moved in to break up the altercation, I approached the sergeant of the MPs in charge and explained that we were attacked first. He immediately ordered his men to stand down and back off.

The altercation was over in short order and we all picked up our bags and walked to our individual departure gates. Soldiers = 1, Protestors = 0!

My destination was JFK where my best friend Joe, his sister Kathy and Kathy's boyfriend Fields (and one of my long time friends) would pick me up and drive me home.

It would be a fateful flight.

CHAPTER 41
AVENEL HERE I COME

The flight home was relatively calm until we hit the east coast and a massive snow storm. Our approach route to JFK was from the south, over Maryland and up into New Jersey. We were at thirty three thousand feet and began a slow descent through the snow and wind when suddenly the DC8 started bouncing around like a Mexican jumping bean. I paid no attention to it until I looked out the window and saw the wings flapping like a Sea Gull in flight. They were bouncing up and down six or seven feet from horizontal. This continued for minutes when suddenly we dropped hundreds or possibly thousands of feet in what seemed like the blink of an eye.

People everywhere started screaming. The man next to me was screaming louder than the women. As we continued our freefall, I had a sinking feeling that I wouldn't make it home. I didn't panic, or scream or show any signs of fear. With the calmness of knowing that my death was imminent, I uttered just one word, "Shit."

I had made it through Vietnam and now I was going to die in a plane crash not more than a few hundred miles from home. The irony of it all could not escape me so I just sat there, calmly and accepted my death just as I did in Vietnam.

Seconds seemed like hours when suddenly we stopped our freefall. Food, food trays and drinks were scattered everywhere and on everyone. The guy next to me looked at me, still with a terrified look on his face and said "what's the matter with you, weren't you afraid?"

"No," I said, "just pissed!" With a confused look on his face, he just stared at me for a few moments then sat back into his seat. We never spoke again.

After landing at JFK and retrieving my duffle bag, I exited the terminal building into Blizzard like conditions. I hoped that my friends might already be there, waiting, but no such luck. The conditions were so harsh outside that it would have frightened a team of experienced sled dogs. Having just come from one hundred plus degree heat just hours before,

I wasn't acclimatized to the cold temperatures. The bitter, biting cold penetrated my wool winter green uniform, overcoat and leather gloves.

Within minutes, my body began to shiver uncontrollably. The first stages of Hypothermia were setting in. My teeth started to chatter like a set of battery powered false teeth.

I was just about to turn around and head back into the terminal when a set of headlights approached and stopped close by. It was them! Getting out of the passenger's seat I recognized my best friend Joe as he walked towards me. I extended an almost frozen hand to him and we shook hands. "Good to see you Ace (he called me Ace and I called him Ace), he said.

"You too" I replied in a rather shaky voice. Words were hard to form on my icy cold lips but I knew that I was safe now and looked forward to the warmth inside the car. Closing the door behind me I got a handshake from Fields and a kiss from Kathy.

Within seconds, I noticed that I could see my breath inside the car. "Hey fields" I yelled out, "turn up the heat, I'm freezing."

"The heater doesn't work Ace," he replied.

Shit, I was nearly frozen and now no heat in the car. At least I was out of the blowing snow…that was something. Two hours later, after driving through a blinding snow storm, we arrived at my grandparent's house. Inside I was greeted with endless kisses, tears and hot chocolate. We all sat around for hours talking and smiling and joking. Although my Vietnam Odyssey was over, my military career still had one more terrible year left to serve in a place called Fort Riley, located in Kansas.

Two days later, after the snow had been plowed and the roads were cleared; I was determined to go back to Upsala College, where I spent my first year and a half after high school. Maybe I could find some of my old friends

CHAPTER 42
HOME

I put on my Class A Uniform complete with ribbons, borrowed my grandfather's Chevy and set out north on the Garden State Parkway to exit 144. It was still bitter cold outside but nothing unusual for New Jersey in late December. As I drove the twelve miles to school, my thoughts were of Vietnam and all of the buddies who I had left behind. I wondered how many would be lucky enough to make it home alive. I thought of the Montgnard Chief who had befriended me and I thought of those friends whom I would never see again.

Parking in the student parking lot, I carefully walked along the snowy sidewalks towards the main entrance of the Student Union. Unlike the throngs who walked there during the warm summer months, the winter snows and cold had limited the sidewalk traffic to a trickle. As I pushed open the door, I wondered what and who I would find. Would I encounter another "Up Close and Personal" hostile reception like that at the Seattle/Tacoma Airport just days before?

There were couches and chairs everywhere, all occupied by students reading, talking or sleeping. A large fire crackled in the immense oval shaped hearth not ten feet from where I was standing. It was a picture perfect setting for a cold, wintry day on a college campus.

I felt like I was once again back in the bush, on ambush! I hoped and prayed that I could just turn off those old feelings that helped me to survive but that was not to be. I hoped for the best but was prepared for the worst.

My eyes slowly scanned the large Student Union room, looking for a friendly face, a familiar face. I was very methodical in my search. I scanned the room from right to left, drawing a few stares as I did so but it seemed as if they were curious stares rather than evil ones. After what I considered to be a thorough look-and-see, I was forced to accept only one possible conclusion...there was no one there who I knew and no one who recognized me. The bottom of my heart fell out onto the floor. It was as if someone had just stabbed with a knife.

One last pass and then I'd head for home.

Half way across the atrium I was stopped dead in my tracks. I spotted a woman with long dark hair, sitting in a large comfortable chair with her legs bent beneath her. How had I missed her on my previous scan?

She was reading a book. Her profile was familiar but it just couldn't be her or could it? During my freshman year, I had a crush on a gorgeous brunette. She was a year or maybe two ahead of me and would have graduated the previous year so it couldn't be her, or could it?

My eyes were fixated on her for seconds or minutes or hours, I don't know which. Slowly, as if something or someone had told her, she raised her head and looked at me. Our eyes met and I smiled. It was her.

She stood up slowly, then broke out into a large smile and started screaming "Oh my God, Oh my God, it's you" as she ran towards me. I held out my arms and she dove into them, wrapping her arms around me and giving me a kiss that seemed to stop time. I could feel a passion and an emotion in her lips that I had never felt while kissing any other girl. That kiss erased all of the suffering and anger and frustration of the past few days. "My God, you're alive," she continued to say as she hugged and kissed me. "One of your friends told me that you went to Vietnam. That was the last that any of us heard from you."

I sat down in the chair where she had been sitting and she sat in my lap, snuggling in ever closer to me. We talked for a long while about old times and old friends. It was wonderful and it was surely nothing that I ever expected. We talked for hours. Just before midnight, she invited me to her room.

I was home!

Jack in Colorado on a pass from 1'st Infantry Division "

CHAPTER 43
DON'T MEAN NUTHIN

**"A floral memorial to the Engineers with whom I served at the
"Vietnam Veterans Wall", on Veterans Day"**

"Boots left at "The Wall"

A Vietnam Odyssey

In this time of Kosovo, Jack Manick remembers how the war his generation fought changed how war itself was fought, from then to now, in his new series in

Insights Of A Veteran

"Vietnam Odyssey…my byline writing a Veterans Column for Comcast in the 1990s"

"Don't Mean Nuthin"

"We used this expression every day in Vietnam when the going got tough… when we lost friends and comrades…when we were so sick that we couldn't stand…when we found ourselves in situations in which we knew we were going to die…when we received mail from girlfriends declaring that they could no longer write to us because their friends said that we were murderers and baby killers…and when protestors threw excrement and animal blood at us at the airports as we returned from Vietnam and were going home."

We said it not because it didn't mean anything to us but because it did, it meant so very much to all of us."

Jack Manick

It is fitting that the last chapter to this book should end on a healing note. A number of years back, ten years to be exact; I was honored to talk to a lady named Julie Weaver. Julie wrote a "Letter of Healing" to Vietnam Veterans. I always look for all that is good and kind and just in a person's heart and soul and because of this, I believe that this letter was written from deep within Julie's Heart and soul. When I first read it, I had to fight back the tears.

Julie's letter was the first indication to me that anyone except for our families, cared about our service in Vietnam. It was also the first and only indication to date that anyone recognized the lifelong harm done to us by our fellow Americans and apologized for it.

In today's world of continuing conflict, we Americans thank, applaud and pray for those who serve in harm's way. We thank them for their service and we try to support them and their families during their Tours of Duty. This is how it should be but it has not always been so. What follows is "The Healing Letter";

.

"Julie Weaver"

AN OPEN LETTER TO
ANYONE WHO SERVED
IN VIETNAM

Dear Hero,

I was in my twenties during the Vietnam era. I was a single mother and, I'm sad to say, I was probably one of the most self-centered people on the planet. To be perfectly honest...I didn't care one way or the other about the war. All I cared about was me—how I looked, what I wore, and where I was going. I worked and I played. I was never politically involved in anything, but I allowed my opinions to be formed by the media. It happened without my ever being aware. I listened to the protest songs and I watch the six o'clock news and I listened to all the people who were talking. After awhile, I began to repeat their words and, if you were to ask me, I'd have told you I was against the war. It was very popular. Everyone was doing it, and we never saw what it was doing to our men. All we were shown was what they were doing to the people of Vietnam.

My brother joined the Navy and then he was sent to Vietnam. When he came home, I repeated the words to him. It surprised me at how angry he became. I hurt him very deeply and there were years of separation—not only of miles, but also of character. I didn't understand.

In fact, I didn't understand anything until one day I opened my newspaper and saw the anguished face of a Vietnam veteran. The picture was taken at the opening of the Vietnam Veterans Memorial in Washington, D.C. His countenance revealed the terrible burden of his soul. As I looked at his picture and his tears, I finally understood a tiny portion of what you had given for us and what we had done to you. I understood that I had been manipulated, but I also knew that I had failed to think for myself. It was like waking up out of a nightmare, except that the nightmare was real. I didn't know what to do.

One day about three years ago, I went to a member of the church I attended at that time, because he had served in Vietnam. I asked him if he had been in Vietnam, and he got a look on his face and said, "Yes." Then, I took his hand, looked him square in the face, and said, "Thank you for going." His jaw dropped, he got an amazed look on his face, and then he said, "No one has ever said that to me." He hugged me and I could see that he was about to get tears in his eyes. It gave me an idea, because there is much more that needs to be said. How do we put into words…all the regret of so many years? I don't know, but when I have an opportunity, I take…so here goes.

Have you been to Vietnam? If so, I have something I want to say to you—Thank you for going! Thank you from the bottom of my heart. Please forgive me for my insensitivity. I don't know how I could have been so blind, but I was. When I woke up, you were wounded and the damage was done, and I don't know how to fix it. I will never stop regretting my actions, and I will never let it happen again.

Please understand that I am speaking for the general public also. We know we blew it and we don't know how to make it up to you. We wish we had been there for you when you came home from Vietnam because you were a hero and you deserved better. Inside of you there is a pain that will never completely go away…and you know what? It's inside of us, too; because when we let you down, we hurt ourselves, too. We all know it… and we suffer guilt and we don't know what to do…so we cheer for our troops and write letters to "any soldier" and we hang out the yellow ribbons and fly the flag and we love America. We love you too, even if it doesn't feel like it to you. I know in my heart that, when we cheer wildly for our troops, part of the reason is trying to make up for Vietnam. And while it may work for us, it does nothing for you. We failed you. You didn't fail us, but we failed you and we lost our only chance to be grateful to you at the time when you needed and deserved it. We have disgraced ourselves and brought shame to our country. We did it and we need your forgiveness. Please say you will forgive us and please take your rightful place as heroes of our country. We have learned a terribly painful lesson at your expense and we don't know how to fix it.

From the heart,

Julie Weaver
237 East Gatewood Circle
Burleson, Texas 76028-8948
(817) 295-6287

Email address: julieweaver@juno.com

CHAPTER 44
IN THE YEARS SINCE

The years pass by ever so silently and almost invisibly. Daily Survival Protocols change from avoiding ambushes, poisonous snakes and booby traps to trying to come up with the money to replace that old Chevy or a down payment for that first house.

The powers to be play many tricks on our minds and bodies. Waistlines seemingly increase overnight. Faces that were once slim and trim, expand out to chubby proportions. My grandmothers always referred to such faces as "Healthy." Memories become spotty and only photos of places gone and past and letters or journals reveal the true story.

I met a man exiting a dermatologist's office who was wearing a WWII baseball cap and I both asked him where he served and thanked him for his service. He couldn't remember all the details until he quickly pulled out his wallet, opened it and asked me to read an index card taped to the inside. On it was written that he served aboard an LCI in the Navy and participated in the Normandy Invasion. As it turned out, he was landing US Troops on Utah Beach(Green Sector) This was about one thousand yards from where my Dad was landing British Soldiers from the 50'th Division on Gold Beach at the very same time in the first attack wave.

I could see the passion in his eyes as I read the index card. He said to me, "Thanks for reading it…I tend to forget what I did."

We shook hands and walked in different directions.

I continue on my path through life, content that a small part of the lives of two units of men have been, at least, partially captured in such a way as to have put the reader in our boots, if only for a few moments. I am content in the knowledge that this small part of history will not be lost when we, the participants pass on.

I was fortunate and surprised to find that the 70th had been reconstituted to Fort Riley in Kansas. I got in touch with the Command

Sergeant Major, Jerry Singletary and the Commanding Officer Colonel Mark Loring. I sent them reams of photos and history of what we were like and what we did there during my Tour of Duty in 1969. They invited me to join them. My visit there was wonderful and I was treated like an honored guest. I returned the following year...for one last visit and one last touch with my past.

Thanks to Colonel Mark Loring and CSM Jerry Singletary for allowing me to share my past...their history...with them.

"Jack receiving an award from Colonel Mark Loring from 70ᵗʰ Combat Engineer Battalion at Fort Riley in the year 2000"

Jack receiving an award from Command Sergeant Major Jerry Singletary from 70th Combat Engineer Battalion in the year 2000 at Fort Riley

Time has a way of silently, almost invisibly catching up with us. Time turns hair gray, enlarges waistlines and inexplicably fattens faces. Our memories of friends and places and events slip away from us like smoke into a cold winter night. We lose a little each day and each night.

Unless it is passed on in some way, these memories or any memories are soon lost...forever! It is my fervent hope that I have passed along some snapshots in time of a small group of men who served in an unpopular war in the Central Highlands of Vietnam.

This book has been my passion and possibly my single minded obsession since the late 1980s when I first put pen to paper and now, with its publishing, I can take a break and do some work around the house, content that I have passed on a bit of history to generation present and future.

Jack at Tom Martin's wedding. Age and time catches up with us all.

Dreams of Days gone by

Chapter 45
Friends made and names lost to time

Jack and the Goat-

Amongst the insanity of war this baby goat wandered into camp and became one of our mascots. He ate almost anything and he could

not run in a straight line. Being an animal lover, I bonded with him instantly. He followed me everywhere. He was a reminder that in amongst the pain and suffering of war ,that good things still happen.

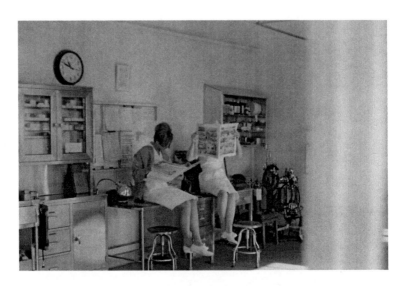

My fondest memories of working in the hospital was the wonderful, professional nurses . Miss Dobbins and Miss ? are the only two who I have photos of.

Sergeant Vinh Thai was a 22 year old advisor and translator. In the time I spent in base camp, we became good friends. I often wonder what became of him when the country fell

Cleon Pidgeon was a member of our sister company...the Vermont National Guard(131'st Engineer Company Light Equipment). He was the nicest, kindest man I'd ever met and a good friend.

Ken Feder a cook and good friend

Jerry. Last name unknown. Where are you now?

John Clark was one of my best friends. We shared the same bunker
along the berm. He was a great guy.

Paul Skerritt one of my best friends passed away 10 years

Paul Skerritt and unknown

Jack and unknown friend

Base camp Jack and unknown friend

Just landed in the USA. Photo of Jack in center, Drury Puckett on far
left the remainder are unknown

Stubby(Robert Stubblefield) on right, Fred in center and unknown

Stubby and Frank Montella

Stubby on right and unknown

I remember that this member of our company was a Radio Operator
but memory forgets his name

The Rat Tent. Although I slept with them(the rats), they never became
my friends

A friend whose name is lost to time at Base Camp

Me on left and my best friend Joe Glydon, who passed away a few years ago

Larry Van Fossen(center) and names lost to time

Jack on left and Tom Martin at the wall. I met Tom in the mid 1980s and we became good friends. Tom is a Silver Star and Purple Heart recipient from the battle for Hamburger Hill in 1969. I never knew him there

Camp Swampy - 1969 - Steamroller left by the French

This old, rusted Steam Roller was a left over from the many conflicts in South East Asia since World War II. It sat in our compound and reminded me of the fact that all wars end and their memories soon turn to rusted relics unless the memories are captured and saved for future generations.

I wonder what happened to the Montgnard after the USA pulled out of the war. Their friendship to us was pure and true and I know in my heart that their fate was horrible at best.

I fell in love with this baby elephant.
If I could have taken him home in my duffel bag, I would have.

Breinigsville, PA USA
28 October 2010
248282BV00002B/1/P